Good Habits for Great Coding

Improving Programming Skills with Examples in Python

Michael Stueben

Apress®

Good Habits for Great Coding

Michael Stueben
Falls Church, Virginia, USA

ISBN-13 (pbk): 978-1-4842-3458-7   ISBN-13 (electronic): 978-1-4842-3459-4
https://doi.org/10.1007/978-1-4842-3459-4

Library of Congress Control Number: 2018934317

Copyright © 2018 by Michael Stueben

This work is subject to copyright. All rights are reserved by the Publisher, whether the whole or part of the material is concerned, specifically the rights of translation, reprinting, reuse of illustrations, recitation, broadcasting, reproduction on microfilms or in any other physical way, and transmission or information storage and retrieval, electronic adaptation, computer software, or by similar or dissimilar methodology now known or hereafter developed.

Trademarked names, logos, and images may appear in this book. Rather than use a trademark symbol with every occurrence of a trademarked name, logo, or image we use the names, logos, and images only in an editorial fashion and to the benefit of the trademark owner, with no intention of infringement of the trademark.

The use in this publication of trade names, trademarks, service marks, and similar terms, even if they are not identified as such, is not to be taken as an expression of opinion as to whether or not they are subject to proprietary rights.

While the advice and information in this book are believed to be true and accurate at the date of publication, neither the authors nor the editors nor the publisher can accept any legal responsibility for any errors or omissions that may be made. The publisher makes no warranty, express or implied, with respect to the material contained herein.

Managing Director, Apress Media LLC: Welmoed Spahr
Acquisitions Editor: Todd Green
Development Editor: James Markham
Coordinating Editor: Jill Balzano

Cover designed by eStudioCalamar

Cover image designed by Freepik (www.freepik.com)

Distributed to the book trade worldwide by Springer Science+Business Media New York, 233 Spring Street, 6th Floor, New York, NY 10013. Phone 1-800-SPRINGER, fax (201) 348-4505, e-mail orders-ny@springer-sbm.com, or visit www.springeronline.com. Apress Media, LLC is a California LLC and the sole member (owner) is Springer Science + Business Media Finance Inc (SSBM Finance Inc). SSBM Finance Inc is a **Delaware** corporation.

For information on translations, please e-mail rights@apress.com, or visit http://www.apress.com/rights-permissions.

Apress titles may be purchased in bulk for academic, corporate, or promotional use. eBook versions and licenses are also available for most titles. For more information, reference our Print and eBook Bulk Sales web page at http://www.apress.com/bulk-sales.

Any source code or other supplementary material referenced by the author in this book is available to readers on GitHub via the book's product page, located at www.apress.com/9781484234587. For more detailed information, please visit http://www.apress.com/source-code.

Printed on acid-free paper

This book is dedicated to the isolated C.S. teacher and student.

Table of Contents

About the Author

Michael Stueben started teaching Fortran at Fairfax High School in Virginia in 1977. Eventually the high school computer science curriculum changed from Fortran to BASIC, Pascal, C, C++, Java, and finally to Python. In the last five years, Stueben taught artificial intelligence at Thomas Jefferson High School for Science and Technology in Alexandria, VA. Along the way, he wrote a regular puzzle column for *Discover Magazine*, published articles in *Mathematics Teacher* and *Mathematics Magazine*, published a book on teaching high school mathematics: *Twenty Years Before the Blackboard* (Mathematical Association of America, 1998). In 2006 he received a Distinguished High School Mathematics Teaching / Edyth May Sliffe Award from the Mathematical Association of America.

About the Technical Reviewer

Michael Thomas has worked in software development for over 20 years as an individual contributor, team lead, program manager, and Vice President of Engineering. Michael has over 10 years experience working with mobile devices. His current focus is in the medical sector using mobile devices to accelerate information transfer between patients and health care providers.

Acknowledgments

Sincere thanks go to the following people: programmer Stephen Drodge for reviewing an earlier draft of this book and for making many useful suggestions; programmer Michael Ames for reviewing an earlier draft of this book; Dr. Stuart Dreyfus (University of California, Berkeley) for his personal thoughts on dynamic programming; Dr. Dana Richards (George Mason University) for mathematical advice on algorithms and puzzles; Dr. James Stanlaw of Illinois State University for discussions of signs, symbols, and semiotics; neurobiologist Paul Cammer (the best teacher I ever met) for years of discussions of effective teaching; hundreds of bright students who accepted my sarcasm and returned it right back to me; my wonderful wife of 40 years, Diane Sandford, for editing several versions of this book; Apress technical reviewer Michael Thomas; Apress editors James Markham, Jill Balzano, and Todd Green for their help in bringing this book into print; and the web site Stack Overflow. Finally, I must thank my two colleagues and master teachers: Dr. Peter Gabor (who reviewed this manuscript and made many suggestions) and Dr. Shane Torbert (who created the A.I. course I taught), both for five years of intense discussions about algorithms. Any mistakes in this book are due to the author, not those who gave me good advice.

Introduction

> For the player who wants to get ahead, he has only
> one piece of advice: get to work. Not with generalities
> taken from books, but in the struggle with concrete
> [chess] positions.—Willy Hendriks, *Move First, Think
> Later* (New in Chess, 2012), page 20.

THIS BOOK IS ABOUT improving coding skills and learning how to write readable code. It is written both for teachers and developing programmers. But I must immediately tell you that we learn how to write computer code only by trying to code many challenging problems, reflecting on the experience, and remembering the lessons we learned. Hence, you will find here more than twenty quizzes and problems. Chess coach Willy Hendriks is right: There is no other way.

INTRODUCTION

I have spent more than 38 years both writing computer code and thinking about how to write code effectively.[1] I can't remember the last time I had a serious bug that I couldn't defeat—eventually. So what is the difference between myself and a novice? Part of it is that I notice details well, and I can stay focused for long periods of time. I can't pass that on to anyone, but I can show you some tricks gleaned from reading experts, talking to fellow programmers, and from analyzing my own mistakes. These tricks are guaranteed to reduce frustrations and failures. [2]

---

[1] I left Northern Illinois University in 1974 as a math major with just two C.S. courses behind me (COBOL and Fortran). Both classes employed optical card readers used with the University's IBM 360/370 computer. It often took 15 minutes of standing in line for the card-punch machine in order to change a single comma. At times there were no seats left in the computer room. I got tired of coding at midnight. The experience was so unpleasant that I vowed never to take another C.S. course. What got me interested in programming—actually the first time—was a TI programmable calculator with magnetic strips for memory. My first program would factor large integers, which I used for recreational mathematics. I started teaching Fortran at Fairfax High School (Virginia) in 1977. The school had three terminals (remotely connected) for the entire class. I tried to give each student about 10 minutes a week on a keyboard. Surprisingly, even under those conditions, some students became addicted to coding. Occasionally I found a student hiding under the tables after school so that he could program for hours after I locked up the room.

Later the H.S. curriculum changed from Fortran to BASIC, Pascal, C, C++, Java, and finally to Python. I discovered that I could not work in two languages at the same time. After six months with Python, I had forgotten my five years of Java. Python is definitely the most fun, with C/C++ second. COBOL was the worst, with Java the second worst. In fact, I think the Java language has discouraged many high school teachers from teaching C.S.

[2] "Essentially every approach works for a small project. Worse, it seems that essentially every approach—however ill-conceived and however cruel to the individuals involved—also works for a large project, provided you are willing to throw indecent amounts of time and money at the problem."—Bjarne Stroustrup, *The C++ Programming Language*, 2nd Ed., (Addison Wesley, 1991), page 385.

The computer code in this book is written in the Python language, which is almost executable pseudo-code. It comes with batteries, as they say. For example, consider the Python min function:

```
print(min(3,5)) # output: 3
```

Most languages have a min function. But look what Python's min can do:

```
paths = [[7,1,1], [5,1,3]]
print(min(paths))              # output: [5,1,3], because 5 < 7
print(min(paths, key = sum)) # output: [7,1,1], because 7+1+1 <
                                                          5+1+3
```

NOTE TO READER: The code examples appearing in this book (62 characters per line) were taken from programs with 80 characters per line. Consequently, some of the longer lines were broken into two (usually indented) lines. This affects their readability in a few cases, but has kept the type larger and easier to scan.

In Python, you can pass a function as a parameter to another function. Why would anyone want to do that? Imagine that you wrote several different functions, each using a different algorithm, to solve the same problem. Then you wrote a test function to test each algorithm. You could change the name of each of your functions, one at a time, to the name the test function expects to call. Or you could just pass the function name as a parameter and not have to change any code, which is much easier. Below is an example.[3]

```
def fn1():
    print('Hello:    ', end ='')
    return (1)
```

---

[3]Alas, if the different algorithms have different function signatures then this method fails—e.g., the bubble sort, the selection sort, and the insertion sort all pass just the array. But the recursive quick sort passes the array *and* the position of the first and last elements.

```python
def fn2():
    print('Goodbye: ', end ='')
    return(2)

def test(func):
    print('testing', func.__name__, 'Output =', func())

def main():
    print('In program',__file__) # output: In program C:\test.py
    test(fn1)                     # output: Hello:   testing fn1
                                  #                  Output = 1

    test(fn2)                     # output: Goodbye: testing fn2
                                  #                  Output = 2
```

In Python, you can make multiple assignments in one line and can do a swap in one line.

```python
a, b, c  = 1, 2, 3 # multiple assignment
a, b = b, a        # swap
```

A list (array) in Python can simultaneously hold different data types. A function can return more than one parameter. The last element in a list has index -1. The second-to-last element has index -2, etc. How convenient is that?[4] The extremely useful associative-array concept exists in Python as a built-in data structure called a "dictionary." The quick sort as shown below can be written in two logical lines. OK, five printed lines, but they are easy-to-understand lines.

```python
def quickSort(array):
    if len(array) <= 1: return array
    return   quickSort([x for x in array[1:] if x <  array[0]]) \
           + [array[0]]                                         \
           + quickSort([x for x in array[1:] if x >= array[0]])
```

---

[4]This attribute can be a problem. I once ran a loop that moved backwards through a list. When it went past 0, the out-of-range error was not caught, because it just started at over at the end.

My point is that the language of Python is nearly ideal for developing algorithms. The main drawback is speed. The language is interpreted, not compiled. But only with graphics have I encountered a speed problem with Python.

You may not understand Python. I have looked at books written in languages that I didn't understand, and (if the code was not too long or too complex) I still understood the main ideas for algorithms. So I'm hoping you can do the same. Let's find out. Consider a function to raise a positive integer to a power. For example, power(5, 23) = 5**23 = 11920928955078125. Of course, there is a built-in function (pow) and a built-in operator (**) in Python to do this for us. But those won't help us in the application I have in mind. Can you understand the following code? I wrote it in two versions.

```python
def power(base, exponent):
    product = 1
    for n in range(exponent):
        product *= base
    return product

def powr(b, exp):
    x = 1
    for n in range(exp):
        x *= b
    return x
```

If you can understand this code, then you can follow much of the code in this book. By the way, there are already a few lessons to be learned here.

1. In my opinion, the second version is easier to understand than the first version. Short identifiers—with obvious meaning—for short scope are more readable than longer identifiers, which are better for function names, class names, and variables in complex code.

2. The reason pow would be a poor function name is because the function would overwrite the built-in pow function of the same name, *for the entire program*. The reason exp is acceptable is because it overwrites the built-in exp function only for the short scope of the function. Good names are sometimes hard to find. Believe it or not, I have had students name their programs random and one student named his program print. Then they were confused when, under Linux, their random and print functions failed to work.

For almost any application, this four-line power function would be ideal. But it could be much more efficient. Again, consider 5**23 = 11920928955078125. We don't need 22 multiplications to do the arithmetic. Notice that we can break up 5**23 like this:

5 * (5*5) * (5*5*5*5) * (5*5*5*5*5*5*5*5*5*5*5*5*5*5*5*5) = 5**23,

and like this:

5 *   5**2   *   5**4   *   5**16   = 5**23,

where the exponents (1, 2, 4, and 16) add up to 23. (Recall $x^a \times x^b = x^{a+b}$.)

Once we calculate a = 5*5, it takes only one more multiplication to produce b = a*a. Then only one more multiplication to produce c = b*b. And only one more multiplication to produce d = c*c. Altogether we can produce 5**23 in only 7 multiplications: (5*a*b*d). The trick is to write the exponent 23 as a binary number: 23 (base 10) = 11101 (base 2). Then multiply each digit (in reverse order) by the base (5 here) raised to a power of 2:

1*(5) * 1*(5**2) * 1*(5**4) * 1*(5**16) = 5**23.

You might try to write this function now, in your own preferred language. The hills make us strong, as they say in cycling. But you may be too busy, and the exercise probably seems both complex and pointless. Who would want such a function anyway? But in a situation we will see later, this binary-jumping type of multiplication will significantly speed up a function. So for the time being I will give you a pass in writing this algorithm. My eight-line solution follows. Python, of course, has built-in features to change an integer into a binary string and to reverse the characters in a string. No wonder people like to code in Python.

```python
def powr(b, exp):
    binStng = str(bin(exp))[2:] # Change integer exp to a
    binary string.
    revStng = reversed(binStng) # Reverse the digits (alt. =
    binStng[::-1]).
    product  = 1
    for ch in revStng:
        if ch == '1':
            product *= b
        b *= b
    return product
```

If you don't know Python, the first two lines will be a mystery, hence the comments. If you do know Python, you still may learn something new and useful in those two lines. The loop should be clear to anyone who has worked with for loops.

I've been programming for nearly four decades, and had written a variation of this function about a month previously. Nevertheless, it took me nine runs to get this function working. (I had placed b *= b above the if statement, and it took me a while to realize the order mattered.) I mention this to make the point that most programmers, certainly the author, fail to write correct code in the first few attempts.

Before we leave this introduction, I want to give you three quizzes that will tell you what this book is all about.

QUIZ 1.

```
# If we optimize the one-line BODY of this for-loop, then
# what is the MINIMUM number of multiplications necessary?
# Do NOT use an exponential operator (**). Do NOT use a built-
# in power function. You MUST use the symbol * to indicate
# multiplication.
#
    total = 0
    for n in range(1, 3000000):
        total += (2*n*n*n + 3*n*n + 4*n) # <--Improve this line.
    print('total =', total)
#------------------------------------------------------------------
```

The answer is at the end of this chapter, but try to solve it now. Passive reading will not take you far. One of my colleagues (the amazing Ria Galanos) was asked the following question in a Google summer interview:

QUIZ 2. Given x, an *unsorted* list of the first 100 positive integers, one of the integers is replaced by 0: x[randint(1,100)] = 0. Write the code—any way you want—to print the missing (replaced) integer. A solution is in the footnote.[5]

---

[5]QUIZ 2 ANSWER: **print(5050-sum(x))**. Where did the 5050 come from? That is the sum of the first 100 positive integers. We can compute this number in our heads. 1+100 = 101, 2+99 = 101, 3+98 = 101, ... 50+51 = 101 (a trick worth remembering). Then, 50* 101 = 5050. I later found this problem in Peter Winkler's *Mathematical Puzzles—A Connoisseur's Collection* (A.K. Peters, 2004), page 102. P.S. She got the job.

There are three main cultures of coding.[6] The people in these cultures all use computers, yet they rarely interact with each other. Perhaps you can tell now which one most interests you.

1. **The software developer (industry)**, who works with libraries of previously developed code to produce new software tools, who devises schemes to manage complexity in software programs, who determines what features make programming tools more useful, or more fun (games), etc.

2. **The computer scientist (theory)**, who develops and analyzes algorithms, who studies the syntax and semantics of computer languages, who designs efficient storage and retrieval strategies, who determines what can be computed efficiently, etc.

3. **The computational scientist (problem solving in other fields)**, who uses the computer as a scientific tool in modeling and simulations, as a way to visualize spatial and temporal patterns, as way to solve equations, as a way to efficiently organize, search, and find patterns in data, etc.

In this book there are references to all three cultures. Most beginners focus on just learning a language, learning data structures, and building coding-specific problem-solving skills. What is missing is learning to write readable code. In my experience, readability is difficult to teach well in both high school and college courses. There are reasons for this, which I will give you later. But I would like you to compare your ability to write

---

[6]Brian Hayes, "Cultures of Code", *American Scientist*, Vol. 103, No. 1, January–February, 2015, pages 10–13. This article is also on the Internet.

readable code with mine. Imagine we are the last two candidates for a summer coding job. The interviewer gives us the following assignment:

QUIZ 3. If I take a 52-card deck and I shuffle it well, then what is the probability that at least one card remains in place?[7] Solve this problem by computer simulation[8] (here, sampling) in your favorite language. That is, shuffle 1,000,000 sorted arrays and determine what percentage of them have at least one element remaining in place. Express this number as a probability. Be sure to make your code as readable as possible. Bring me your code tomorrow morning. I'll have one of our programmers look at your two programs and tell me whose code he prefers.

Quiz 3 is the most important quiz in this book. If you attempt no other problem in this book, try to write this short program—and a complete program is expected, not just a function. My code follows, with notes as to why I made some design decisions. Before you compare your code to mine, what can you tell me about the programmer who will judge our code? My answer is in the footnote.[9]

How would you answer this interview question: "So, what will you do this summer if you don't get this job?" My suggested answer-to-impress is in the footnote.[10]

---

[7]This is known as Montmort's Matching Problem. See Isaac Todhunter, *Theory of Probability* (London: Macmillan, 1865), (Chelsea Reprint, 1965), page 91 (online). Curiously, for a deck of any number of cards greater than 5 the answer is almost the same.

[8]*Tech. Note. Wikipedia* states that a **computer model** is the set of algorithms capturing the essence of a process or system, and that a **computer simulation** is the running of those algorithms. That being said, the terms *simulation* and *model* are often interchanged in both writing and speaking. Random sampling to obtain numerical approximations by ratios is called the **Monte Carlo Method.**

[9]He wants someone who pays attention to detail, who has some maturity in his/her coding skills, and who wants this job so much that the candidate will try to impress the code reviewer. Will your code show this?

[10]"I'll have to go back to reading computer books and working problems on my own. I would much rather gain some experience this summer by working in industry."

QUIZ 3 ANSWER.

```
"""+==========+=========-========*========-========+==========+
   ||                 A SHUFFLING PROBLEM                    ||
   ||            by M. Stueben (October 8, 2017)             ||
   ||      Interview Question, Mr. Jones, XYZ Corporation    ||
   ||                                                        ||
   || Description: By computer stimulation this program      ||
   ||              determines the probability of a deck of   ||
   ||              52 cards having at least one unmoved card ||
   ||              element after shuffling. (Answer: 0.63,   ||
   ||              rounded.)                                 ||
   ||                                                        ||
   || Language:  Python Ver. 3.4                             ||
   || Graphics:  None                                        ||
   || Downloads: None                                        ||
   || Run time:  Approx. 43 seconds for 1,000,000 runs of a  ||
   || 52-element array.                                      ||
   +========================================================+
"""

#####################<START OF PROGRAM>###################
def printHeading():
    print('                    A SHUFFLING PROBLEM')
    print('                    (currently calculating)')
#-------------------------------------------------------------

def shuffleArrays():
    totalArrays = 0 # Arrays with at least one unmoved element
    after shuffling.
    for trial in range(TRIAL_RUNS):
        array = list(range(LIST_SIZE))
        shuffle(array)
```

```python
        for num in range(LIST_SIZE):
            if array[num] == num:
                totalArrays += 1
                break
    probability = round(totalArrays/TRIAL_RUNS, 2)
    return probability
#------------------------------------------------------------

def printResult(probability):
    print('   Result:', probability ,'is the probability of an
    array having at')
    print('   least one unmoved element after shuffling. This
    is based')
    print('   on a computer simulation with an array size =',
    LIST_SIZE, 'and')
    print('  ', TRIAL_RUNS, 'trial runs.')
#============<GLOBAL CONSTANTS and GLOBAL IMPORTS>=============

from random import shuffle
TRIAL_RUNS = 1000000
LIST_SIZE  =       52
assert LIST_SIZE > 1, 'LIST_SIZE must be greater than 1.'
#=============================================================

def main():
    printHeading()
    probability = shuffleArrays()
    printResult(probability)
#------------------------------------------------------------
```

```
if __name__ == '__main__':
    from time import clock; START_TIME = clock();main();
    print('\n    '+'- '*12);
    print('   PROGRAM RUN TIME:%6.2f'%(clock()-START_TIME),
    'seconds.');
##################<END OF PROGRAM>###########################
```

Output:

```
                A SHUFFLING PROBLEM
                (currently calculating)
Result: 0.63 is the probability of an array having at
least one unmoved element after shuffling. This is based
on a computer simulation with an array size = 52 and
1000000 trial runs.


- - - - - - - - - - - - -

PROGRAM RUN TIME:  43 seconds.
```

What was I thinking when I wrote this code?

1. The pretty box, the centering, the vertical alignment are all just window dressing. Is this fancy stuff necessary? Like it or not, looks matter.

2. The minimum information is a title, your name, the date, and a program description. The other information in the box is optional, but shows attention to detail. I want to look like I am trying to impress the interviewer.

3. There are no spelling, punctuation, or grammatical errors (important). I used complete sentences in both the description and the program output.

4. This program is so simple, why not place all of the code in the main function? Two reasons: 1) major code chunks need descriptive, self-documenting names, and 2) the main function is expected to be mostly a list of calls to other functions (stepwise refinement).

5. Comments are almost unnecessary, because the code is self-documented and well organized. Docstrings in a program this short are unnecessary. Still, some interviewers may expect them in an interview program.

6. The variable names are descriptive. Over-abbreviation, to save a few keystrokes, was avoided. In particular `array` was used, not `a` or `arr`.

7. The output is well-labeled.

8. The two constants are in all caps.

9. The import and global constants are placed above the main function. It is usual to place them at the top of the program in large commercial programs. In extremely small programs I think they are better placed above the main function.

10. An `assert` is used to catch ridiculous cases. Error traps should be common in student code.

11. The indenting is everywhere consistent: 4 spaces.

12. Some output is printed immediately. I do not want the user to stare at an empty screen for 43 seconds and wonder if the program is running.

13. The following two lines could have been combined into one line, but then the descriptive variable `probability` would not be part of the code.

```
probability = round(totalArrays/TRIAL_RUNS, 2)
return probability
```

14. The run-time is printed. (Every program I write prints its run time.) Some text editors and IDEs automatically print the runtime. That is how important this statistic is.

15. The answer is correct.

Did you learn anything? Readability is a hot topic with conflicting opinions. What you are used to seeing will look more readable than what I am used to seeing. But it is always good to know how other people think, even if we disagree. I hope that I have interested you in reading the rest of the book. If not, at least start the next chapter. Much of this book is text, not code. Good luck.

> Documentation and readability are as important to software quality in the long run as speed of creation, correct functioning, and performance are in the short run.—L. Peter Deutsch, (ACM Fellow), Found on the Internet (ACM SigSoft, Software Engineering Notes, Vol. 24, Issue 1, January, 1999).

* * *

QUIZ 1 ANSWER: `total += ((n+n + 3)*n + 4)*n`. (Only <u>two</u> multiplications are necessary.) Here are some running times (of repeated calls) for six different versions:

1. `2*n*n*n + 3*n*n + 4*n` -->. . . . . . .1.09 seconds (original)

2. $((n+n+3)*n+4)*n$ -->. 0.76
    seconds   (<u>fastest</u>)

3. n*((n + n + 1) * (n + 1) + 3)-->....0.86
    seconds. (2nd fastest)

4. ((n+n)*n + (n+n+n))*n + n+n+n+n --> 1.39
    seconds. (also two stars)

5. 2*n**3 + 3*n**2 + 4*n -->. 2.85
    seconds. (poor)

6. 2*pow(n,3) + 3*pow(n,2) + 4*n --> . 3.23
    seconds. (worst)

For non-Python people, please excuse this digression into the Python language. When I showed my powr function to my colleague Peter Gabor, he suggested the following improvements:

```python
def powr1(b, exp):
    myPowr = 1
    while exp > 0:
        myPowr *= ((~exp)&1) or b
        b *= b
        exp >>= 1  # Shift one bit right.
    return myPowr
```

Explanation: The Python tilde (pronounced TIL-da) operator (~) is a bitwise operator. The expression ~x is the same as -(x+1). It is only employed here because it will flip the right-most bit. The expression (~exp)&1 is equivalent to the rightmost bit of ~exp. The expression ((~exp)&1) or b will be either 1 or b. In Python the or operator returns the value of the last expression evaluated, not True or False. His powr1 function can also be written like this:

```python
def powr2(b, exp):
    myPowr = 1
    while exp > 0:
        if exp%2 == 1:     # An odd exp means right-most bit is 1.
            myPowr *= b
        b *= b
        exp //= 2
    return myPowr
```

Or even like this (a form I would not want to debug):

```python
def powr3(b, exp):
    return (not exp) or ((powr3(b, exp >> 1)**2) * (((~exp)&1)
    or b))
```

PART I

Not Learned in School

CHAPTER 1

A Coding Fantasy

ONCE UPON A TIME, a talented young programmer was in a situation where he did not have the resources to seek more education. He had a dead-end job that would never allow any promotion. Further, his family could not help him, and he lived in a decaying and unsafe part of town. Our programmer had four friends who had developed similar programming skills and who also felt limited by their opportunities. They were all slightly depressed and worried about their futures.

Suddenly, the five programmers discovered an amazing opportunity. If they could team up and write a particular computer application, then the attention they would receive would immediately open doors for better jobs.

Of course, anyone in this situation would want to attempt to write the application. But it was not so simple. Previously, the most challenging program each of them had written took three weeks of time at 1-2 hours a day. Most of the time was spent in debugging. Some of those bugs were so difficult to track down that they had twice given up on their programs, only to come back to them out of curiosity. In fact, those three weeks of time were actually spread over six weeks. They all had the same experience.

Upon reviewing the work for this new project, it appeared that the job naturally could be divided into five equal parts. The problem was that each part was five times longer than anything any one of them had worked on before. They had 40 weeks to finish the project. In theory, if all could stay focused, that was more than enough time to finish. But in practice, the complexity was beyond what anyone thought he or she could

© Michael Stueben 2018
M. Stueben, *Good Habits for Great Coding*, https://doi.org/10.1007/978-1-4842-3459-4_1

do. The tantalizing prize was also an invitation to failure. Briefly each thought that the quiet go-nowhere life they were currently living might be preferable to 40 weeks of misery that almost certainly would lead to failure. Who needed that? Maybe something else would come along. Eventually in conversation, the five friends realized that this defeatist thinking is a common reason why people do not climb out of their poor situations in life. Yet, as each one currently understood the project, it was too difficult for them to complete. If they could increase the likelihood of success, then it might be worth a try. So, what to do?

First, the five programmers had to accept the fact that they would have to turn themselves into programming robots. Many of the pleasures that were part of their everyday lives would have to be replaced with hours of coding. This would require a change of both habits and perspective on life. Could they do this? The prize dangling in front of them just might be enough.

The real problem was debugging. Although all parts of the code seemed reasonable enough, there were so many parts that debugging problems would arise en masse. They didn't see how any one of them could be successful. Then someone suggested a solution: For almost every key function written, a companion function could be written to test that function. After each session of coding, the testing functions would be run. Another program would import most of the important functions and run several sets of data through each function. The data would test, for example, almost every **if** statement in a function.

This meant that if a redesign occurred, the functions adversely affected would be flagged immediately. Writing two functions for every one function needed in the application would be extra work, but the testing functions would be simple to write, and mostly similar to each other. This scheme, called *unit testing*, seemed to offer hope.

Another member suggested that the group get together every week to read each other's code, to discuss problems, and to suggest solutions coming from fresh eyes. In these *code reviews* they would share both problems and hard-learned solutions. Another suggestion was to document almost every key function with an English description (*docstrings*), so that any of the other members could more easily follow the code. Another suggestion was that they should occasionally try to work in pairs (*pair programming*): one typing and the other thinking about what is being typed.

The group felt that their only chance at success was to adopt these conventions. One of the members later described working with these conventions as writing code in a straightjacket.

Soon after the coding began, the members noticed that progress was slow but steady. The inevitable redesigns, usually based on overlooked special cases and poorly chosen data structures, almost always caused a domino effect of other changes. These changes were all quickly noticed and located by unit testing.

The members also began discussing small differences in coding styles—e.g., should one write

```
if (x and y) == True: print(x)
```

or

```
if x and y: print(x)?
```

Because of differing opinions, they decided to vote on a group style and stick to the group's decision. Eventually, their conventions, which were often arbitrary, began to look correct and any different convention looked wrong. Because the same style was used by everyone, they all became efficient at reading code written in their *shop style*.

To make a long story short, their combination of sacrifices, commitment, and good decisions about writing code enabled them to complete the project and win a better life. Eventually, they were hired by employers seeking expert programmers.

Their new employers appreciated the members of this group for several reasons. First, the programmers had put so much of their lives into writing code that their skills were excellent. They wrote code quickly and with few bugs. They understood their language, and used its constructs efficiently. Second, and just as important, their code was easily readable by anyone else. Third, they were flexible. They adopted the current house style in coding, even when they personally preferred to write code differently.

In some of the companies where these coders worked, there were layoffs. Our five original coders were never let go. As one employer said, "They always give more than is expected. Who would let an employee like that go?"

Years passed and they all retired from the business of writing code. One of the younger programmers was a little bored. He missed the coding experience, but was too old to return to full-time work. His spouse noticed that the neighboring high school needed a part-time teacher for a single one-semester class of advanced programming. He took the job.

The previous teacher expected the students to understand different algorithms and build their programming skills by correctly implementing the algorithms in computer code. The old programmer-turned-replacement teacher agreed, and realized that many of the conventions that were necessary for success in business would not apply to students writing small programs. Still, he thought, writing code that was readable was something that should be taught along with algorithms, language instructions, and data structures. Halfway through the course, he had lectured on and had posted the following guidelines.

Advice for Developing Programmers (pain management)

1. Limit functions to a single task, or to simple and highly related tasks (cohesion vs. coupling).

2. Label and align your output.

3. Document your programs at the top: name, date, class period (maybe course and instructor), title, and program description. Watch your spelling, grammar, and punctuation.

4. Code with line numbers and never indent less than three spaces.

5. Use vertical alignment in your code if it will emphasize significant relationships.

6. Do not use Python language names (reserved words and built-in names) for identifiers or file names— e.g., `random`, `max`, `print`, `factorial`, etc.

7. Refactor (= redesign) your programs after they work to be more readable. This is when and how program design is learned.

8. Use step-wise refinement: function calls that outline your program's work. Limit the `main()` function to calls to other functions. In short programs you may add initialization and maybe some output lines to the `main` function.

9. Write self-documenting code (descriptive identifiers, usually verb-object function names) and thereby minimize comments. Avoid over-abbreviating identifiers to save typing a few letters.

10. Always print the runtime, and perhaps some other statistics, for every program.

11. Avoid magic numbers, unless they make the code significantly simpler to work with.

12. Avoid global variables, but global constants are acceptable.

13. Do *not* write clever code (code that doesn't immediately look like what it does), when simpler code will do.

14. Choose readability over both optimization for speed and optimization for memory use.

15. Anticipate bugs by using defensive measures (asserts, error traps, **try/except** blocks, and intermediate prints). Just don't overdo it.

16. Test every key function upon completion. Consider untested code to be broken code.

17. For a complicated algorithm, consider writing some simple tests *before* you write the code, not *after* you write the code.

* * *

18. Do not start on the next assignment or function until you have finished the previous one.

19. When coding, you need total focus. Avoid the chatty classmate. (The purpose of sometimes isolating yourself is to force you to solve problems on your own. Do not become dependent upon your classmates.)

20. Save every assignment on at least two different physical devices.

* * *

21. Write some code every week. Do not regress. You may have to push yourself.

22. Spend time with smart people and try to get them to talk shop.

23. Read the code of other programmers.

24. Learn programming tools on your own: a sophisticated editor, language idioms and tricks, built-in functions, and data structures.

25. Come to your problems with a history of attempting challenging problems.

26. Try hard to avoid cheating.

27. Do not let grades and outside activities sabotage your education. You, not the school, are responsible for your learning.

Unfortunately, the list was not only ignored, it was disputed by the students. He overheard many disparaging comments:

> "I don't see why my code must be readable to others when is it readable to me and nobody else will ever read it. Getting the program to work was hard enough. I need time for other classes."

> "I can't believe he asked us not to write clever code. Is he trying to stifle us?"

> "I think my code is descriptive enough. He is being too picky asking for better descriptors."

> "The other C.S. teacher is not so picky. I wish I were in her class."

> "My code is exactly like Paul's because we worked together. He is always saying we need to help each other. He better not say I cheated."

> "He tells us to help each other, but not to get help. That makes no sense."

"There are no errors in my program, so why did he want me to have error traps in my code?"

"My code works for my input. It doesn't work for his input, because he tests with weird data, like the empty set."

"I still don't understand how focusing on grades could adversely affect my education."

"Why should we learn the tools on our own time? Shouldn't he teach them to us?"

"There are lots of programs on the Internet that don't follow his rules. So, who does he think he is?"

The old programmer was sensitive enough to eventually realize that the classroom atmosphere had gone from enthusiasm to dislike. Consequently, he changed his priorities. Only a few short programs would be checked for style. The others were accepted if they worked. The assignments became shorter and easier. He praised the students for simple successes. He started most classes with an interesting YouTube video, and allowed lively discussions to go on, even when they robbed the class of practice time. In the end the students were amazed at how much the teacher had improved. Several students gave the teacher parting notes and small gifts.

Just before the end of the school year, he reflected over what had happened. The ideas, habits, and perspectives that he was trying to pass on to the students were just beyond them. They were quick in picking up details, but did not have the maturity or motivation to appreciate any sort of big picture. Years ago, he and his friends were forced to change themselves by desperation. Teaching their kind of meta-thinking could not be done by talking. It had to be experienced in some manner to be believed. He did, however, leave them with a warning. He told them the following story.

THE OLD PROGRAMMER'S STORY

Students, something amazing happened to me last night, and I want to share it with you. I talked with God. Yes, that's right God visited me. Admittedly, He came to me in a dream, but I know it was God. And we talked about your futures. Not for all of you, but for many of you. And I want to tell you what the future holds for you. Your futures are going to be wonderful. You are going to go to college, graduate, and find a nice job. You will have a number of interesting vacations and adventures before you meet your significant other. You'll get a nice house, enjoy your job, have some great kids, and enjoy good health. You are going to have the kinds of futures that everyone wants to have. And I thought I should tell you now, while you're young, just how great your futures will be—at least until about the age of 45.

At that time you will be fired from your job. Not for anything you did wrong. It is just that businesses change and merge. The employment sector is in constant flux. Since you did not stand out in your profession, you were let go.

Naturally you tried to find another job. After all, you had years of experience. Unfortunately, the coding shops preferred to hire young programmers whom they did not have to pay as much. The different managements felt that after a few years the younger programmers would have almost as much experience as the older programmers anyway. The younger programmers might become great programmers, whereas you had only been an average programmer. So you went on many interviews and never got a job offer. That meant your spouse was supporting the family. You stayed home most days and did the chores. The vacations were cut, summer camps for the kids were canceled, electronic devices could not be upgraded, and when the main TV broke, your family moved the little TV in from the den to the living room. Any money that you spent on yourself was immediately noticed and harshly criticized. Your spouse did not expect this austere lifestyle when he or she married you. Resentment led to arguments. Your spouse criticized you in front of the children, who also began to lose respect for you. Your family relationships were becoming toxic. Finally, your spouse filed for divorce and asked you to move out.

In the divorce, you got some money for the house and from your joint savings, but your spouse got the kids—you couldn't support them. Eventually your money ran out and you ended up taking a cleaning job just to pay for your rent and food. You began to get depressed and started to take comfort in the cheap euphoria of drink. You didn't become an alcoholic, but you drank every day. Several years later you happened to look into a mirror and noticed that you looked older than you should. You had a tooth missing and couldn't afford to replace it. You looked up towards the ceiling and said, "Why did this happen to me? What did I do to end up like this?" Suddenly, you heard a sound behind you and noticed some movement in the mirror. You turned around and, guess what, you happened to see me, your old computer science teacher.

"Mr. S., I thought you died years ago. What are you doing here?"

"I did die years ago. But now I have become an instrument of the cosmic forces. And I am here to help you out of your predicament."

"I can't believe my luck," you say. "Are you going to find me a good job so that I can support a family and get my self-respect back?"

"No, the cosmic forces don't work that way."

"Then are you going to give me money?"

"No, the cosmic forces don't work that way either."

"Well then what? How are you going to help me?"

"First of all, I want to tell you how you got yourself in this predicament. You sinned by being average. You never stood out. You didn't study any more than you needed to get by. You did just the minimum of what was asked. You didn't try to learn new skills. You didn't try to improve your current skills, because you didn't have to. When potential employers called your old employer, all the management could do was to verify your previous employment. They had nothing really good to say about you. No wonder you were the first to be fired and are the last to be re-hired. Once you understand that, then there is hope for success"

"Ok," you say. "That seems true enough. In my defense, I never thought my future would come to this. I thought average was good enough. And I had other interests outside of work. I didn't want to become a workaholic. But OK, I've learned my lesson. Just get me out of this life."

"Have you learned your lesson? Well, we'll find out. I'm going to rewind time and send you back to when you were in my class. You will forget about your future, except for this short story of your life, which I am telling you now. I am like the ghost of Christmas future. The future is not fixed, or else I would not be telling you this. Your warning is to be better than average. Always continue to learn more and improve your skills. Always give more than is expected, in your job, and in your personal relationships. Yet, know this: You will not get another chance. Good luck."

The students thought the story was cute, and they appreciated a teacher who could entertain them. Most of them soon forgot the story. Only a few were bothered by it. For them, the story supported what they had already come to believe: That terrible traps lay in their futures—traps in jobs, traps in marriages, and even traps for the children that eventually they would try to protect. He never knew it, but the old programmer had done all that was possible for his students.

CHAPTER 2

Coding Tricks

> Mastering the skill of analyzing [chess positions]
> requires a massive amount of practice and hard
> work. But once you get it down, you will not regret
> the investment.—Joel Johnson (U.S. chess master)
> *Formation Attacks* (privately published, 2010), page 15.

THIS CHAPTER will take a simple—almost trivial—function and write it in 12 different ways. Most of these tricks are not taught in school. You need to learn them on your own.

DEFINITION: The Fibonacci[1] numbers are numbers in a sequence that begins 1, 1, ... and thereafter each new number is the sum of the previous two numbers. Following are the first 17 Fibonacci numbers:

```
+----------------------------------------------------------------------------+
| Fibonacci numbers: 1, 1, 2, 3, 5, 8, 13, 21, 34, 55, 89, 144, 233, 377, 610, 987, 1597 |
| The nth position   1  2  3  4  5  6   7   8   9  10  11   12   13   14   15   16    17 |
+----------------------------------------------------------------------------+
```

Here, the 1000th Fibonacci number is 4346655...228875 (209 digits). Sometimes this sequence is initially indexed at zero, and sometimes it

---

[1] I believe the preferred pronunciation is FEE buh naht chee, but this has been Anglicized to an acceptable FIB uh naht chee. My source is the useful *Webster's New Biographical Dictionary* (Merriam-Webster).

© Michael Stueben 2018
M. Stueben, *Good Habits for Great Coding*, https://doi.org/10.1007/978-1-4842-3459-4_2

begins with the initial value of zero. If you asked a beginning programmer to write a function to print the nth Fibonacci number, he\she would probably write a simple iteration function like this:

```
def fibA(num): # This function took 7.45 seconds to find
                  the 1000th
                  # Fibonacci number 100,000 times in Python
                  Ver. 3.4.
    if num < 3:
       return 1
    a = b = 1
    for i in range(2, num):
        a, b = b, a+b
    return b
```

If you asked the same programmer to solve the problem recursively, the result would be something like the function fibB below.

```
def fibB(num): # Too slow.
    if num < 3:
       return 1
    return fibB(num-1) + fibB(num-2)
```

This is the only function in this collection of Fibonacci functions that is too slow for practical work. It may appear that the only justification for fibB is to introduce recursion to beginners. Not so. It can also serve as an example of a poor way to do recursion. If the recursion were done better (fibH shown later or maybe by using a memorizing decorator, also shown later), it would be much faster.

You might say fibB is the worst function in this collection. It is also the simplest function. So we have learned two ways to evaluate functions: by speed and by simplicity. How many other ways are there? At least four more ways. We will return to this question later.

The fibB function took 313.48 seconds (5 minutes, 13 seconds) just to calculate the 45th Fibonacci number one time. I am interested in calculating the 1000th Fibonacci number one-hundred thousand times. Of course, to make fibB faster, we could provide more base cases. Introducing a look-up table is a standard trick in programming. In Python sometimes it can be done with the clever indexing method shown below.

```
def fibBB(num): # Still too slow to compare.
    if num < 18:
        return [0,1,1,2,3,5,8,13,21,34,55,89,144,233,377,610,
                987,1597,][num]#17 base cases
    return fibBB(num-1) + fibBB(num-2)
```

The 313.45 seconds are reduced to about a half second in fibBB. Unfortunately, the fibBB function took 51.08 seconds just to calculate the 55th Fibonacci number: still too slow. Read and check all technical material closely. Did you notice the 17 base cases required 18 numbers?

We can improve the twins fibB and fibBB by introducing a dynamic (changing) look-up table. This is called **memoization**. Although memoization can speed up the recursion of overlapping subcases, this improved function (fibC) is still more than seven times slower than fibA (iteration). When the 17-base-case look-up table was appended, the time INCREASED (how strange) by almost 24% (from 57.11 seconds to 70.69 seconds). Coding ideas that sound good sometimes do not turn out that way.

```
def fibC(num, dict): # 57.11 seconds to find the 1000th
Fibonacci number
                    # 100,000 times.
    if num in dict:
        return dict[num]
    dict[num] = fibC(num-1, dict) + fibC(num-2, dict)
    return dict[num]
# The call to fibC looks like this: print(' C.', fibC(n,
{1:1, 2:1}))
```

The functions fibA and fibC are both examples of "dynamic programming," a difficult topic, which we will consider in the final chapter. Making the dictionary global in fibC saves us from passing the dictionary. Nevertheless, using a global dictionary does NOT decrease the speed, and global variables are to be avoided where possible. So, can we avoid passing the dictionary without a global variable? Yes. Python functions are classes; they have class variables.

```
def fibD(num): # 73.96 seconds.
    if num in fibD.dict:
        return fibD.dict[num]
    fibD.dict[num] = fibD(num-1) + fibD(num-2)
    return fibD.dict[num]
fibD.dict = {1:1, 2:1}
# A Python function's class variable must be declared BELOW the
# function.
```

Unfortunately, fibD is significantly slower than fibC, even though the fibD code is identical to the fibC code, except for fibC doing the extra work in passing an address. How is such a speed change, especially a time *increase*, possible? Evidently, accessing a class variable (fibD.dict) takes significantly more time than accessing either a global variable or a parameter (dict).

The design of fibD makes me uncomfortable, because we have a look-up table floating around in the code. Suppose they get separated? And looking at one function while trying to find one of its references reduces readability. My suggestion is to embed them together in another function. But the time is still slow. In fact, a nested function is always slower to execute than a non-nested function.

```
def fibE(num): # 76.35 seconds.
    def fib(num):
        if num in fib.dict:
            return fib.dict[num]
```

```
        fib.dict[num] = fib(num-1) + fib(num-2)
        return fib.dict[num]
    fib.dict = {1:1, 2:1}
    return (fib(num))
```

Can we do better? Yes by using a default value for the initial dictionary. This is a standard trick in programming. Remember it.

```
def fibF(num, dict = {1:1, 2:1}): # 59.99 seconds.
    if num in dict:
        return dict[num]
    dict[num] = fibF(num-1, dict) + fibF(num-2, dict)
    return dict[num]
```

Shouldn't there be an assert statement, something like this:

```
assert type(num) == int and num > 1, 'Bad data: num = ' + str(num)
```

Yes, but for these examples I have simplified the code.

Now I want to introduce a tricky concept: decorators. Recall the slow fibB.

```
def fibB(num): # Simple code, but too slow, or is it?.
    if num < 3: return 1
    return fibB(num-1) + fibB(num-2)
```

If only fibB had a memoization dictionary it would run dramatically faster, but that would complicate the code. So can we have it both ways? Well, almost. The designers of Python have introduced a way to do this without most of the disadvantages. Alas, the code will reside in two places. Here is how you do it.

```
def memoize(function):      # function = fibB.
    dict = {}               # This line is executed only
                              once.
```

```
    def wrapper(num):              # num came from fibB(num).
        if num not in dict:
            dict[num] = function(num)# The return of fibB is
                                     always to dict[num].
        return dict[num]           # The return is to function,
                                     except for final.
    return wrapper                 # This line  is executed
                                     only once.

@memoize
def fibB(num):
    if num < 3: return 1
    return fibB(num-1) + fibB(num-2)
```

This process is called "decorating a function." It not only saves us from introducing a new dictionary in every one-parameter function that needs memoization, but a decorator also simplifies the decorated function by extracting the memoization code. Unfortunately, the designers could not find a simple design for decorating a function. Programmers have to study and write many decorators to get a feel for what is going on.

Occasionally you may want to time a function. Why not just put @timer above the function's definition and pull this decorator up from your personal library?

```
def timer(function):
    from time import clock
    from sys  import setrecursionlimit; setrecursionlimit(100)
# default = 1000
    startTime = clock()
    def wrapper(*args, **kwargs):
        result = function(*args, **kwargs)
        return result
```

```
elapsedTime = round(clock()-startTime, 2)
print('-->', function.__name__ +"'s time =", elapsedTime,
'seconds.')
return wrapper
```

The `clock` could be imported elsewhere. The optional `setrecursionlimit` is sometimes useful for recursive functions. The (`*args, **kwargs`) means that any set of normal arguments and keyword arguments will be accepted. The `function.__name__` just pulls up the name of the function. So you see decorators can sometimes simplify code. Note well: 1) Recursive decorated functions seem to require much more recursion than if not decorated. 2) Decorators will not be used much in this book.

Having looked at several Fibonacci functions, we ask again if there is yet another way? What do you think of using formulas: No loops and no recursion? How did we overlook this? Formulas are both simple and fast.

```
def fibG(num):
    from math import sqrt
    phi1 = (1 + sqrt(5))/2
    phi2 = (1 - sqrt(5))/2
    return round((phi1**num - phi2**num) / sqrt(5))
# fibG(70) = 190392490709135
```

Hist. Note: These equations are called Binet's formulas, named after the French scholar who published them in 1843.[2] As an exercise, improve the speed of `fibG`. My version is in the footnote.[3]

---

[2]See Ross Honsberger's *Mathematical Gems II* (MAA, 1985), page 108.
[3]
```
def fibG(num): # Faster version
    from math import sqrt
    sqrt5 = sqrt(5) # Do not compute this number more than once.
    phi   = (1 + sqrt5)/2
    return round((phi**num)/sqrt5)
```

However, using formulas with floats to produce large numbers is a terrible idea, because floats are limited in precision, and therefore eventually will output INCORRECT values. Integers in Python are limited only by the available memory of the computer. Staying with integers, we can accurately generate the ten-millionth Fibonacci number, which has 2,089,877 digits. Computer arithmetic is not always the same as mathematical arithmetic for at least four reasons.

1. Computers—due to binary representation—only approximate floating point numbers:

```
print( (1/3) == 0.3333333333333333 ) # = True
print(1.0e+309)                        # = 'inf'
print(1.4/10)                          # = 0.1399
9999999999999
```

2. Past the limits of significant digits (16 digits (53 bits) in Python), computations can't be trusted:

```
print('2.0**53-1 =', 2.0**53-1) # = 2.0**53-1 =
9007199254740991.0
print('2.0**53-0 =', 2.0**53-0) # = 2.0**53-0 =
9007199254740992.0 (limit)
print('2.0**53+1 =', 2.0**53+1) # = 2.0**53+1 =
9007199254740992.0
```

3. Round-off errors accumulate:

```
print(0.1 + 0.1 + 0.1 == 0.3) # = False
print(0.1 + 0.1 + 0.1)        # = 0.3000000
0000000004
```

4. Rollover. In many languages, if you add 1 to the largest integer, it becomes a negative number with almost the same absolute value. This does not occur with Python integers. But this and other conveniences (mixed data types in lists) make Python slower than other languages.

Python does have a decimal format for large floats. Unfortunately, it is slow.

```
def fibGG(num): # 1153 seconds = 19 minutes and 13 seconds.
    from decimal import Decimal, getcontext
    from math import sqrt
    if num > 70:
        getcontext().prec = 2*num
    phi1 = (Decimal(1) + Decimal(5).sqrt())/Decimal(2)
    phi2 = (Decimal(1) - Decimal(5).sqrt())/Decimal(2)
    return round((phi1**Decimal(num) - phi2**Decimal(num)) /
            Decimal(5).sqrt())
```

At this point most people would probably choose fibA over the other functions, because it is easy to understand and faster than the other functions we have seen. The function fibA can find the 10-millionth Fibonacci number in just under 16 minutes.

Perhaps an even better solution is to just save the first gazillion Fibonacci numbers on a disk, and then read off the one we want. The code below will create a file holding the first max = 78125 Fibonacci numbers in 933 seconds (= 15 minutes and 33 seconds).

```
#---Create file containing the first max Fibonacci numbers.
    from time import clock
    max = 78125
    print('max =', max)
    print('start')
```

```
start = clock()
file1 = open('g:\\junk.txt', 'w')
file1.write('1\n')
a = b = 1
for i in range(1, max):
    file1.write(str(a)+'\n')
    a, b = b, a+b
file1.close()
stop = clock()
print('stop')
print('time =', round(stop-start, 2), 'seconds.')
```

Doubling the range of numbers seems to slightly more than quadruple the time. This may be because the Fibonacci numbers grow in size. If doubling the range multiplies the time by four (probably an underestimate), then we roughly estimate the time needed to create a file of the first ten-million Fibonacci numbers by timing $10,000,000/(2**7) = 78125$ numbers and multiplying the time by $4**7 = 16384$. Consequently, the time to create a file for the first ten-million Fibonacci numbers is estimated to be at least $933*16384$ seconds $= 15286272$ seconds, which is almost 177 days. Note: You should not read technical material passively. You need to check the logic and math behind these calculations.[4]

Once the file is built, extracting a *small* number is fast, but a *large* number takes time.

```
#---Extract a number from of a file of numbers.
    file1 = open('g:\\junk.txt', 'r')
    print('start')
```

---

[4]If we double the number 78125 seven times then we obtain 10,000,000. Consequently, if it takes t seconds to generate the first 78125 Fibonacci numbers, then it will take $(4**7)$ t seconds $= 16384$ t seconds to generate the first 10,000,000 Fibonacci numbers.

```
start = clock()
for n in range(78124):
    file1.readline()
num = (file1.readline())
file1.close()
stop = clock()
print('stop')
print('time =', round(stop-start, 2), 'seconds.')
# 8.94 seconds.
```

Now comes a surprise. The code above takes 9 seconds to extract the 78124th Fibonacci number. The function fibA will generate the 78124th Fibonacci number in just 0.3 seconds. The idea of a look-up table (here stored on a disk) is a useful idea. We have already seen it dramatically increase the speed in fibBB over fibB. However, accessing a large Python file can be slower than direct calculation.

So maybe you have learned a few programming tricks (memoization, class variables, embedded functions, default values, preferring integers to floats for accuracy with large numbers, and the value of look-up tables). Remembering tricks will help you mature as a programmer. Forgetting tricks is almost like never learning them. So how do we remember them? We write code that uses what we have recently learned.

These examples, as simple as they are, give us a natural opportunity to look at the coding style of most beginners. We will return to coding tricks in Chapter 4.

CHAPTER 3

Style

> The hard-science people rarely know how to write,
> and most of them don't know how to program
> either; they're taught how to code up an algorithm,
> not how to write a maintainable computer
> program.—Allen I. Holub, *Enough Rope to Shoot*
> *Yourself in the Foot* (McGraw-Hill, 1995), page 18.

* * *

> Readability, I have been told, is not everything.
> Neither is breathing, but it does come before
> whatever comes next.—William Sloane, *The Craft of*
> *Writing*, (W.W. Norton, 1979), page 11.

STYLE IS ANTICIPATING the difficulty others will have understanding, debugging, modifying, and using your code in their programs, and then addressing these difficulties in your constructions. It is a form of good manners.[1] I gave the previous chapter to all of the students in several of my programming classes, and we discussed it in detail. Then I collected the handout, and gave the following assignment.

---

[1]Best definition: Good manners is making the people around you feel comfortable. Here is the same thought again: "Good writers have developed an abiding empathy for their readers, while bad ones haven't."—Bryan Garner, *Legal Writing in Plain English* (University of Chicago, 2001), page 145.

© Michael Stueben 2018
M. Stueben, *Good Habits for Great Coding*, https://doi.org/10.1007/978-1-4842-3459-4_3

ASSIGNMENT: Write the following seven Fibonacci functions:

1. fibA simple iterative.

2. fibB simple recursive.

3. fibBD simple recursive with a decorator.

4. fibC recursion and memoization, with a dictionary passed as a parameter.

5. fibD recursion and memoization, with a dictionary as a class variable.

6. fibE recursion and memoization, with an embedded function.

7. fibF recursion and memoization, with a default dictionary parameter.

8. fibG formulas you must find on the Internet.

The range of ability in any computer science class is enormous. Some students finished this assignment in 30-45 minutes. Others took another 30 minutes and needed much help from their classmates. Some could not finish and had to work on the assignment at home.

I began looking at the working functions that were offered as copies of my functions. I was in for a surprise. Special purpose syntactic constructs in programming languages are known as "idioms". In Python, the preferred way (idiom) to assign one value to two variables is like this: a = b = 1. The preferred way to swap two variables is like this: a, b = b, a.

Here is the Fibonacci function that I had shown my students 15 minutes earlier. It uses the two idioms described above.

```python
def fibA(num):
    if num < 3: return 1
    a = b = 1
```

```
    for i in range(2, num):
        a, b = b, a+b
    return b
```

One of my students wrote the iterative Fibonacci function using Java/C/C++ idioms.

```
def fibA(n):
    if n <= 2: return n
    a = 1
    b = 1
    tmp = 0
    for i in range(n-2):
        tmp = b
        b   += a
        a   = tmp
    return b
```

There is a natural tendency not to learn a new idiom. If an old way works, then why not continue to use it? These Python idioms are so simple, common, and useful, and had been demonstrated in my own public code for months that I was surprised that this student had not adopted them.

When I looked at his fourth function, I could not easily understand his code until I indented it. The student was trying to reproduce this code:

```
def fibC(num, Dict):
if num in Dict:
    return Dict[num]
Dict[num] = fibC(num-1, Dict) + fibC(num-2, Dict)
return Dict[num]
```

Here is what he came up with, and it does work:

```
def fibC(n, d:dict):
    if n <= 2: return 1
    if n-1 in d: a=d[n-1]
    else: a = fibC(n-1,d)
    if n-2 in d: b = d[n-2]
    else: b = fibC(n-2,d)
    d[n] = a+b
    return a+b
```

Here is the same function indented:

```
def fibC(n, d:dict):
    if n <= 2:
        return 1

    if n-1 in d:
        a=d[n-1]
    else:
        a = fibC(n-1,d)

    if n-2 in d:
        b = d[n-2]
    else:
        b = fibC(n-2,d)

    d[n] = a+b
    return a+b
```

This particular student was one of my brighter students and often was one of the first students to finish a quiz. Nevertheless, this student and some of his classmates made no attempt to adopt a readable style. Getting the code to work was their only goal. This was at the end of the year in at least their third programming course.

Students do not understand style due to their inexperience in coding. They do not write long complicated programs. They do not modify and debug legacy code written by others. Consequently, their natural style for writing a program never evolves beyond that of writing short programs. The teacher insists on a style which is beneficial for long programs to be read by others, which is to be applied to short programs to be read only by the student and maybe the teacher. Trying to teach style can easily put the student, who thinks the teacher is being too pedantic, in conflict with a teacher.

Years ago, I asked my students to solve a problem with the most readable code possible, code that they would be proud to show during an interview. To my surprise, even strong students produced ugly and over-commented code. They simply had no idea what readable code was. After that I began showing examples of both easy-to-read code and hard-to-read code.

Now, about five or six times a year I insist that my students write short programs in readable style. When they print out their little programs and give them to me, I point out the first style error that I see and make them print it again. Some students need to print out their programs six or more times. I always see a few students conferring with each other trying to anticipate what my next criticism will be so that they will not have to print their programs again. At least they get some experience with writing readable code. But unless they know that I will inspect their code, most students will not take the time to write readable code.

The problem in getting students in the habit of refactoring (cleaning up their code to make it more readable) is the same as getting students to write competent essays. Attention to grammar, punctuation, rhetoric (effective use of sentences), diction (word choice), substance, and even proofreading will mostly be ignored unless the teacher demands them. Demanding quality requires close inspection of each student's work. I asked a highly respected member of the English department if she repeatedly read and returned the same essay until it was acceptable.

She said that she did this as a beginning teacher, but discontinued the practice, because it took too much personal time. It is the same with most teachers in most subjects. We do not have the time to regularly inspect our students' work to ensure quality. Ultimately, each student must be his or her own teacher.

> Where do scientists learn how to develop software and use computers in their research? Almost all [of nearly 2000 academic respondents of a Web-based survey in 2008] said *that informal self-study had been most important.* Peer mentoring came second, with formal instruction at school or on the job trailing well behind.—Greg Wilson, *American Scientist*, Vol. 97 (September-October 2009), pages 361-362.

Here is a check list I used to automate the refactoring process a little:

IS YOUR PROGRAM FINISHED BEFORE THE DEADLINE? IF YES,

---

a.   Did you use step-wise refinement? [If no, then go back and fix.]

b.   Did you refactor when you finished? [If no, then go back and fix.]

c.   Did you write self-documenting code? [If no, then go back and fix.]

d.   Did you limit functions to single tasks? [If no, then go back and fix.]

e.   Did you use the idioms of your language? [If no, then go back and fix.]

f.   Did you use asserts and other error traps? [If no, then go back and fix.]

g.   Did you use vertical alignment where useful? [If no, then go back and fix.]

h. Did you create labeled and attractive output? [If no, then go
    back and fix.]

i. Did you print the time your program took to run? [If no, then go
    back and fix.]

j. Did you test the final product well, especially special cases and
    borderline cases? [If no, then go back and fix.]

k. Did you test each major function immediately after you wrote
    it? [If no, don't do this again. Adopt the habits of professionals.]

l. Did you avoid writing clever code, doing needless optimizing,
    and coding for unimportant cases? [If no, don't do this again.
    Adopt the habits of professionals.]

Now back to more coding tricks.

CHAPTER 4

More Coding Tricks

It has often been said that a person does not
really understand something until he teaches it to
someone else. Actually, a person does not really
understand something until he can teach it to
a computer, i.e., express it as an algorithm. The
attempt to formalize things as algorithms leads to
much deeper understanding than if we simply try to
comprehend things in the traditional way.—Donald
E. Knuth (1974 Turing Award[1] winner) "Computer

---

[1]In case the reader is unaware, the highest award given in the field of computer
science is the Turing Award. It is given annually by the ACM (Association for
Computing Machinery) for lasting and important contributions of a technical
nature to the computer field. The Turing Award was named for the early
computer pioneer Alan Turing (1912–1954). Today Turing is considered to be
the father of both computer science and artificial intelligence. In 1945 Turing
was awarded the OBE (Order of the British Empire) for his code-breaking efforts
during WWII. In 1952 Alan Turing was arrested for a homosexual encounter with
a 19-year-old male. To stay out of prison, he submitted to a hormone "treatment"
that had a detrimental effect on his body and mind. Two years later, at age 41, he
was found dead by cyanide poisoning. The post-mortem ruled it a suicide, but his
mother and many of his close friends believed it was an accident. See *Wikipedia*.
In 1966 the Turing Award was established. In 1999, *Time* magazine declared Alan
Turing one of the 100 most important people to live in the twentieth century.
On December 24, 2013, Turing was granted a posthumous pardon by the Queen
of England (only the fourth since WWII). In 2014, the Hollywood movie *The
Imitation Game* was released. It chronicled Turing's life as code breaker and his
difficulties at the end of his life.

© Michael Stueben 2018
M. Stueben, *Good Habits for Great Coding*, https://doi.org/10.1007/978-1-4842-3459-4_4

Science and Its Relation to Mathematics," *American Mathematical Monthly*, Vol. 81, April, 1974, page 327.

BELOW, THE *RECURSIVE* FUNCTION (fibH) is an improvement over fibB.

```
def fibH(num, a = 0, b = 1): # 31.91 seconds.
    if num == 1:
        return b
    return fibH(num - 1, b, a+b)
```

We could write fibH in one line as shown below (no speed increase).

```
def fibHH(n, a = 0, b = 1): # 31.91 seconds.
    return fibHH(n-1, b, a+b) if n > 1 else b
```

Since Python allows anonymous functions to be written on the fly, we can use lambda, but the result is slower.

```
f = lambda n, a=1, b=1: int(n<3) or a+f(n-1,b,a+b)
# 56.08 seconds.
```

The question is always this: Which of the three versions is easiest to debug.

Digression. Any recursive function can be written iteratively. In fact. recursion itself is not recursive. Recursion is implemented as a stack of calls with their parameters, local variables, and address back to the calling routine. All of this information for each item on the **call stack** is a **stack frame**.

Notice that in fibH the recursive call stands alone, unlike return fib(x-1) + x, where an addition is appended *after* the recursion call. This standing alone or making the recursion the last action before the return (e.g., return x + fib(x-1)) is called "tail recursion." The advantage is that a smart compiler—i.e., an optimized compiler—will recognize tail recursion and change it to a goto, so that the enormous stack memory demands of recursion are reduced. Curiously, Python compilers do *not* optimize for tail recursion.

Even without optimization by a compiler, tail recursion may vastly improve the speed of a function by eliminating recursive calls, as fibH does here.

Instead of a Fibonacci function, consider a factorial function. Here there is no sum of previously solved cases to reach a final number. Below we compare five different forms of the factorial function. We see tail recursion is no faster than non-tail recursion, because tail recursion does not eliminate a recursive call in the factorial function. Even a look-up table does not help.

```python
def factorial1(n):           # Tail recursion 1 = 12.25 seconds
    if n == 1: return 1
    return n*factorial1(n-1)

def factorial2(n, x = 1):    # Tail recursion 2 = 13.72 seconds
    if n == 1: return x
    return factorial2(n-1, n*x)

def factorial3(n):           # non-Tail recursion = 11.88 seconds
    if n == 1: return 1
    return factorial3(n-1)*n

def factorial4(n):           # Iteration = 5.51 seconds
    t = 1
    for n in range(1,n+1):
        t = t*n
    return t

def factorial5(n):           # Tail recursion with look-up
                             # table = 12.36 seconds
    if n <=11:
        return [0,1,2,3,24, 120, 720, 5040, 40320,362880,
        3628800, 39916800][n]
    return n*factorial5(n-1)
```

Unrelated to this discussion is the following curiosity: The two single-line functions below will both compute n factorial using the Python "and/or trick" which probably should never be used. (For this trick to work, the middle expression must *always* evaluate to True.)

```
def factorialA(n):
    return (n>1) and (n*factorialA(n-1)) or 1
#-------------------------------------------------
def factorialB(n, x = 1):
    return (n>1) and factorialB(n-1, n*x) or x
```

End of digression.

Can we do this better, or faster, or at least differently with building a Fibonacci function? Searching the Internet, I discovered the curious "Fibonacci matrix" (aka the Q matrix), where

$$\mathbf{A}^n = \begin{pmatrix} 1 & 1 \\ 1 & 0 \end{pmatrix}^n = \begin{pmatrix} \text{fib}(n+1) & \text{fib}(n) \\ \text{fib}(n) & \text{fib}(n-1) \end{pmatrix}$$

Or in code:

```
A**n  =  [ [1,1], [1,0] ]**n  =  [ [fib(n+1),fib(n)],
[fib(n),fib(n-1)] ],
```

At this point you should do what I did when I first encountered this equation. Work out a few examples by hand to convince yourself that the matrix equation is true. For example:

$$\begin{pmatrix} 1 & 1 \\ 1 & 0 \end{pmatrix}^1 = \begin{pmatrix} 1 & 1 \\ \mathbf{1} & 0 \end{pmatrix}, \begin{pmatrix} 1 & 1 \\ 1 & 0 \end{pmatrix}^2 = \begin{pmatrix} 2 & 1 \\ \mathbf{1} & 1 \end{pmatrix}, \begin{pmatrix} 1 & 1 \\ 1 & 0 \end{pmatrix}^3 = \begin{pmatrix} 3 & 2 \\ \mathbf{2} & 1 \end{pmatrix}, \begin{pmatrix} 1 & 1 \\ 1 & 0 \end{pmatrix}^4 = \begin{pmatrix} 5 & 3 \\ \mathbf{3} & 2 \end{pmatrix}, \dots,$$

$$\begin{pmatrix} 1 & 1 \\ 1 & 0 \end{pmatrix}^{12} = \begin{pmatrix} 233 & 144 \\ \mathbf{144} & 89 \end{pmatrix}, \dots, \begin{pmatrix} 1 & 1 \\ 1 & 0 \end{pmatrix}^{23} = \begin{pmatrix} 46368 & 28657 \\ \mathbf{28657} & 17711 \end{pmatrix}$$

This is not a proof, but will give you a feeling for why Fibonacci numbers are popping out of these matrices.

Matrix multiplication may seem to be a slow way to generate Fibonacci numbers, and it is if we need to multiply A by itself 22 times to produce the 23rd Fibonacci number (28657). [Note: 23 = 10111 in base 2.] But suppose after generating the second Fibonacci number, A**2 = [[2,1],[1,1]], we multiply A**2 by itself to get A**4 = [[5,3],[3,2]]. Then we multiply A**4 by itself and generate A**8 = [[34,21],[21,13]]. Then we multiply A**8 by itself and generate A**16 =[[1597,987],[987,610]]. It turns out that

```
X = A**23 = (A**16) * (A**4) * (A**2) * (A**1) =
[[46368,28657],[28657, 17711]].
```

Our answer is X[0][1] = 28657 = the 23rd Fibonacci number, with only 7 (= 4 + 3) matrix multiplications instead of 22 matrix multiplications. You still may not be impressed at the speed of this scheme. But imagine trying to calculate the ten-millionth Fibonacci number.

Instead of calculating ten-million Fibonacci numbers (requiring almost 10,000,000 additions), we need only to calculate 23 (= 24-1) Fibonacci numbers (requiring only 30 = 23+7 matrix multiplications). Where did the 24 come from? The number 10,000,000 expressed in base 2 has 24 digits.

```
print(bin(10000000)) # = 100,110,001,001,011,010,000,000 in
base 2.
```

Also, 24 is log-base-two of ten-million, rounded up, using the change-of-base formula. Calculate this number now to check my work. Look up the change-of-base formula for logarithms if you cannot remember it. Still can't do it? Then find someone who can show you how. Logarithms are useful. You need some skill with them. The computation is in the footnote.[2]

---

[2]Answer: $\text{ceil}\left(\log_2\left(10{,}000{,}000\right)\right) = \text{ceil}\left(\dfrac{\log_{10}\left(10{,}000{,}000\right)}{\log_{10}\left(2\right)}\right) = 24.$

We first need a utility function `mul(A,B)` that will multiply two 2x2 matrices. Then to find `fib(23)`, we set A =`[1,1,1,0]` (not `[[1,1],[1,0]]`, because we wish to reduce the use of square brackets). Next, using `mul()` we produce `A**1`, `A**2`, `A**4`, `A**8`, and `A**16`. We let X = `A**23` = `A**16` * `A**4` * `A**2` * `A**1`. How do we do this? In other words, how did we decide to ignore `A**8` in the calculation of X? And how do we find a sum of powers of 2 equal to an arbitrary positive integer? And are we sure that it we can always find such a sum?

Here is a question I like to ask students before introducing the binary system: An eccentric rich man liked to go shopping, but always wanted to pay the *exact* amount (up to $100 with checks and 99 pennies) so that he received no change back. Question: What is the fewest number of checks he needed to write out before he went shopping? The answer is in the footnote.[3]

Since 23 in binary is 10111, reversing the digits and changing its type to a string, we get '11101'. If we let X = the product of the (`A**p`) expressions, for all positions p (the initial position is 1, not 0) where there is a 1 in the reversed string, then the 23rd Fibonacci number is the answer. This scheme always works, partly because any positive integer can be represented as a binary number.

> I have deeply regretted that I did not proceed far
> enough at least to understand something of the great
> leading principles of mathematics, for men thus
> endowed seem to have an extra sense.—Charles
> Darwin, *Autobiography* (recollections from
> Cambridge 1828-1831).

---

[3]Answer: 7 checks. The eccentric shopper must have a $1 check. Then if the next check is for $2, he can buy anything up to $3. So his third check should be for $4. Then he can buy anything up to $7. So his fourth check should be for $8. You see the pattern: $1, $2, $4, $8, $16, $32, $64. By this argument *any* positive integer can be expressed as the sum of distinct powers of two. So 23 is expressed as the sum 1 + 2 + 4 + 16.

```
def fibIII(n): # 1.61 seconds. (Remember, fibA took 7.45 seconds.)
    def mul(A, B): # multiply two 2x2 matrices
        a, b, c, d = A
        e, f, g, h = B
        return a*e+b*g, a*f+b*h, c*e+d*g, c*f+d*h
    A = [1,1,1,0]           # = Fibonacci matrix. We will
                                generate A, A**2, A**4, A**8,
                                A**16,
                        #    etc., some of which can be
                             combined to produce matrix X.
    X = [1,0,0,1]           # = identity  matrix, which will
                             later contains the answer:
    s = str(bin(n))[2:]     #    x[1] = fibIII(n). The str(bin(n))
                             [2:] will change fibIII
    s = s[::-1]             #    number to a binary string--e.g.,
                             n = 12 --> '1100'.
    for n in range(len(s)): # The s[::-1]will reverse digits in
                             a binary string.
        if s[n] == '1':
            X = mul(X, A) # Matrix X accumulates some of the
                             powers of matrix A--
        A = mul(A, A)       # e.g., X = A**12 = A**4 + A**8.
    return X[1]
```

This is an impressive decrease in time. It does not use recursion and simply strides toward the target number by making each step twice as big as the previous step. But why not re-write fibIII and remove the call to the embedded function? Surely that would make the function faster.

```
def fibII(n): # 2.10 seconds
    A = [1,1,1,0]           # = Fibonacci matrix.

    X = [1,0,0,1]           # = identity  matrix.
```

```
s = str(bin(n))[2:]    # Change fibII number to a binary
string--e.g., n = 12 --> 1100.
s = s[::-1]            # Reverse digits in binary
string--e.g., 1100 --> 0011.
for n in range(len(s)):
    if s[n] == '1':
        X = X[0]*A[0] + X[1]*A[2], X[0]*A[1] + X[1]*A[3],
            X[2]*A[0] + X[3]*A[2], X[2]*A[1] + X[3]*A[3]
        A = A[0]*A[0] + A[1]*A[2], A[0]*A[1] + A[1]*A[3],
            A[2]*A[0] + A[3]*A[2], A[2]*A[1] + A[3]*A[3]
return X[1]
```

To my surprise, the fibII function is a little slower than fibIII. Can you determine the cause by inspection? The mystery is explained in the next function.

```
def fibI(n): # 1.37 seconds.
    a,b,c,d = 1,1,1,0    # = Fibonacci matrix.
    e,f,g,h = 1,0,0,1    # = identity  matrix.
    s = str(bin(n))[2:] # = base 2 representation of n--e.g.,
    if n = 12, then s= "1100".
    r = s[::-1]          # = reversed version of s--e.g.,
                           if s = "1100", then r= "0011".
    for n in range(len(r)):
        if r[n] == '1':
            e,f,g,h = a*e+b*g, a*f+b*h, c*e+d*g, c*f+d*h
            # = X*Y (2x2 matrix mult).
        a,b,c,d = a*a + b*c, a*b + b*d, c*a + d*c, c*b + d*d
        # = Y*Y (2x2 matrix mult).
    return f
```

The function fibI is exactly the same as fibII, except that fewer list indices (with square brackets) were needed. Recall that a primitive identifier (like a or x) is just a memory address. But each element in a list (not an array of consecutive places in memory) is both a value and the address of the following element. Thus to find x[3], the computer goes to address x. Then it reads and moves to the next address: x[1]. Then it reads and moves to the next address: x[2]. Finally, it reads and moves to the next address: x[3]. The code in fibII required 12 of these read-and-move operations. It is more efficient to look them up once, and then assign the values to non-subscripted identifiers, than to keep looking up chained addresses. Anyway, the speed improvement is small. Perhaps fibIII is to be preferred, because it is simpler to understand.

The following formulas can be derived from the Fibonacci matrix. Can you derive them?

```
fib(2*k)   = fib(k)*(2*fib(k+1)-fib(k)) [= fib(k)*(fib(k+1)+
fib(k-1))],

fib(2*k+1) = fib(k+1)**2 + fib(k)**2.
```

Initially, I could not derive these formulas, but I used them anyway. Then it annoyed me—really annoyed me—that I could not derive these linear algebra formulas. What kind of precalculus teacher was I? So I went back and fiddled with A**n * A**n = A**(2n). Twenty minutes later, out popped the answer. (Actually I worked backwards from the answer to find the derivation.)

Many mathematicians use classical theorems that they themselves cannot prove. There is no problem in using mathematics that has been verified by experts, even if we can't follow their proofs. However, you need to be aware of constraints/restrictions/limits/riders/provisions/boundaries/special cases, etc.

Both computer scientists and physicists often do what is called non-rigorous mathematics—i.e., mathematical thinking based on analogies and apparent patterns, reasoning that would not be acceptable to a mathematician. This works in computer science because the computer scientist then writes a program that works, based on the math, and thereby confirms (to a degree accepted by some) the mathematics. In a similar way, the physicist builds stuff that works, thereby confirming (to a degree accepted by some) the mathematics. Of course, it would be better to prove the mathematics rigorously, but that often requires symbol-manipulation skills a researcher does not have. And to develop those skills (if even possible) would take time away from research. Most modern research is done with teams, partly because ambitious projects take too much time for one person, but also because too few people have all the skills needed for a big project. By the way, what is the definition of "proof"?[4]

Notice below that 1) no else or elif is necessary in fibJJ. Some people like to put them in anyway, and 2) we prefer fibJ(k)**2 to fibJ(k)*fibJ(k) to cut the recursive calls in half.

```
def fibJJ(n): # 3158.00 seconds
    if n < 3:
        return 1

    if (n%2) == 0:
        k = n//2
        return fibJJ(k)*(2*fibJJ(k+1)-fibJJ(k))

    k = (n-1)//2
    return fibJJ(k+1)*fibJJ(k+1) + fibJJ(k)*fibJJ(k)
```

---

[4]My definition: A proof is a convincing argument. Consequently, a proof can be wrong. There are several famous cases of this in the history of mathematics. Kempe's published proof and Tait's published proof of the four-color theorem come to mind. Each went unchallenged for 11 years. Also, what is accepted as a proof for one generation is sometimes not sufficient for a later generation. "Sufficient unto the day is the rigor thereof."—E.H. Moore (1903).

I was surprised at how slowly the fibJJ code executed, but I had been concentrating on just getting the function to return correct values. A few days later, I came back to it with fresh eyes, and immediately realized how inefficiently I had written this code. I rewrote the code and reduced the time from 3158 seconds to 38 seconds. Then I replaced the 2-value base case with a 17-value base case look-up table and reduced the time down to 5 seconds (fibJ). Never fail to consider the power of a look-up table.

```
def fibJ(n): # 5.00 seconds
    if n < 18:
        return [0,1,1,2,3,5,8,13,21,34,55,89,
                144,233,377,610,987,1597,][n]
    if (n%2) == 0:
        k = n//2
        f = fibJ(k)
        g = fibJ(k+1)
        return f*(2*g-f) # = fibJ(k)*(2*fibJ(k+1)-fibJ(k))
    k = (n-1)//2
    f = fibJ(k)
    g = fibJ(k+1)
    return g*g + f*f # = fibJ(k+1)*fibJ(k+1) + fibJ(k)*fibJ(k)
```

And now maybe you see why I chose *not* to use the formula fib(2*k) = fib(k)*(fib(k+1)+fib(k-1))]. That formula would require the code to make three recursive calls, not two calls.

The fibJ() function still recalculates a few of the same Fibonacci numbers. So, we introduce memoization to avoid recalculating the same numbers. But the code now becomes more complicated. Do we ever want to write code like this? Only when we MUST have speed, and this function is indeed fast.

```
def fibK(n, dict = {}): # 1.19 seconds
    if n < 18:
        return [0,1,1,2,3,5,8,13,21,34,55,89,
                144,233,377,610,987,1597,][n]

    if (n%2) == 0:
        k = n//2
        if k not in dict:
            dict[k] = fibK(k, dict)
        A = dict[k]
        if (k+1) not in dict:
            dict[k+1] = fibK(k+1, dict)
        B = dict[k+1]
        return 2*A*B-A*A
    else:
        k = (n-1)//2
        if (k+1) not in dict:
            dict[k+1] = fibK(k+1, dict)
        A = dict[k+1]
        if k not in dict:
            dict[k] = fibK(k, dict)
        B = dict[k]
        return A*A + B*B
```

Digression: Please note that in Python a default parameter usually should *not* be set to the empty set (or empty list) as I did above: dict = {}. Even though the code works fine, a second run of fibK, without the program ending will *not* reset dict = {}. Consequently the dictionary will not need to be re-built on the second call, which will make the function appear faster than it is in repeating tests. I have been caught by this Python peculiarity more than once. Look at this code:

```
def doIt(dict ={}):
    print(dict)
    dict['A'] = 1

def main():
    doIt() # output: {}
    doIt() # output: {'A': 1}
```

Here are two ways to fix the problem.

```
def doIt(Lst = None):
    if Lst == None: Lst = []
    Lst.append('x')
    return Lst

def main():
    print(doIt()) # output: main ['x']
    print(doIt()) # output: main ['x']

def doIt(Lst = None):
    Lst = Lst or []
    return Lst

def main():
    print(doIt()) # output: main ['x']
    print(doIt()) # output: main ['x']
```

Recall that Python or and and both return the last value examined. Thus, if Lst = None (= False), then the computer is forced to examine [ ] and return [ ]. To keep fibK simple, I left it the way I initially wrote it. End of digression.

Function fibK is one of the most complicated functions in this list. Can we clean it up? Yes, by returning two values. Unfortunately, this makes the function more difficult to use. On two occasions I took the answer to be the second value, not the first. The function fibL is both simpler to look at than fibK, and faster. Appending the 17-value look-up table only increases the speed by about 25%. Maybe I should have tried a 100-value look-up table.

```
def fibL(n): # 0.63 seconds [0.46 seconds with the look-up
table.]
    if n == 0:
        return (0, 1)
##    if n < 18: # Optional base case look-up table.
##        return [(0,1),(1,1),(1,2),(2,3),(3,5),(5,8),(8,13),
        (13,21),(21,34),(34,55),
##                (55,89),(89,144),(144,233),(233,377),
        (377,610),(610,987),(987,1597),
##                (1597,2584),][n]
    else:
        a, b = fibL(n // 2)    # a = fibL(2*k); b = fibL(2*k+1).
        c = a*(2*b - a)        # fibL(2*k  ) =
                               fibL(k)*(2*fibL(k+1) - fibL(k))
        d = a*a + b*b          # fibL(2*k+1) = fibL(k+1)**2 +
                               fibL(k)**2

        if (n%2) == 0:
            return (c, d)      # return fibL(k), fibL(k+1)
        else:
            return (d, c + d)  # return fibL(k), fibL(k+1)
```

We have not yet discussed memory usage. So we ask each function to calculate the ten-millionth Fibonacci number, which ends in 380546875 and has 2089877 digits. We are in for a surprise. The function fibK is now slightly faster than fibL.

1. fibA = 949.76 seconds (almost 16 minutes).

2. fibB = impossible

3. fibC = maximum recursion depth exceeded.

4. fibD = maximum recursion depth exceeded.

5. fibE = maximum recursion depth exceeded.

6. fibF = maximum recursion depth exceeded.

7. fibG = overflow, result too large.

8. fibH = maximum recursion depth exceeded.

9. fibI = 24.09 seconds

10. fibJ = 3.23 seconds

11. fibK = 2.32 seconds

12. fibL = 2.55 seconds

Overall, which function is the best?

> fibA is easy to understand, but too slow for big numbers.

> fibI is slow compared to others, but easier to understand.

> fibJ is 5 times faster than fibI, but uses formulas some programmers can't derive.

> fibK is fastest, but it is complicated.

fibL is shorter than fibK, almost as fast as fibK, but returns two values, which have tripped me up twice in testing the code.

The question of which is best, like many questions in life, turns out to be senseless, because we do not have a single standard for "best."

Recall that algorithms, along with their instantiation as functions, are evaluated traditionally by THREE criteria:

1. **speed** ("Better" is the enemy of "good enough." You might not need super speed.) To confuse matters, functions that are second best on one set of data sometimes turn out to be best on a different set of data.

2. **readability** (ease in debugging, modifying, and understanding). Of course, some functions are difficult to understand no matter how they are written.

3. **memory** (memory hogs are impractical).

Years ago, as a student, I wrote the quick sort. My code sorted almost all the numbers, but a few were left unsorted. I had used a "<" when I should have used a "<=". Lucky for me that I tested the code with a large number of integers (not floats), in a small range (two-digits), and with a checking routine so that I did not have to visually inspect the output for correctness. If I had not done all of this, then it is unlikely that any of the test cases would have failed. My code only failed when I had duplicate numbers, and sometimes not even then. So imagine that my flawed quick sort was a small part of a large student program. I would have been convinced that my sort was correct. And because of limited time and energy, I might never have re-tested the sort.

My point is this: There is more to evaluating an algorithm than the three criteria stated previously. The ease of **understanding** an algorithm, its level of difficulty **in translating** into computer code, and the difficulty of **using** that code in other programs also are significant properties of an algorithm.

My definition of technology: hardware, software, and *algorithms*.

PART II

Coding Advice

CHAPTER 5

Function Design

I CLAIM THAT using functions effectively is tricky, and will try to convince you of this claim with the following examples.

Most of the time you want to create functions that do only one task. No multi-purpose functions—most of the time. I once wrote a graphics program to read in an image file and print it in color (one function) or print it in gray-scale (another function). Much of the code in two functions was the same, or almost the same. Using a Boolean parameter (colorFlag), both the gray and color functions could be combined into one function. Thus, I had one less function for the price of four extra lines. See below.

AN EXAMPLE OF MULTI-PURPOSE CODE

```
WIDTH = 512
HEIGHT = 512
class ImageFrame:
    def __init__(self, colors, wd = WIDTH, ht = HEIGHT,
    colorFlag= False):
        self.img = PhotoImage(width = wd, height = ht)
        for row in range(ht):
            for col in range(wd):
                num = colors[row*wd + col]
                if colorFlag == True:
                    kolor ='#%02x%02x%02x' % (num[0], num[1],
                    num[2]) # = color
```

© Michael Stueben 2018
M. Stueben, *Good Habits for Great Coding*, https://doi.org/10.1007/978-1-4842-3459-4_5

```
    else:
        kolor ='#%02x%02x%02x' % (num, num, num)
        # = gray-scale
    self.img.put(kolor, (col,row))
c = Canvas(root, width = wd, height = ht); c.pack()
c.create_image(0,0, image = self.img, anchor = NW)
printElapsedTime ('displayed image')
```

When I reviewed my work a year later, I had to read the code—not just the name of the function—before I could understand what colorFlag did. If the code had been kept as two functions with descriptive names ImageFrameForColorList and ImageFrameForGrayScaleList, then there would be no colorFlag to understand. The common code in both functions could be extracted into a third function, which could be called by both the gray-scale function and the color function. The justification for this third function is that any change in the common code would need to be done only once (DRY: don't repeat yourself). The danger with repeated code is that you may change it in one place without realizing that it needs to be changed in another place.

This example is a nice illustration of **cohesion** vs. **coupling**. Placing all the code to solve these two related tasks in one function increases the cohesion (usually good). Spreading it out to two or three functions increases the coupling of the functions (usually bad). So which scheme is better—the single function, the two functions, or the three functions? My feeling is that because of the simplicity of the code (at least to me) keeping it all in one function makes the code easier to understand and to debug. Often when we follow one guideline (maximize cohesion and thereby minimize coupling) we violate another principle (limit functions to single tasks). Whatever your decision, be aware of the issues involved. Programming expert Ward Cunningham stated this perfectly: "If you don't think carefully, you might think that programming is just typing statements in a programming language."[1]

How long should a function be? Programmers Brian Kernigham and P.J. Plauger once mentioned that the median size of their functions was 15 lines, and the mean was 19 lines.[2] It seems that rarely should a function contain more lines than will fit on a screen. My text-editing screen holds 38 lines with the type size I like. But, of course, we never seek small; we seek readability. Here are my 34 lines of code to determine if an $n \times n$ Sudoku board is a solution.

```python
def solutionIsCorrect(matrix):
#---Build lists of rows and columns.
    rows = [[]] * MAX
    cols = [[]] * MAX
    for r in range(MAX):
        for c in range(MAX):
            rows[r].append(matrix[r][c].value)
            cols[c].append(matrix[r][c].value)

#---Build list of blocks.
    block = []
    for n in range(MAX):
        block.append([])
    for n in range(MAX):
        for r in range(blockHeight):
            for c in range(blockWidth):
                row = (n//blockWidth)*blockHeight+r
                col = (n%blockHeight*blockWidth) +c
                block[n].append(matrix[row][col].value)
```

---

[1]Found in Andrew Hunt and David Thomas, *The Pragmatic Programmer* (Addison Wesley, 2000), page xiii.

[2]*Software Tools in Pascal* (Addison-Wesley, 1981), page 189.

```
#---Check all rows for all n digits.
    for r in rows:
        for n in range(1, MAX+1):
            if {n,} not in r:  # <--The type must be set({n}),
            not int (n).
                return False

#---Check all columns for all n digits.
    for c in cols:
        for n in range(1, MAX+1):
            if {n,} not in c:
                return False

#---Check all blocks for all n digits.
    for b in block:
        for n in range(1, MAX+1):
            if {n,} not in b:
                return False
    return True # True means NO errors in the matrix.
```

Why not push the little parts into their own functions and call them from this function? The answer is that the parts are pretty simple to debug. There is not much complexity to reduce, so I chose cohesion over coupling. Notice that comments are used as function headers. This works well when the multi-tasked function can be broken into a set of *related* and *simple* single-tasked parts.

Why would anyone bother to create a one-line function, instead of using the one line of code itself? The answer is that the name of the function is easier to understand than the single line of code. But doesn't the single line of code eventually have to be understood? Not unless we are debugging or modifying that particular line of code. Wouldn't you rather encounter the Boolean expression (in the Nelder-Mead algorithm)

```
if triangleHasNotConverged(count, A, B, C):
    return
```

which references this function

```
def triangleHasNotConverged(count, A, B, C): # Boolean result
    return (count < MAX_TRIANGLE_COUNT and
            SMALLEST_TRIANGLE_SIZE < max(B.dist(C), A.dist(B),
            A.dist(C)))
```

rather than this ugly line:

```
If (count < MAX_TRIANGLE_COUNT and
  SMALLEST_TRIANGLE_SIZE < max(B.dist(C), A.dist(B), A.dist(C))):
      return
```

I once wrote the function makeComputerReply() to make a game move (in Othello) on the screen. That was a short function that performed just one task, or so I thought. But what the function actually did was 1) calculate where the move should be, 2) call another function to make the move in an internal matrix, and then 3) display the move on the screen. Since 2) and 3) always occur together, maybe they can be considered to be one task. Still, that is *two* tasks, not three. If someone had pointed this out to me, I would have said that breaking up the function would have added complexity to the program, not reduced it: cohesion over coupling. The function call would need to be changed from the simple

```
makeComputerReply()
```

to the more complicated

```
bestCol, bestRow, finalPieces = makeComputerReply()
makeMoveInMatrixAndOnScreen (bestCol, bestRow, finalPieces,
COMPUTER)
```

I later returned to my program and realized that the code that calculated the computer's best one-ply move, with a small modification, could also calculate the human's best one-ply counter-reply. Thus, the computer could think ahead two-ply instead of one-ply. And if it could do two-ply then it could do four-ply and make some deeply thought-out moves. All this could be accomplished by redesigning the makeComputerReply() function.

But as I said, the function I was trying to modify also inserted each move in a matrix and printed the move on the screen. So I had to remove the insert-and-print code from the function, and place it underneath the call to the now-renamed bestResponse(player). The original design decreased complexity for *understanding* the code, but increased the complexity for *modifying* the code. Previously, I didn't know that such a situation was possible. What a surprise.

Now assume you are writing a program which needs both a 2D- and a 3D-distance function. Which of the *three* methods below would you choose?

```
# METHOD 1 (two functions)
def distance2D(x,y):
    assert len(x) == len(y) == 2
    return sqrt( (x[0]-y[0])**2 + (x[1]-y[1])**2 )

def distance3D(x,y):
    assert len(x) == len(y) == 3
    return sqrt( (x[0]-y[0])**2 + (x[1]-y[1])**2 +
    (x[2]-y[2])**2)
#-------------------------------------------------------------------

# METHOD 2 (one function with a for loop)
def distance(x,y):
    assert len(x) == len(y) and len(x) in {2,3}
    total = 0
```

```
    for n in range(len(x)):
        total += (x[n]-y[n])**2
    return sqrt( total)
#-------------------------------------------------------------

# METHOD 3 (one function with a loop comprehension)
def distance(x,y):
    assert len(x) == len(y) and len(x) in {2,3}
    return sqrt(sum([(x[n]-y[n])**2 for n in range(len(x))])))
```

Why would you write two functions when one function would work? A reasonable reply is that the two function names are more descriptive than the single-function names. And the two functions are easier to debug than the more powerful single functions. Nevertheless, because calculation of a distance is simple, and because I am used to list comps, I prefer Method 3. BTW, unless you know that you are likely to extend a function, do *not* make it general. Even if you know, you may still prefer to get your program working with simpler functions.

That being said, I actually think Method 3 can be improved by unrolling the for loop, which I show below. This brings us to another question. Which of the four error messages shown below do you prefer to finish Method 4?

```
# METHOD 4 (one function with no loops)
def distance(x,y):
    if len(x) == len(y) == 2:
        return sqrt((x[0]-y[0])**2 + (x[1]-y[1])**2)

    if len(x) == len(y) == 3:
        return sqrt((x[0]-y[0])**2 + (x[1]-y[1])**2 +
        (x[2]-y[2])**2)
```

Finish this function by choosing an error trap below.

```
#---Exit message A
    exit('Error in distance function.')

#---Exit message B
    assert(False), 'Error in distance function.'

#---Exit message C
    msg = 'len(x) = '+ str(len(x)) + ' and len(y) = '+
    str(len(y))
    assert False, 'Error in distance function: ' + msg

#---Exit message D
    msg = 'len(x) = '+ str(len(x)) + ' and len(y) = '+
    str(len(y))
    exit('Error in distance function: ' + msg)
```

My answer is in the footnote. [3]

Recall the old alphametic puzzle SEND + MORE = MONEY,[4] where each letter represents a different digit. The unique solution is 9567 + 1085 = 10652. I once assigned a class to write a program that would find all solutions of *any* alphametic—e.g., DOG * CAT = FIGHT has 16 solutions. I did this because I wanted the students to become familiar with the powerful Python commands eval, maketrans, and translate commands. The code I produced (shown below) surprised me.

---

[3]My choice is B. Exit messages C and D take too much time and code for an error that I expect rarely will be made. Message A simply exits the program with an error message. Message B does the same as A, but also causes the cursor to be placed on the assert line in the function.

[4]The alphametic was invented by Henry Dudeney, and first published in the July 1924 issue of the British *Strand* magazine.

```
#                       Teacher's solution
#######################<BEGIN PROGRAM>#######################
def createAlphametic():
    from itertools import permutations
    from re          import findall  # re stands for regular
                      expressions.
    puzzle = 'SEND + MORE == MONEY' # Notice we use '==', not '='.
    puzzle = 'OOOH + FOOD == FIGHT' # 8886 + 1883 == 10769
    print(' NOW ATTEMPTING TO FIND ALL\n SOLUTIONS FOR THIS
    ALPHAMETIC\n PUZZLE:', puzzle)
    solutionFound = False
    count = 0

    words = findall('[A-Z]+', puzzle.upper())
                          # words = ['SEND', 'MORE', 'MONEY']
    keys = set(''.join(words))
            # keys  = {'Y', 'S', 'R', 'M', 'O', 'N', 'E', 'D'}
    if len(keys) > 10:
        print('--- ERROR: The puzzle has MORE than ten letters.')
        exit()
    initialLetters = {word[0] for word in words}
                      # Example: initialLetters = {'M', 'S'}
    numberOfInitials = len(initialLetters)
    keys             = ''.join(initialLetters) + ''.join(keys -
    initialLetters) # Example: keys = 'MSEDONRY'

    for values in permutations('1234567890', len(keys)):
        values = ''.join(values)        # Example: ('1', '2',
        '3', '4', '5', '6', '7', '8') becomes '12345678'
        if '0' in values[0:numberOfInitials]:
                # No zeros are allowed in initial letters.
```

```
            continue                 # If eval() finds a number
            beginning with zero, it will throw an exception.
                                     # 'M': 3,  'S':  8,  'E':
                                     5, ...}
        table     = str.maketrans(keys, values)
                    # table = {77: 51,   83: 56,   69: 53, ...}
        equation = puzzle.translate(table)
                    # Example: equation = 8514 + 3275 == 32156
        if eval(equation):
            solutionFound = True
            if count == 0:
                print('-----------------------------------')
                print('All solutions are listed below:')
            count += 1
            print(count,'. ', equation, sep = '')

    if not solutionFound:
        print('No solutions exist.')
#-----------------------ALPHAMETICS------------------------

def main():
    createAlphametic()
#-----------------------ALPHAMETICS------------------------
if __name__ == '__main__':
    from time import clock; START_TIME = clock();  main();
    print('\n+===<RUN TIME>===+');
    print('|  %5.2f'%(clock()-START_TIME), 'seconds |');
    print('+================+')
######################<END OF PROGRAM>####################
```

Why did I not use stepwise refinement, and break the code into single-task functions? For example, why not break it up like this:

```
def main():
    puzzle      = createAlphametic()
    solutionSet = solveAlphametic(puzzle)
    printResults(solutionSet)
```

This, in fact, is how I started to code the assignment. However, the program generally took 30 seconds or longer to run, and I wanted to see the results as they were discovered, and not printed out all at once at the end. This meant I would have only two calls in the main function. But the `createAlphametic()` function was so simple that it didn't add much clarity by being separated from the other function. The result is that this complicated code does *not* become more readable by being broken up into several small functions. Then why not stuff all the code into the main function? My policy is to call any key block of code with a descriptive name. The main function should call at least one other function. My only exception to this policy is teaching-code that is designed to illustrate syntax.

Here is another exception. When I designed a toy neural network, I wrote a function that created both training data and random weight values. (See below.) This is two tasks. The tasks were so short, simple, and related that it only made sense to stuff them into the same function: again, cohesion over coupling.

```
def createNetwork(iMax = 8, jMax = 3, kMax = 8):
#---Create the training data.
    inputs = [[1,0,0,0,0,0,0,0,-1], [0,1,0,0,0,0,0,0,-1],
             [0,0,1,0,0,0,0,0,-1],
             [0,0,0,1,0,0,0,0,-1], [0,0,0,0,1,0,0,0,-1],
             [0,0,0,0,0,1,0,0,-1],
             [0,0,0,0,0,0,1,0,-1], [0,0,0,0,0,0,0,1,-1],]
```

```
#---Create the w and v weights.
    w = [ [uniform(-2,2) for col in range(jMax)] for row in
    range(iMax+1)]  # = 9 rows & 3 cols
    v = [ [uniform(-2,2) for col in range(iMax)] for row in
    range(jMax+1)]  # = 4 rows & 8 cols
    return inputs, w, v, h
```

Here is my point: The rules of limiting a function to a single task and breaking up its parts by using stepwise refinement are important and need to be followed—*usually*. Rules are human constructions and are not perfect. They are just guides. One oft-quoted expert rule about coding is "special cases aren't special enough to break the rules." I disagree; different environments and different situations require different policies.

I first encountered the warning to be wary of rules in a philosophy book: "Morality is valuable so long as it is recognized as a means to an end; it is a good servant, but a terrible master."[5] Are there no absolute rules in life or programming? After a lifetime of thinking, I'm still not sure. Consider this: In writing code, readability comes first, if optimization is not necessary, and if the time cannot be better spent elsewhere. Is that an absolute rule?

---

[5]Alan W. Watts, *The Spirit of Zen* (Grove Press, 1958), page 61.

CHAPTER 6

Self-Documenting Code

I feel disloyal but dauntlessly truthful in saying that most scientists do *not* know how to write, insofar as style does betray *l'homme même* [the man himself], they write as if they hated writing and wanted above all else to have done with it.—Sir Peter B. Medwar (Nobel Laureate), *Advice to a Young Scientist* (Harper & Row, 1979), page 63.

It is remarkable that nearly all scientists, at the point where they turn from mathematical or chemical language to English, seem to feel relieved of any further obligation to precise terminology.—Robert Graves and Alan Hodge, *The Use and Abuse of the English Language* (Paragon, 1970), page 227.

Few people realize how badly they write.—William Zinsser, *On Writing Well,* 5th ed. (Harper, 1994), page 19.

© Michael Stueben 2018
M. Stueben, *Good Habits for Great Coding*, https://doi.org/10.1007/978-1-4842-3459-4_6

> All good writing is self-taught. The truth remains
> that the would-be writer, using a book or critic, must
> teach himself.—Jacques Barzun, *Simple & Direct*
> (Harper & Row, 1975), page 3. [In 2003, Professor
> Jacques Barzun (Columbia University) received the
> Presidential Medal of Freedom for his influential
> writings.]

THE POINT OF the above quotations is that clear communication is difficult. If we change the language from English to a computer language, does the difficulty reduce to the point that anyone who tries will do well? I don't believe so, and my proof is the poorly named, over-abbreviated, awkwardly structured code we can find on the Internet and in some computer books.

The key to readability in computer code is ***self-documenting*** code, code that reveals its intent by careful structuring (cohesion with related tasks, coupling of single tasks) and choice of identifiers (descriptive names for both functions and data).

As a general convention, class and variable names should be nouns or noun phrases, and function names should be action verbs or verb-object phrases. I sometimes name a function as a noun describing the returned item—e.g., `result` (for a tic-tac-toe win, lose, or draw), `symbol` (for a character that is returned). Someone suggested that all Boolean functions should begin with **is**. Thus, `allVowels` should be `isAllVowels`. Initially, I didn't think much of this advice, but then I noticed that it actually made some of my code read like English sentences. So now I follow this suggestion. My advice is to avoid using joke names, cute words, and offensive words. I have always found the names **foo, bar, baz,** and **spam** to make examples *less clear*. Their use seems to be showing off with an insider's joke.[1] I prefer the generic function name doIt (verb-object).

Of course, creating descriptive names is difficult at the beginning when you are more focused on just getting the code to work and function tasks are still being modified. Perhaps a good example to look at is a set of identifiers that tell us nothing:

```
def process(argument, parameter, data, whatIsIt):
    ...
    something  = action(value)
    entity     = call(variable)
    stuff      = phunction(identifier)
    ...
```

How about the easy-to-write variables bug, cat, cow, dog, fly, fox, hen, hog, pig, and rat, or even it? (I've seen thingy, stringy, and obscene terms in student code.) Can you think of worse names? Yes, that's easy: identifiers that can't be pronounced, like 1010, o000o, and a bunch of underscores: ____.That being said, the single underscore (_) actually has at least two uses as a variable. Consider the goal of printing the sum of the numbers in this list:

```
Lst = [('A', 1), ('B',2), ('C', 3), ('D',4),]
```

---

[1]These place-holders are technically known as "metasyntactic variables." See *Wikipedia*. The *foo* and *bar* terms have unknown origin, but may be related to the military slang *Fubar*, "fouled (sic) up beyond all recognition." The *spam* term (possibly "spiced ham" introduced in 1937) is in reference to a Monty Python comedy skit, which is available on YouTube ("Monty Python Spam"). As the reader may already know, the name "Python" was chosen in reference to the six-member British comedy group known as Monty Python's Flying Circus (45 TV episodes from 1969 to 1974, and five movies, the last in 1983). The humor of this group strikes different people in different ways. When I showed the YouTube "Monty Python Argument Clinic" to my students, some thought it was hilarious, while others were clearly bored.

Following are two methods to do this. Which is better?

```
#---Method 1
    total = 0
    for (ch,num) in Lst:
        total += num
    print('total =', total) # output: total = 10

#---Method 2
    print('total =', sum([num for (_,num) in Lst]))
    # output: total = 10
```

Notice that the underscore is used as a throwaway variable in the second method. If this is the first time you have seen it, this will seem a poor choice for an identifier, but I have seen it used in commercial code on several occasions. It says to the reader that this is a place-holder variable—i.e., we have to have it, but we never use it.

I find Method 1 more readable, yet I recommend Method 2. Why? Because Method 2 is more Pythonic, more professional. We need to get comfortable reading code the way professionals prefer to write it, as in this case with a list comprehension and with the underscore used as a dummy variable.

Here is another use for an underscore:

```
_ = 0 # <-- The underscore is the constant 0.


#     Easy to read
M = [[3, _, 4, _, _, 6,],
     [_, 7, _, _, _, _,],
     [_, _, _, 9, _, _,],
     [_, _, 5, _, _, _,],
     [2, _, _, _, 1, _,],]
```

```
#      Less easy to read.
M = [[3, 0, 4, 0, 0, 6,],
     [0, 7, 0, 0, 0, 0,],
     [0, 0, 0, 9, 0, 0,],
     [0, 0, 5, 0, 0, 0,],
     [2, 0, 0, 0, 1, 0,],]
```

Somewhere I read we should avoid similar names like str1 and str2, because it is too easy to type one for the other, and the difference between the names is not meaningful. It seems to me that this idea is not true in a small scope.

Now for a little experiment. I wrote some code where I needed two random numbers chosen between 0 and 1, with the first number less than or equal to the second number. I thought of four choices for their names: (randomNum1, randomNum2), (r1, r2), (x, y), and (a, b). Which code segment below would you prefer to debug?

Version 1
```
    for n in range(totalRuns):
        randomNum1, randomNum2  = random(), random()
        if randomNum1 > randomNum2:
            randomNum1, randomNum2 = randomNum2, randomNum1
        if (randomNum1 > 0.5 or randomNum2-randomNum1 > 0.5
                            or randomNum2 < 0.5):
            noTriangleCount += 1
        else:
            triangleCount += 1
```

Version 2
```
    for n in range(totalRuns):
        r1, r2  = random(), random()
        if r1 > r2:
            r1, r2 = r2, r1
```

71

```
      if (r1 > 0.5 or r2-r1 > 0.5 or r2 < 0.5):
          noTriangleCount += 1
      else:
          triangleCount += 1
```

Version 3.

```
  for n in range(totalRuns):
      x, y  = random(), random()
      if x > y:
          x, y = y, x
      if (x > 0.5 or y-x > 0.5 or y < 0.5):
          noTriangleCount += 1
      else:
          triangleCount += 1
```

Version 4.

```
  for n in range(totalRuns):
      a, b  = random(), random()
      if a > b:
          a, b = b, a
      if (a > 0.5 or b-a > 0.5 or b < 0.5):
          noTriangleCount += 1
      else:
          triangleCount += 1
```

I chose Version 4 (a and b), because single-letter identifiers are the easiest to read, and a and b have a psychological order (a < b). So do x and y, but they also come with a history of y being a function of x (not here). The only other common pair I know is p and q, which are used for pointers or positions in a list. The following two functions do the same task: They flatten a list—e.g., they both will turn

```
[0, [1, [2, 3, [4, 5]], 6, [7]], [8, 9]]
```

into

```
[0, 1, 2, 3, 4, 5, 6, 7, 8, 9]
```

So, which function below is more readable: the first using the *descriptive* newLst, or the second using the *ambiguous* y?

```
def flatten(Lst): # Recursive
    newLst = []
    for x in Lst:
        if type(x) == list:
            newLst.extend(flatten(x))
        else:
            newLst.append(x)
    return newLst

def flatten(Lst): # Recursive
    y = []
    for x in Lst:
        if type(x) == list:
            y.extend(flatten(x))
        else:
            y.append(x)
    return y
```

Again, I think y.append(x) is easier to understand than the newLst. append(x), even though newLst is more descriptive than y. How can a variable that is more readable in isolation be less readable in code? Well, usually it can't, but this code is simple enough that the information in the name newLst is not needed. What is helpful is that we expect y to be a function of x, and that is exactly the case here. When we have *small* fragments of *simple* code, one-letter variables can be more readable than multi-word descriptive variables. The general rule is the greater the scope the longer the identifier. That is a *general* rule, not an absolute, dogmatic law.

73

The biggest trap in naming variables is not making them descriptive enough. The second biggest trap is to over-abbreviate their names. That being said, short and single-letter identifiers are acceptable for loop indices and temporary variables of short scope. Even these tiny tots can be descriptive. Of course, <u>never</u> use o[2] or O (they both look like zero: 0), and avoid the letter l (it looks like one: 1). Here are some descriptive single-letter identifiers.

b for Boolean (bool is built-in)

c and maybe k for constant (maybe const1 and const2 are better)

f for function, not for flag (use flag for flag)

g for function (after using f)

h for heuristic function

i and j and maybe k for loop indices[3] (and maybe sometimes n, num or indx)

p for position or pointer

Q for queue (but why not use queue, or even que?)

r for random (maybe rand is better), but not the module name random.

t for total (or tot, or even total, but *not* the built-in function sum). Perhaps use t for time, or tictoc for time, but not the module name time.

---

[2]I have a C++ textbook in which the author uses o for output. Wouldn't output be better?

[3]Both *indexes* and *indices* are equally acceptable plurals, but *indices* is preferred for mathematical and technical use. The for loop i probably stands for index, not integer.

M for matrix (maybe `matrix` is better)

`(r,c)` for row and column (maybe `row` and `col` are better)

`(x,y,` and maybe `z)` for coordinates

`(a,b)` for first and second values

`x[n]`, `y[n]`, and `z[n]` for arrays, but `arrayX`, `arrayY`, and `arrayZ` may be better

`ch` and `kh` for characters, etc.

I try to avoid the following:

d for distance (`dist` is better)

m for maximum (`big` or `maximum` is better, but not the built-in `max`)

p for probability (`prob` is better)

s or `s1` for string (`stng` and `str1` are better)

Even neutral identifiers like `args`, `other`, `data`, `info`, `collection` and `result` are acceptable for a short scope where their meaning is either obvious or explained in an inline comment. For example,

```
data = ['-',0,0,0,0,0,0,0,0,0,] # Distances to goal node from
                                          nodes 1-9.
```

In the following code, I shortened an identifier and made the code more readable.

Original version:

```
def fb(node):
    if node == 9: return 0
    shortestDistanceFromNodeToGoal =
```

```
    min([dist + fb(neighbor) for (dist, neighbor) in
    graph[node]])
return  shortestDistanceFromNodeToGoal
```

Improved version:

```
def fb(node):
    if node == 9: return 0
    shortest = min([dist + fb(neighbor) for (dist, neighbor) in
            graph[node]])
    return  shortest # = shortest distance from current node to
                goal node
```

Follow mathematical notation where possible. In math books, we write linear vector equations like this: $\vec{y} = m\vec{x} + \vec{b}$ or like this $\mathbf{Y} = m\mathbf{X} + b$,[4] *not* like this (unless we have no choice):

```
outputVector = matrix*inputVector + auxiliaryVector.
```

We do this because the first two expressions are more readable than the third expression. The rules for naming mathematical constants/variables/parameters are different from naming program variables/functions/modules/libraries/files/directories. Try to go with the math conventions when programing mathematical expressions.

I saw one program author use the identifiers start and end for two positions in a list. That is clear enough, but I would have preferred English idioms—e.g., begin and end, or start and stop, or first and last, or even left and right. He also used piv for pivot. Why not spell it out?

Suppose we have a list of men's heights. A reasonable identifier for the list is mensHeights. But when we choose just one element we must use mensHeights[n] for a *single* man's height. The identifier is fine for the

---

[4]In the linear equation $y = mx + b$, the m can be thought of standing for "matrix." A scalar can be thought of a 1×1 matrix.

list, but less so for an element in the list. No language is perfect. So, which identifier should we choose? I prefer mensHeights over mansHeight.

The following line of Python code, where A is a Vector object, caused an error (aka raising, throwing, and generating an exception):

```
print(A*2)
```

The error resided in this Python method found in a student's Vector class:

```
def __rmu1__(self, entity):
return self*entity
```

I could not find the error, because the code is actually correct. So what was causing the error? Here is the corrected code:

```
def __rmul__(self, entity):
return self*entity
```

Does the corrected code look *exactly* like the bad code? That is because the error is almost impossible to see. The rmul looks almost like rmul. The student had typed the *number* '1' for the lower-case *letter* 'l'. So, what does a programmer's typeface look like? It is monospaced (useful for vertical alignment) and makes different letters look different—e.g., the number 105 does *not* look like the letters 10S.[5] By the way, this example remains in my mind cemented by the pain it took me to find it.

0	0	1	I	l
uppercase o	number zero	number one	uppercase i	lowercase l

---

[5]A great programming type is **Vera Sans Mono.** Look it up on the Internet.

Which is the best function name:

```
createMatrix(),⁶
createPopulation(),
createPopulationMatrix(),
popMat(), or
coffee()?
```

Rarely are we interested in the data type of a variable. So I prefer `createPopulation()` to `createMatrix()`.⁷ The `createPopulationMatrix()` seems needlessly long. The shorter `popMat()` is too abbreviated for my taste. Why would someone name a function `coffee`? Thinking of descriptive names is difficult for some people. The isolated programmer knows what his own variables mean, so why not pick *any* name, or at least a quickly chosen reasonable name? The main practical reason for me is that I have too often lost my grasp on large complicated programs. The program intricacies were so many and so complicated that I began to forget both what and how I did something last week. I have been forced to re-write programs in a more readable style just to understand my own work. And as a C.S. teacher, I want my code to be understood by others, not intimidated by it.

> People sometimes ask me what length I look for in
> a method. To me length is not the issue. The key is
> the semantic distance between the method name
> and the method body.—Martin Fowler, *Refactoring*
> (Addison Wesley, 1999), page 77.

---

⁶CamelCase (aka CapWords aka studlyCaps) notation is slightly easier to write than under_score (aka snake case) notation, which is slightly easier to read—e.g.,
   def extractXandYCoordinatesFromChromosome(row):
   def extract_X_and_Y_Coordinates_From_Chromosome(row):
   Both styles are acceptable for coding.
⁷The study of names, especially in technical fields, is called *onomastics*.

Prefixing the data type as a tag to the name of a variable or constant is called *Hungarian notation*. Occasionally there is some justification for it, but not often in school problems.

Certainly functions should be separated by at least a blank line. Should you place a line of dashes or stars between functions? I don't know anyone who does this but me. On the screen most coders don't think it is worth the trouble, but on paper (no color), separating lines helps in reading handouts of code.

Which example below is preferable (aligned or irregularly spaced equal signs)?

```
version 1:
    bestX         = x
    bestY         = y
    bestDirection = f(x,y)
    step          = 2*pi/64  # = 64 directions
    radius        = 0.01     # = the distance of the step.
------------------------------------------------------------

version 2:
    bestX = x
    bestY = y
    bestDirection = f(x,y)
    step = 2*pi/64  # = 64 directions
    radius = 0.01 # = the distance of the step.
```

Answer: Either is acceptable, because they are both readable. [Note: The Python PEP 0008 style guide discourages version 1.] Some people don't see much benefit from attempting to make code visually attractive (version 1). In fact, they are bothered by the fussiness of others in this matter. Vertical alignment does take more time to set up and more effort to maintain. Yet, others are bothered by a lack of visual organization.

So, again, I think it is a personal style. Incidentally, I recall two great math department heads whose offices were always a mess (lack of visual organization). It didn't matter, because they were effective in their jobs.

In some languages the programmer has the option of using named arguments received as named parameters (aka keyword arguments received as keyword parameters). And in Python, if the receiving set of parameters begins with a star, then keywords arguments are *required*.[8] Below are two examples. [Note: You pass *arguments* (aka *actual* parameters) and receive *parameters* (aka *formal* parameters).]

```
def fn(*,a,b,c,d):
    print(a,b,c,d)
#---------------------
fn(a=1, b=2, d=3, c=4) # output:1 2 4 3

fn(a=1, b=2, d=3, 4)    # output:ERROR (missing keyword)
```

Is this a good idea? The extra effort makes good sense with a long list of parameters, or where the reader needs the extra help. Also using a named argument can save space. Instead of this:

```
def createArray(arraySize):
    array = []
    ...
def main():
    arraySize = 100
    array      = createArray(arraySize)
```

---

[8]*Reserved words* aka *keywords* (one word) cannot be used as identifiers—e.g., `for = 3` causes a compiler error, because the compiler thinks `for` is the start of a loop. However keyword arguments and keyword parameters are simply named identifiers in function calls.

Rewrite it with one less line:

```python
def createArray(arraySize):
    array = []
    ...
def main():
    array = createArray(arraySize = 100)
```

If we pass just the 100, we lose the descriptor.

If you have many parameters, use named arguments and vertical alignment. Here is a line of code from the fourth edition of an O'Reilly Python programming book:

```python
threadtools.startThread(
    action     = self.cache.deleteMessages,
    args       = (msgnumlist,),
    context    = (popup,),
    onExit     = self.onDeleteExit,
    onFail     = self.onDeleteFail,
    onProgress = self.onDeleteProgress)
```

Notice the use of named arguments, vertical alignment and the stacking of parameters. I have never stacked parameters in a function header, because I have never had a function this verbose. Nevertheless, stacking seems to be a good idea for lengthy parameter sets.

Which of the following three examples is the most readable?

```python
Method 1.
netSalary = (jobIncome + hobbyIncome + stockDividends +     \
            (rents - utilities) - personalLivingExpenses - \
             mortgagePayments - medicalExpenses)
print(netSalary)
```

Method 2.

```
netSalary = (jobIncome              +
             hobbyIncome            +
             stockDividends         +
             (rents - utilities)    -
             personalLivingExpenses -
             mortgagePayments       -
             medicalExpenses)
print(netSalary)
```

Method 3.

```
netSalary =  (jobIncome
              + hobbyIncome
              + stockDividends
              + (rents - utilities)
              - personalLivingExpenses
              - mortgagePayments
              - medicalExpenses)
print(netSalary)
```

My preference is for Method 3. In text, most math books break *after* an operator. In code, it is sometimes better to break *before* an operator.

Use **external documentation**. By this I mean at the top of your program, in a neat box, place *some* of the following information:

1. *a title for your program

2. *a program description and maybe some program requirements

3. *your name

4. *the date (including the year) the document is turned in

5. *the course name, class period/section

6. the programming language

7. imported packages, modules, and libraries, especially graphics

8. key algorithms used

9. strategy or design implemented in the program

10. external files

Here is an example from my own code:

```
"""+===============+=====-========*========-======+===========+
   ||                   CIRCLE DETECTION                     ||
   ||             by M. Stueben (October 8, 2017)            ||
   ||           Artificial Intelligence; Mr. Stueben,        ||
   ||             Periods 1, 2, and 7                        ||
   ||                                                        ||
   || Description: This program detects a circle (radius     ||
   ||              and center) in a 512x512 gray-scale       ||
   ||              image of a circle and 500 random points   ||
   ||              (aka snow, noise).                        ||
   ||              It then draws a new circle in red over the||
   ||              initial circle. The circles almost match. ||
   || Algorithms:  Gaussian smoothing, Sobel operator/filter,||
   ||              Canny edge detection, and a vote accumulator-||
   ||              matrix equal to the size of the image.    ||
   || Downloads:   None                                      ||
   || Language:    Python Ver. 3.3                           ||
   || Graphics:    Tkinter Graphics                          ||
   +========================================================+
"""
```

Next is a topic that drives some people crazy: small coding conventions. Which expression below is the most readable?

```
ANN = inputs,w,h,v
```

```
ANN = inputs, w, h, v
```

I slightly prefer the second, unless there is a shop style with which everyone needs to conform. Should you write

```
y = 2 * (x + y)
```

or

```
y=2*(x+y)?
```

What someone suggested is

```
y = 2*(x + y).
```

Why? Maybe because multiplication in textbooks is often implied: $2a$, not $2 \times a$.[9] Consequently, we place spaces around '+' and '—', but not around '*'. Write what you think is most clear.

---

[9]Recall that multiplication and division are of equal precedence in interpreting *arithmetical* mathematical expressions—i.e., you perform those two operations in the order that they appear: $8/2 \times 4 = 16$. Now, move to algebra and let $a = 4$. Modern algebra books have $8/2a = 1$. So we see that in algebra implicit multiplication (implied grouping) has a different precedence than explicit multiplication. In coding, implicit multiplication is (usually) not possible. But, it is possible on my programmable TI-84 calculator, which interprets both expressions as 16.

Below is a function to determine the area of a triangle given its vertices.[10] I placed spaces around only one operator and not the seven others. Also the parameter pairs are separated by three spaces.

```python
def triangleArea (x1,y1,   x2,y2,   x3,y3): # vertices
    return abs((x1-x3)*(y2-y3) - (x2-x3)*(y1-y3))/2
```

The Python PEP 0008 style guide suggests *usually* surrounding assignments and relations with white space : x = 5, not x=5. But allow no spaces for named argument/parameter assignments—e.g., doIt (a=1, b=2). It also recommends no spaces following function names: print(x), not print (x). I try to follow these rules, but occasionally slip up. The wonderful VIM code editor will flag code not following PEP 0008 guidelines.

Should we place each statement on its own line or is that is being too dogmatic? From an old 1981 book on computer science[11]: "Successive commands can be written on the same line provided that, logically, they belong together." The question, as always, is readability. All methods below are fine, because they are all readable.

---

[10] Why does this work? The determinant $\begin{vmatrix} x_1 & y_1 \\ x_2 & y_2 \end{vmatrix}$ is the area (possibly negative) of the parallelogram with adjacent sides made up of position vectors $\langle x_1, y_1 \rangle$ and $\langle x_2, y_2 \rangle$. This is easy to prove with a geometric diagram. Do it now. (A position vector has its initial point at the origin.) The vector from point $(x3, y3)$ to point $(x1, y1)$ is position vector $x1 - x3,\ y1 - y3$. The vector from point $(x3, y3)$ to point $(x2, y2)$ is position vector $x2 - x3,\ y2 - y3$. So the area of the triangle with these two vectors as sides must be $\dfrac{1}{2}\begin{vmatrix} x1-x3 & y1-y3 \\ x2-x3 & y2-y3 \end{vmatrix} = \big((x1-x3)(y2-y3)-(x2-x3)(y-y3)\big)/2$.

I found this computation in an article by Brian Hayes in Andy Oram and Greg Wilson's *Beautiful Code* (O'Reilly, 2007). The author was trying to determine if three points were collinear (if area of the triangle they formed as vertices is zero).

[11] David Gries, *The Science of Programming* (Springer-Verlag, 1981), page 276.

```
#--Method 1 (acceptable, but discouraged in Python)
a = 1; b = 2; c = 3; d = 4

#--Method 2 (common in Python)
a, b, c, d = 1, 2, 3, 4

#--Method 3 (bulky, but this is the most readable)
a = 1
b = 2
c = 3
d = 4
```

According to PEP 0008, nothing should follow a colon. In other words, this is what most code readers should expect:

```
    if a == b:
        doIt(c)
#--------------------

    if a == b:
        doIt(c)
    else:
        runIt(c)
#--------------------

    for i in range(5):
        print(i)
```

But if you look at code on the Internet, you will find the following.

```
if a == b: doIt(c)
else: runIt(c)

for n in range(5): doIt(n)

while type(x) == int: (p, x) = (x, array[x])
```

From a beginner's Python textbook:

```python
def fib(num):
    return 1 if num < 3 else fib(num-1) + fib(num-2)
```

Yes, the previous items are all readable. It is just that they are unexpected, and strike some coders as ugly. That being said, list comprehensions, which we are all expected to use in Python, are written exactly in this so-called ugly way.

```python
print( [x*x for x in range(5)])              # = [0, 1, 4, 9, 16]
print( [x*x for x in range(5) if x%2 == 0])  # = [0, 4, 16]
print( [x*x if x%2 == 0 else -1 for x in range(5)] )
                                             # = [0, -1, 4, -1, 16]
```

Generally a list comprehension is faster than a `for` loop. Yet, exchanging a `for` loop (with an `if-else-if-else`) for a list comprehension (with an `if-else-if-else`) actually makes the code slower. That was a surprise to me.

The following is extremely readable code that breaks the colon rule and even places multiple statements on the same line:

```python
for x in dataSet:
    if -10 <= x <  0: print('Case   I'); continue
    if   0 <= x < 10: print('Case  II'); continue
    if  10 <= x < 20: print('Case III'); continue
    print(x)
```

Because it uses vertical alignment to such good effect, I don't think this code block can be made more readable.

Confession: I sometimes use the one-line form (if a == b: doIt (c)), but never with an else. One respected Python author suggested that functions, loops, and if statements, all with single-line bodies, are acceptable in being written on one line. I don't like to see code like this, but it is readable.

The following is a controversial example. Both versions use the genetic crossover method to generate two genetically new children from the chromosomes (strings, here) of two parents. Which is more readable?

Version 1:
```
def produceTwoChildren(parent1, parent2):
    r  = randint (0, MAX)
    child1 = parent1[0:r] + parent2[r:MAX]
    child2 = parent2[0:r] + parent1[r:MAX]
    return (child1, child2)
```

Version 2:
```
def produceTwoChildren(parent1, parent2):
    r  = randint (0, MAX)
    return (parent1[0:r] + parent2[r:MAX], parent2[0:r] +
    parent1[r:MAX])
```

Version 1 is more readable because it uses vertical alignment for the computations, contains the descriptive identifiers child1 and child2, and places the two computations on separate lines, which makes them easier to understand.

Version 2 is more readable because it is shorter and the code is so simple we don't need it broken up, we don't need it vertically aligned, and we don't need descriptive names.

I prefer Version 1, but cannot argue against the reasons for preferring Version 2. That being said, let's look at the same problem again. A straight stick is one unit in length. Two marks are randomly made on the stick. What is the probability that that these marks are within a tenth of a unit of each other? Solve by simulation with max = 10000000 runs.

```
from random import random
max     = 10000000
```

```
#---Method 1 (one line, broken into two lines)
    print ('Answer1 =', round(sum([abs(random()-random()) <= 0.1
                            for n in range (max)])/max, 2))
```

```
#---Method 2 (five lines)
    total = 0
    for n in range (max):
        total += abs(random()-random()) <= 0.1
    answer = round(total/max, 2)
    print ('Answer2 =', answer)
```

I can understand the code in Method 1 almost as easily as the code in Method 2. Method 1 also has the advantage of being only one logical line long. Nevertheless Method 2 is preferred because it is easier to debug. In writing Method 1 I had accidentally placed the 2 next to the final parenthesis. No compiler error was generated, and the code looked correct. The output was 0 2, instead of the correct 0.19.

So what can we say about all of these examples? First, never break with shop style. If there is no shop style, and if you break with PEP 0008 or some other coding convention, at least have some justification for doing so. If someone else does not follow your small coding conventions, don't start a religious argument.

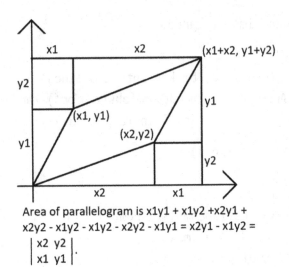

Area of parallelogram is x1y1 + x1y2 +x2y1 + x2y2 - x1y2 - x1y2 - x2y2 - x1y1 = x2y1 - x1y2 =
$$\begin{vmatrix} x2 & y2 \\ x1 & y1 \end{vmatrix}.$$

CHAPTER 7

Step-Wise Refinement

> Only stories are really readable.—Rudolf Flesch, *The Art of Readable Writing* (Collier MacMillan, 1949), page 74.

ONE WAY TO SELF-DOCUMENT your code is to use **top-down design**, a form of **structured programming** also called **step-wise refinement**.[1] In this style,[2] the main function contains function calls with descriptive English names—e.g., enterData(), computeData(), and printData(). The function calls will form an outline of what the code does. They tell a story.

When you follow one of these calls, you again may get mostly an outline of sub-calls that describe what the child function does. For example, computeData() may lead us to calculateDistances() and FindSmallestDistance(). Of course, this cannot go on forever, and eventually the reader must encounter actual computer instructions. The goal is to choose function names so descriptive that a reader can easily

---

[1] I equate structured programming with procedural programming (programming with functions, procedures, subroutines, and methods), with step-wise refinement as its goal. The opposite of *structured code* is *spaghetti code*.

[2] "Style is the art of choosing."—Winston Weathers, "The Rhetoric of the Series," Found in *Contemporary Essays on Style* by Glen A. Love and Michael Payne (Scott Foresman, 1969), page 21.

© Michael Stueben 2018
M. Stueben, *Good Habits for Great Coding*, https://doi.org/10.1007/978-1-4842-3459-4_7

understand the design of a program without reading much computer code or comments. Here is another example:

```python
def main():
    matrix = createSudoku()
    matrix = solveTheSudoku(matrix)
    printVerification(matrix)
    root.mainloop() # Required for Tk graphics.
```

In contrast, the **bottom-up design** is a stream-of-consciousness coding, aka cowboy coding, aka coding by the seat of your pants—i.e., we code the next part of the program that occurs to us, while the big picture is vaguely kept in our heads. This style works well with small programs.

It doesn't matter if a program is written bottom-up, top-down, or is a mixture of both. The goal is that the program *reads* top-down. This allows for program verification on different levels (forest level and tree level), and makes reading the program easier for the reviewer, which could be its author in three months.

Below is one of my top-down (step-wise refined) main functions in Python:

If you look closely, you will notice that most lines accept the output from the previous line.

```python
def main():
    image = list(readPixelColorsFromImageFile\
            (IMAGE_FILE_NAME = 'e:\\lena_rgb_p3.ppm'))
    displayImageInWindow(image, False)

    saveTheImageGrayScaleNumbersToFile\
            (image, GRAY_SCALE_NUMBERS_FILE_NAME =
            'e:\\grayScale.ppm')
    image = extractTheImageGrayScaleNumbersFromFile\
            (GRAY_SCALE_NUMBERS_FILE_NAME = 'e:\\grayScale.ppm')
    displayImageInWindow(image, False)
```

```
image = smoothTheImage\
        (image, NUMBER_OF_TIMES_TO_SMOOTH_IMAGE = 4)
saveTheImageGrayScaleNumbersToFile\
        (image, GRAY_SCALE_NUMBERS_FILE_NAME =
        'e:\\smoothed.ppm')
image = extractTheImageGrayScaleNumbersFromFile\
        (GRAY_SCALE_NUMBERS_FILE_NAME = 'e:\\smoothed.ppm')
displayImageInWindow(image, False)

image = sobelTransformation(image)  # image = [...(mag,
angle)...]

sobelMagnitudes = normalize([x[0] for x in image])

displayImageInWindow(sobelMagnitudes, False)

imageWithGrayValuesTransformedToLists = cannyTransform(image)

image = doubleThresholdImageListsInToGrayScaleValues\
        (imageWithGrayValuesTransformedToLists)

displayImageInWindow(image, True)

root.mainloop()
```

Only some weeks later, after I pulled up the program to check some detail, did I suspect that the main function was too big. Here is my rewrite:

```
def main():
    imageFileName              = 'g:\\lena_rgb_p3.ppm'
    grayScaleNumbersFileName = convertColorFileToGrayScaleFile
                               (imageFileName)
    smoothedFileName = extractSmoothAndSaveImage(grayScale
                       NumbersFileName)
```

```
imageLists        = sobelTransformSmoothedImage(smoothedFile
                    Name)
printNormalizedImageLists(imageLists)
imageLists        = cannyTransform(imageLists)
image             = doubleThresholdImageListsInToGrayScale
                    Values(imageLists)
displayImageInWindow(image)
root.mainloop()
```

This version is more readable because it is shorter. Can it be written more clearly? Maybe, but this is my best effort after two tries.

An important style of programming is called **incremental** (aka *iterative*, aka *evolutionary*) development. In this style, the programmer first writes the program with only a small subset of the requirements (a "walking skeleton"). Once that is working, a new set of requirements is added. Then, when the improved program is working, another set of requirements is added, etc. Reorganization of design will probably need to be implemented multiple times during the development. Sometimes the evolutionary approach is called the **MoSCoW** method: *Must have, Should have, Could have and Won't have, but would like to have.* Sometimes it is referred to as **time boxing**.

There are advantages to this approach. A working—admittedly incomplete—program is always finished. This gives a psychological boost to the programmer(s). There is much less stress and uncertainty at the end of the project than is typically the case with large projects. The graphical layout, the interface, and user directions tend to become better due to early user feedback. The early versions of the program become prototypes that guide the final design. Is this the best way to program? Possibly for programs with many features, but most school programs just develop algorithms.

CHAPTER 8

Comments

*U*SE COMMENTS WITH CARE. The 5-line Boolean function below is my revision of 13 lines of code with nine more comment lines. The longer version was an Internet instructor's example, with the direction to comment nearly every line of code (terrible idea, even for beginners). Self-documentation is better.

```python
def isAllVowels(stng):
    for ch in stng.lower():
        if ch not in ['a', 'e', 'i', 'o', 'u']:
            return False
    return True
```

Self-documenting code eliminates the need for many comments. But we still need comments for the following reasons:

a. to show organization (break the code into cases),

b. to give the *insights*—i.e., to make subtle observations explicit,

c. to state some assumptions, especially pre-conditions, post-conditions, invariants, and boundary limits, or

d. to give examples (useful when writing classes).

© Michael Stueben 2018
M. Stueben, *Good Habits for Great Coding*, https://doi.org/10.1007/978-1-4842-3459-4_8

The code below prints out a chess board with eight queens. The first line shows the benefit of an example comment.

```python
def printBoard(board):      # Example: board = [3,5,7,2,0,6,4,1]
    print("##################")
    for col in board:
        s = ['- '] * len(board)           # build a list of
                                          #   strings with no 'Q '
        s[col] = 'Q '                     # insert 'Q 's in the
                                          #   correct places
        print('# ' + ''.join(s) + "#") # make the list into one
                                          #   string.
    print("##################")
```

Should comments be written in complete sentences as suggested by PEP 0008? Yes, if you can, but a comment is readable either way. Should comments be written in-line as in the printBoard() example? Some experts say no. But I prefer to do this for short comments. This is the advantage of 110-character line lengths, not for long code lines, but for the occasional in-line comments following the code. Also, lining up comments, as shown above, makes the code more inviting to read.

Comments should tell you *why* (if the code isn't clear), not *how*. You don't need to explain how or even what, because that is done in the code. And if you write a comment about how, and the how is changed, then the comment needs to be changed. But what often can't be understood through the code alone is the why-are-we-doing-this?

What do you think about these two comments concerning a method in a vector class?

```python
def dist(self, other): # Return the distance between two points
(position vectors).
    return (self-other).mag()  # Vector.dist(A,B) and A.dist(B)
                                #   both work
```

Is the "`Return the distance ...`" comment necessary? I think so. Classes, especially complicated classes, should be documented like a manual, and should contain redundancy. As a Python beginner, I did not realize that a Python class automatically allowed both notations. So, I now try to make optional notations explicit. Notice that the minus sign in "`self-other`" looks like a hyphen. Maybe it should have been written "`self - other.`"

I suspect that exceptionally talented programmers rarely feel commenting and reorganizing code are necessary for their high school programs. They almost never get lost in their own code, and badly written code is still easy for them to understand. That is one reason average workers have difficulty following the talented. They don't make much effort to be clear, just concise. And that is why talented students are sometimes contemptuous of readability requirements. They honestly don't understand our difficulties.

Do comments indicate bad code? While this can be true, a statement like that can cause beginning coders to shun comments. The goal is to write readable code. If comments help, then they should be used. Consider the comments in this depth-first search function.

```
def DFS_FewestNodesPath(node, goalNode, path=[]):
# Notes: 1. We avoid loops by reference to the path itself.
#        2. The recursion will be unwound just below the
              recursive call at (*).

#---Append current node.
    path = path + [node]

#---base case
    if node == goalNode:
        return path
```

```
#---recursive case
    bestPathSoFar = []
    for (child, dist) in graph[node]: # dist is a dummy
    variable that is never used.
        if child not in path:
            newPath = DFS_FewestNodesPath(child, goalNode, path)
            # <-- (*)
            if newPath and (len(newPath) < len(bestPathSoFar) or
            bestPathSoFar == []):
                bestPathSoFar = newPath

#---Return best path, which could be [].
    return bestPathSoFar
```

I think the eight comments are needed in this ten-line body, because the function is recursive and for me the algorithm is complicated. Industry tries to avoid recursion unless it is absolutely necessary, because it is too hard to maintain.

Here is advice from a programming contest training manual: "Write comments first. If you can't *easily* write these comments, you probably don't really understand what the program does. We find it much easier to debug our comments than our programs."[1] (I think by "comments" they include an outline of the program by function calls.) Unfortunately, we *cannot* write comments correctly until we understand the solution. We begin to understand the solution when we discover that our program fails, and we trace through the code. Let me give you an example. I was writing the code to implement the minimax decision-rule for a game of Othello. Here is my original comment:

```
#---Return best board score for white
```

---

[1]Steven S. Skiena (Stony Brook) and Miguel A. Revilla (Valladolis, Spain), *Programming Challenges* (Springer, 2003), page 9. Today this is called CDD (comment driven development).

Days later I changed the code and revised the comment to this:

```
#---Three cases: 1. Return (usually) the move with the minimum
                    boardScore value (COMPUTER's choice), or
#                2. if there is no legal move AND depth is
                    zero, then return
#                   boardScore(), or
#                3. if there is no legal move AND depth != 0,
                    then return maxValue(depth-1, alpha, beta)
```

Until I traced through my failing program and discovered my simple-minded code failed in some circumstances, I never thought about the positions where one side has no legal move. So the comment was as wrong as the code. Still, writing comments first may be a good idea. I just have never tried it. The authors made the insightful observation that "bugs tend to infest code that is too ugly to read or too clever to understand."[2] Amen.

Below are two versions of a function that receives a list and a number r, and then returns the rth permutation of the list.

```
# VERSION 1.
def permute(Lst, r):
 #--initialize
    Lst = Lst[:]
    L = len(Lst)

 #--check data
    assert L>=1 and r>=0 and r<factorial(L) and \
          type(Lst) == list and type(r)==int
```

---

[2]Steven S. Skiena and Miguel A. Revilla, *Programming Challenges* (Springer, 2003), page 40.

```
#--base case
    if L == 1: return Lst

#--recursive case
    d     = factorial(L-1)
    digit = Lst[r//d]
    Lst.remove(digit)
    return [digit] + permute(Lst, r%d)

# VERSION 2.
def permute(Lst, r):
    Lst = Lst[:]
    L = len(Lst)
    assert L>=1 and r>=0 and r<factorial(L) and \
            type(Lst) == list and type(r)==int
    if L == 1: return Lst
    d     = factorial(L-1)
    digit = Lst[r//d]
    Lst.remove(digit)
return [digit] + permute(Lst, r%d)
```

I originally wrote version 1. But later I came to see that the comments were not only unnecessary, but that they made the code harder to read. So why the change in my perspective? Answer: I got more comfortable with reading Python code. The comments necessary for a beginner are not necessary for the more experienced programmer.

The first comment below was helpful a year later when I needed to print a matrix in the Cell class. At that time I worked with classes so rarely that I could not immediately remember the call format.

```
#---The call looks like this: Cell.print(matrix)
#    def print(matrix): # DEBUGGING UTILITY: Print the matrix/
                             board to the console.
         .  .  .
#------------------------Cell Class------------------------
```

I consider coding the algorithm to change a repeating decimal into a fraction to be difficult. Curiously, the examples are easy to understand. To make this clear to a student programmer, the code below has the same example worked out twice: algebraically and in computer code. If I introduced a small error, you could probably find it in a minute or two. This is well-documented code, but who has the time to write comments like this? My answer is that in special circumstances, this kind of detail is necessary.

```
#      EXAMPLE:
#      Let             x =       12.345676767...
#      Then       100000x = 1234567.676767676...
#      And           1000x =    12345.676767676...
#      So 100000x - 1000x = 1234567 - 12345 =   1222222.
         <-- Notice that we can ignore the decimal parts.
#      Thus, x = 1222222/99000

def repeatingDecimalToFraction(number, repLength):
#---Preconditions: number is float type, repLength is integer and 0 <
repLength <= length of decimal portion.
    numberCastToString    = str(number)
    decimalPointPosition  = numberCastToString.find('.')
    lengthOfDecimalPortion = len(numberCastToString) -
                            decimalPointPosition - 1
```

```
                           # == AN EXAMPLE IS GIVEN TO MAKE THIS
                           ALGORITHM CLEAR. ==
                           # number            = 12.34567 <-- Here,
                                               the 67 repeats.
                     # repLength          = 2, the length of 67
numberlength = len(numberCastToString) # numberlength = 8, the
                                       total length
lengthOfIntegerPart = len(str(int(number)))  # lengthOfIntegerPart =
                                             2, the length of 12
shiftLength = numberlength - (lengthOfIntegerPart + 1 + repLength)
# 1 is for the decimal point.
                     # shiftLength        = 8 - (2 + 1 + 2) = 3,
                                          the distance
                     # from the decimal point in 12.34567 to
                     the repeating part (67)
factor1 = int (10**(shiftLength+repLength)) # factor1    =   100000
factor2 = int (10**shiftLength)             # factor2 =    1000
numberTimesFactor1 = int(number * factor1)  #    = 1234567.676767
numberTimesFactor2  = int(number * factor2)  #   =   12345.676767
numerator = numberTimesFactor1 - numberTimesFactor2
               #    = 1234567.676767 - 12345.676767= 1222222
denominator = factor1 - factor2         # = 99000 (= 100000x -
                                        1000x = (100000 - 1000)x
return numerator, denominator      # postcondition: integer types
                                   are returned.
```

Some programmers will see this as too much detail, but too much
for them is not too much for others. If you look closely you will notice the
variables factor1 and factor2. Generally, we prefer more descriptive
and less similar variable names. I know this, but I couldn't think of better
names.

According to PEP 0008, "You should use two spaces after a sentence-ending period." I remember being given the same advice in a 1961 high school typing class. When word processors arrived, the general advice was changed to one space between sentences. I don't think the two-space rule matters much.

Industry expects a comment to begin each Python function (docstrings). This makes sense for legacy code. And since it is the world standard, you might consider getting into the habit of doing this for complex functions. I have seen many functions on the Internet that were so poorly named and used such abbreviated cryptic parameters that I wished the authors had used docstrings.

CHAPTER 9

Stop Coding

> When I code, I sometimes write lines hoping they
> will work without really understanding what they
> are doing.—A high school senior taking his fourth
> programming class (December 2011).

THE MOMENT YOU START *to feel confused, stop coding.* When I first assigned
the Traveling Salesman Problem to my students, I appended the following
advice:

> The data in your program will be a list of
> xy-coordinates. Make it a list of lists, not tuples.
> And append an id in the zeroth position—e.g.,

```
city = [[id, x-value, y-value], [id, x-value, y-value], ...,
[id, x-value, y-value]]
```

> Why make a list of lists instead of a list of tuples?
> Because you don't know if you will later need to
> modify the components, and tuples are immutable.
> Why append an id? Because you don't know if
> you will later need to give your xy-coordinates an
> attribute—e.g., visited and not-visited—or a tuple of
> attributes.

© Michael Stueben 2018
M. Stueben, *Good Habits for Great Coding*, https://doi.org/10.1007/978-1-4842-3459-4_9

When I first came to write the Traveling Salesman Problem, I worked in tuples with no `id`. Eventually I began to lose control of the program. The functions were becoming so complicated (triply subscripted brackets) that modifications were painful. It was time to start over. Based on my failures, I knew that mutable lists and attributes would simplify the program. Why didn't I realize this at the beginning? Because I was so focused on conceptual details, I could not think well about implementation. Only when my coding became difficult did I realize my design mistakes.

If your program starts to get so complicated that you can't understand it, then you must refactor or start over completely. When you have to start over, the good news is that you are smarter, and some of your code is salvageable.

Do you need to outline an entire program or an algorithm before you start? If the program/algorithm is exceptionally complicated, then you need at least some outlining.[1] You will know this because you will immediately feel uncomfortable with the assignment. Let me make this explicit: You _must_ spend time thinking-before-coding about a project that you find complicated. For most school problems, I usually design and type code at the same time. Anybody can do this with simple programs, but there is a level of difficulty beyond which coding-on-the-fly does not work well. You need to find your own level, and know when you can and cannot get away with the quick-and-dirty style.[2] This is not easy, because habits

---

[1] In 2003, at ARML, the premier H.S. mathematics competition, the captain of our school's math team gave his teammates a pep talk before the final round. He said that he had noticed in practice many of his teammates missed problems that they were capable of solving. Why? They had failed to read the problems carefully enough to detect subtle relationships in the given information. His advice was to "read each problem closely _before_ starting to solve it." Our school won ARML that year.

[2] Search the Internet for BDUF (big design up front), RDUF (rough design up front), and "emergent design." There are significant problems with designing a complex program, without the experience of having written a prototype (scaled-down version) of the same program.

are hard to break, our egos get involved, and we want to keep up with our classmates. Typing lines of code that do not work well together is not coding, except in name. Perhaps we have learned a lesson. Pay attention to the psychology of coding.

One way to outline on a keyboard is to just write the function names (**stubs** with no code inside, or **mocks**, which return bogus data).[3]

```
def doIt(x): # <--STUB
    pass

def doIt(x): # <--MOCK
    return 0
```

There are two competing design philosophies in computer programming: *Do the right thing* and *worse is better*. The *do the right thing* philosophy is equally concerned with the completeness, consistency, correctness, ease-of-use, and simplicity of software design. It is an attempt to build perfect programs. And why shouldn't we make this attempt? This is the philosophy of professional software designers. Why would anyone claim that *worse is better*? Here is why:

a.   *Completeness* refers to special cases *not* being ignored in the program. If those special cases are of little interest to the user, why pay a heavy cost to code them up? Sometimes completeness is a waste of time.

b.   Consistency is useful and necessary for teams, but for the lone programmer, semi-consistency is good enough. Our limited time can be better spent elsewhere.

---

[3]The definitions of *stubs* and *mocks* vary. Safer is to use the term "fakes."

   c.   Ease-of-use is important if other people will use the program you wrote. But school programs are usually executed only by the designer. Unless ease-of-use is the goal of an assignment, it may get in the way of other goals.

   d.   Even the desire of having a program be correct may be sacrificed for good reason. I once saw some code where the distance formula $\sqrt{x^2 + y^2}$ was replaced by $x + y$ to speed up the program.[4] If my approximation program runs in 10 seconds, and your accurate program runs in 3 minutes, is your accurate program the one people will want to use? Sometimes we can pay too high a price for correctness.

At this point the *do the right thing* people will want to interrupt. They will point out that I have only reasoned from exceptions. Since every philosophy has exceptions, my objections are worthless. Worse, these exceptions are trying to tear down a positive philosophy. Where is the replacement philosophy? Fair enough. The *worse is better* school does have a replacement philosophy. Here it is: The *worse is better* philosophy advocates simplicity of design as primary. It suggests that consistency, completeness, ease of use, and correctness, and other positive attributes are more likely to evolve from a simple design kept simple than from a first attempt at perfection. If these characteristics do not occur by themselves, then we can insert them by modifying a simple-and-working program. The do-the-right-thing philosophy may work for teams that can spend months designing a program, but it is not the way a lone coder should write a program.

---

[4]How bad could the error be? Let $z = x + y$, where x and y are both non-negative, and $w = \sqrt{x^2 + y^2}$. Then what is the largest $\frac{z}{w}$ will ever become? The answer is $\sqrt{2}$.

My take on this tiny debate is that the goal of perfection in school programs can be pedantic. The standards for excellence in programming also must be measured in terms of resources (time mainly), and the motivation behind the assignment. Now for an example.

Students who program long enough will notice that they have repeatedly written debugging code to print a matrix, as well as other data structures. So why not write a universal matrix printer and keep it in a personal library? My version is below. Give it a matrix with integers, floats, strings, Booleans, and None all mixed together (this is Python, remember), and the code will neatly print all the data with vertical alignment.

```python
def printMatrix(Lst, decimalAccuracy = 2):
    print('---MATRIX:')
    if type (Lst) != list or type (Lst[0]) != list:
        print('*' * 45)
        print(' WARNING: The received parameter is NOT a \n',
                'matrix type. No printing was done.          ')
        print('*' * 45)
        return
    maxLength = 0
    for row in Lst:
        for x in row:
            if type(x) == float: x = round(x, decimalAccuracy)
            maxLength = max(len(str(x)), maxLength)
            if type(x) == float:
                print('%11.2f'%x,         end='')
            elif type(x) == int:
                print('%8d   '%x,         end='')
            elif type(x) == str:
                print('%8s   '%x,         end='')
            elif type(x) == bool:
                print('%8s   '%str(x), end='')
```

```
        elif x == None:
            print('%8s    '%str(x), end='')
        else:
            print(x, ' ')
    print()
print('==============================')
print('cell maxlength =', maxLength, '(8 is limit)')
```

Big question: Is a universal printer (this code) ever needed? The only matrices I have ever printed contained floats and integers. It now seems to me that I got carried away by the coolness of this tiny project: a *universal* matrix printer. It is over-engineered. I violated the YAGNI principle (don't write code if **y**ou **a**ren't **g**oing to **n**eed **i**t). Here, worse is definitely better.

By the way, here is a Python trick to pretty print a list:

```
Lst = ['A', 2, [1,2,3], 4000, 0.123]
print('', *Lst, sep='\n....')
"""
Output:
....A
....2
....[1, 2, 3]
....4000
....0.123
"""
```

The following advice actually contains some wisdom: Failing to plan is planning to fail. Think twice, code once. Code in haste and debug forever.[5] Remember that one week of debugging can save an entire hour of planning.

---

[5]Robert L. Kruse, *Data Structures & Program Design*, 2nd Ed. (Prentice-Hall, 1987), page 55.

CHAPTER 10

Testing

It is said that "eternal vigilance is the price of liberty."[1] Yes, because eternal vigilance is the price of all quality. When writing code this means test as you go, test each key function immediately after it is written, not waiting until the entire program is written. CABTAB: code a bit; test a bit. Early testing is probably the best idea ever for reducing coding errors. If we don't catch the bugs in each code chunk as we write it, then later we will be less familiar with the code when we try to debug it.

We test for the expected output of known input. We test for out-of-range values, off-by-one values, nonsense/interchanged data, empty sets, zero-length steps, bad game moves (illegal move or no legal move), division by zero, pre-conditions, post-conditions, invariants, proper relationships, and especially ***boundary conditions***. Testing as you go is called ***systematic testing*** and ***incremental prototyping***.

Recall that the 2-D video screen is internally represented by a 1-D list. Consequently, if we wish to draw a circle on a rectangular (`WIDTH × HEIGTH`) screen by pixel poking, then a 2-D image must be translated into a 1-D representation. I tried to do this directly. Look at the code below. The 1-D list is called `image`. Only one of the three lines (A, B, and C) is correct, yet they all look correct. Which one is correct?

---

[1]Paraphrased from a speech in 1790 by the Irish orator and politician John Philpot Curran. See *Wikipedia*.

© Michael Stueben 2018
M. Stueben, *Good Habits for Great Coding*, https://doi.org/10.1007/978-1-4842-3459-4_10

```
def frange(start, stop, step = 1):
    i = start
    while i < stop:
        yield i # <-- not return i
        i += step

def drawCircle(cx, cy, radius, image):
    from math import cos, sin
    for t in frange(0, 6.28, 0.01): # range will not allow
    float steps.
        x = cx + radius*cos(t)
        y = cy + radius*sin(t)
        image[int(y)*WIDTH  + int(x)] = 255 # <--A
        image[int(y *WIDTH) + int(x)] = 255 # <--B
        image[int(y *WIDTH  +     x)] = 255 # <--C
    return image
```

The only correct line is B. I spent several minutes looking at this code (with line A) trying to discover why the circle was spread out into waves. The expression y*WIDTH first must be rounded down. The point of this example is that errors are impossible to avoid without testing the code.

The following trap caught one of my brighter students:

```
v = [0]*2
print('v =', v)  # v = [0, 0]
m = [v]*2 #
print('m =', m)  # m = [[0, 0], [0, 0]]
m[0][0] = 8
print('m =',m)   # m = [[8, 0], [8, 0]]
#--Surprise: m[0][0] and m[1][0] share the same memory address.
```

Years ago I devised with a single question to determine which of my high school juniors and seniors were mathematically weak. Try it with any high school student.

Solve for y in terms of the other letters: $x - a = \dfrac{by - c}{d - y}$. [3 minutes]

Later I realized that coding up the solution to this problem gave an instructive example about how difficult it is to remove logical errors.

QUIZ 4. In your favorite language, write the following short function, and then compare your code with mine.

```
def solveEquation(a,b,c,d,x):
#    +---------------------------------------------------------+
#    | Given: (x-a) = (b*y-c)/(d-y)                            |
#    | Return the unique value for y, if it exists.           |
#    |          if no value for y exists, then print an       |
#    |            error message and exit the program.         |
#    |          if multiple values for y exist, then print    |
#    |            a warning and return a valid value for y.    |
#    +---------------------------------------------------------+
#... Finish writing this function.
```

Good luck.

```
#                   QUIZ 4 (My Solution)
def solveEquation(a,b,c,d,x):
#    +---------------------------------------------------------+
#    | Given: (x-a) = (by-c)/(d-y)                             |
#    | Return the unique value for y, if it exists.           |
#    |          [y = (x*d - a*d + c)/(x-a+b).]                 |
#    |            If no value for y exists, then print an      |
#    |              error message and exit the program.       |
#    |            If multiple values for y exist, then print   |
#    |              a warning and return a valid value for y.  |
#    +---------------------------------------------------------+
```

```
    if (x == (a-b) and (c != b*d)):
        exit('ERROR: No solution. The expression reduces to c =
        b*d.')

    if (x == (a-b) and (c == b*d)):
        print('WARNING: y is NOT unique: y may take ANY value,
        except d.')
        return int(not d) # y = 0 or 1

    if (x != (a-b) and (c == b*d)):
        exit('ERROR: No solution. The expression reduces to
        y = d.')
#---Note: x != (a-b) and c != b*d).
    y = (x*d - a*d + c)/(x-a+b)    # <-- No division by zero and
    no y = d.
    return y
```

Unfortunately, this problem is so difficult that it is limited in its educational use. Still, this is the kind of exercise that builds problem-solving skills.

You would think that A += B is only a shorthand notation for A = A + B. This is not true in Python and perhaps some other languages.

```
def append1(A): #
    A += [3]    #
#-----------------------
def append2(A):
    A = A + [3] # The two As are different objects.
#-----------------------
def main():
    A = [1,2]
    append1(A)
    print(A) # output: [1, 2, 3]
```

```
A = [1,2]
append2(A)
print(A) # output: [1, 2] ß Surprise!
```

So how can we protect ourselves from such syntactic poison?[2] The answer is to keep our code simple, and test as we go.

To fix an error, the first tool everyone tries is the guess, because that takes no effort, and many times that is successful. It is only when we can't fix a bug by guessing that we have to stop and think. But sometimes we don't stop—we just keep changing stuff in the hope that our problem will go away. At this point, our efficiency may actually drop *below* zero. We may start changing code that should not be changed.

The main way to discover errors in school programs is to run test data through the programs and check the results (**tracing**). Sometimes, for tricky algorithms, it is helpful to write a testing program that runs random data through a function and checks the answers.

Another way to find errors is to place error traps that will print only if an error is discovered. This gives us a self-debugging program to some extent. One reason to do this is that a bug correction in one part of a program may cause a failure in a different part.

Misko Hevery in a YouTube video asked an interesting question: Could you reconstruct source code from its tests? My initial reaction was "of course not." Then he suggested that a set of tests should tell a story. Suppose the tests looked like this:

```
Test1_ItShouldDoThis()
Test2_ItShouldDoThat()
Test3_ItShouldDoSomethingElse()
Test4_ItShouldDoThisToo()
Test5_ItShouldExitLikeThis()
```

---

[2]If a language provides convenient, compact shortcuts, then those shortcuts may be described as *syntactical sugar*, a term coined in 1964. The built-in dictionary data structure in Python is syntactic sugar for an associative matrix/list. I suspect that Python has more syntactic sugar than any other language.

So maybe he is right, and maybe our tests should be laid out to tell a story.

QUIZ 5. (IMPORTANT) Recall that the dot product of two vectors is the sum of their pair-wise products. For example, the dot product of x = [1,2,3,4] and y = [2, -3, 0, 5] is

1×2 + 2×(-3) + 3×0 + 4×5 = 16.

The four functions below all correctly calculate and return the dot product of two vectors (aka lists, aka arrays) x and y. The only difference is the error traps. Which is the preferred error trap: A, B, C, or D?

```
#---Method A.
def dotProd(x,y):
    return sum(x[n]*y[n] for n in range(len(x)))
```

```
#---Method B.
def dotprod(x,y):
    assert type(x) == type(y) == list
    return sum(x[n]*y[n] for n in range(len(x)))
```

```
#---Method C.
def dotprod(x,y):
    assert len(x) == len(y)
    return sum(x[n]*y[n] for n in range(len(x)))
```

```
#---Method D.
def dotprod(x,y):
    assert type(x) == type(y) == list
    assert len(x)   == len(y)
    return sum(x[n]*y[n] for n in range(len(x)))
```

My answer is in the footnote.[3]

When you write a function, consider testing for any pre-condition and boundary condition that will not generate a compile or run-time error. Making this a habit will save you hours of debugging time. The following is a fancy assert, which is probably not worth the time to code when a simpler form will do. Still, you should know such forms are possible.

```
import sys
assert x>0, 'in function ' + sys._getframe().f_code.co_name + \
          ' x = ' + str(x)
```

Output: `AssertionError: in function doIt x =  -1`

Also, do not put parentheses or brackets around a Python assert. A non-empty tuple or list is always evaluated as true (syntactical poison).

A programmer-built error trap can print much more information than an assert, can close files, and can save information in an error file. So why would anyone prefer to use the built-in assert statement instead of writing an error trap? Answer:

1. The assert is immediately seen as an error trap, not part of the function's task.

2. The assert is faster and easier to write than a user-built error trap.

---

[3]QUIZ 5 ANSWER: I choose C because without `len(x)` == `len(y)`, an error can pass undetected into the rest of the program. I consider the function not properly written without this error trap. However, we do NOT need to check the data types of x and y, because the compiler will do this for us. The compiler checks to be sure both x and y are subscriptable, and that they are collections of numbers, not strings or objects. Keep in mind that the times operator (*) is overloaded in Python—e.g., `'cat'*3` = `'catcatcat'`. Occasionally strange errors will slip through. Would a world-class programmer test for this possibility? My opinion: It is not cost-effective to protect our code from every extremely rare possibility.

3. The IDE will place the cursor on the assert line in
    your program; an error trap will usually just print an
    error message and exit the program.

QUIZ 6. Write a function that expects to receive two strings of the same
size and returns the number of letters that are different but in the same
relative places—e.g., the function receiving "ab<u>cd</u>ef" and "a<u>x</u>c<u>x</u>fe" would
return 4. My answer is at the end of this chapter. There is a clever way to do
this, at least in Python.

Consider printing some statistics (fancy term: **dynamic performance
analysis**) while your program is running, or after it finishes. Certainly,
always print the run time for *every* program—no exceptions. This can help
you determine the big O of your program. You may also want to print

1. the number of recursive calls made and the
    recursive depth reached,

2. the number of nodes accessed in a tree (I did this to
    measure the performance of alpha-beta pruning. My
    program looked at 2/3 fewer nodes with pruning.),

3. the maximum tree-level depth reached,

4. the maximum size of a queue or of some other
    dynamic data structure,

5. the number of items written into or read out of a file,

6. or the time taken per move and maybe the average
    time-per-move during a game.

There are several advantages to writing tests and debugging utilities
before you write your code.

1. When you finish writing your code, you can
    immediately test it while it is fresh in your mind,
    instead of taking some minutes to create a test.

2. You actually write the tests rather than moving on to another function.

3. Writing the tests first helps outline the function before you write it.

Some reasons NOT to test your code are 1) it's boring/stressful/tiring, 2) it apparently slows our progress, 3) we are not used to testing, and 4) we are afraid we might actually find a bug. All of these excuses are forms of self-delusion. To put it bluntly, not testing as you go signals sloppiness, laziness, and incompetence.

> Student programmer: "Is there any way out of this misery?"

> C.S. teacher: "Yes. Don't get into it in the first place: Test as you go, and write code defensively."

```
#------------------------------------------------------------------
```

QUIZ 6 ANSWER:

```
different sameLettersInSamePlaceCount(stng1, stng2):
    return sum(ch1 != ch2 for (ch1, ch2) in zip(stng1, stng2))
```

OK, if you didn't know about the zip function then you couldn't have used it. The instruction

```
print(list(zip(stng1, stng2)))
```

produces

```
[('a', 'a'), ('b', 'x'), ('c', 'c'), ('d', 'x'), ('e', 'f'),
('f', 'e')]
```

The zip function is worth remembering. In fact, this example is worth remembering. Notice that this comprehension is a generator comprehension, not a list comprehension (no square brackets). Notice how long the function name is. A glance at this simple code will tell the reader what it does. So why not use the name letters Count or something simpler? Answer: Because we want the reader to know exactly what the function calculates and returns without having to inspect function code.

* * *

A lifetime of looking at high school math/c.s. problems has motivated me to offer three more math problems for computer science students:

1. Given $g(x)$ in terms of $f(x)$, can we write $f(x)$ in terms of $g(x)$? Sometimes, <u>if you see the trick</u>. Given $g(x)=af(bx+c)+d$, with $a\neq 0$ and $b\neq 0$, write $f(x)$ as a function of $g(x)$ and the parameters $a,\ b,\ c,$ and d.

2. Given $a\leq x\leq b$, with $a<b$, find $f(x)$ such that $c\leq f(x)\leq d$, and $f(x)$ increases uniformly as x increases uniformly—e.g., if x is $\frac{3}{4}$ of the way between a and b, then $f(x)$ is $\frac{3}{4}$ of the way between c and d. The need for this formula is common in graphics. For example, you need this formula to draw the fancy web shape on the right. As x ranges from G to C, y must uniformly range from H to D.

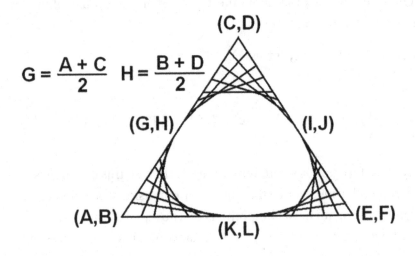

3. An automobile radiator holds quartCap quarts. It
    is filled with a pct1 percent solution of anti-freeze.
    Write a function antifreeze to return the correct
    number of quarts (rounded to at most 2 decimal
    places) of the solution that should be drained and
    refilled with pure antifreeze to bring the strength up
    to pct2 percent. Exit your program in an impossible
    situation—e.g., we assume that pct1 and pct2 are
    numbers between 0 and 1 inclusive.

* * *

ANSWER 1. $f(x) = \dfrac{g\left(\dfrac{x-c}{b}\right)-d}{a}$, where x is in the domain of f. Since

the x on both sides of the original equation represents the same value,
replace it on both sides with $\dfrac{x-c}{b}$, then simplify.

ANSWER 2. $f(x)=\dfrac{(x-a)(d-c)}{b-a}+c$.

Algebra: The simplest derivation I know is shown below.

$$a \le x \le b$$

$$0 \le x-a \le b-a$$

$$0 \le \frac{x-a}{b-a} \le 1$$

$$0 \le \frac{(x-a)(d-c)}{b-a} \le (d-c)$$

$$c \le \frac{(x-a)(d-c)}{b-a}+c \le d$$

Analytic Geometry: The problem naturally reduces to finding the line $y = mx + b'$ passing through the points (a, c) and (b, d). The slope for such a line is $m = \dfrac{d-c}{b-a}$, and b' is found by substitution of (a, c) into $y = mx + b'$, which gives us $b' = c - \dfrac{d-c}{b-a}a$. Thus, $y = \dfrac{d-c}{b-a}x - \dfrac{d-c}{b-a}a + c$. This expression simplifies to $y = \dfrac{(x-a)(d-c)}{b-a} + c$.

ANSWER 3.

```
def antifreeze (quartCap, pct1, pct2):
    assert 0<= pct1 <=1 and 0<= pct2 <=1 and pct1 <= pct2 and
            quartCap > 0, \
            ["ERROR (bad input):", quartCap, pct1, pct2] # Note
            the FOUR cases.

    return round(quartCap*(pct2-pct1)/(1-pct1), 2)
```

CHAPTER 11

Defensive Programming

By June 1949 people had begun to realize that it was not so easy to get a program right as had one time appeared. I well remember when I was trying to get working my first non-trivial program [in assembler code or perhaps machine language]. The realization came over me with full force that a good part of the remainder of my life was going to be spent in finding errors in my own programs. Turing had evidently realized this too, for he spoke at the conference on "checking a large routine."—Maurice Wilkes (Turing Award winner, 1967), *Memoirs of a Computer Pioneer* (MIT, 1985), page 145.

USE DEFENSIVE PROGRAMMING. Since we know in advance that there will be bugs, we can become proactive in several ways. We can write functions that

a. print passed parameters after they arrive in functions (tracing),

b. print intermediate computation values, and

© Michael Stueben 2018
M. Stueben, *Good Habits for Great Coding*, https://doi.org/10.1007/978-1-4842-3459-4_11

c.   print error messages to catch bad data (wrong type, wrong size, wrong order, division by zero, and out-of-bounds errors). This is called **error handling** and **crash reporting**. The try/except construct is sometimes useful here.

All of this is known as **defensive programming** or **scaffolding** because most of it will be removed eventually.

Here is a trick from Industry: Have a global constant called, say, errorCheck or debug. Preceding every block of error code (asserts, traces, printouts, try/excepts, type checks, etc.) is

```
if errorCheck:...
```

Then we don't erase the error code; we just turn it off with errorCheck = False. In industry, they sometimes set errorCheck to 0 (turn off all checking), 1 = turn on some checking, 2 = turn on more checking, etc.

I recently wrote a few lines of code to catch a variable that got out of bounds. I was proceeding by habit and even said to myself, "Well, this is a waste of time. This variable will never be out of bounds," only to discover on the next run that the variable was out of bounds. Repeated experiences like this have made me a believer in cautious coding.[1]

There is one danger to defensive coding: It can bury errors. Consider the following code:

```
def drawLine(m, b, image, start = 0, stop = WIDTH):
    step = 1
    start = int(start)
    stop =  int(stop)
```

---

[1]Placing too many error traps in a function can obscure what the function is supposed to do. In that case, sometimes, the traps should be moved into their own function.

```
if stop-start < 0:
    step = -1
    print('WARNING: drawLine parameters were reversed.')
for x in range(start, stop, step):
    index = int(m*x + b) * WIDTH + x
    if 0 <= index < len(image):
        image[index] = 255 # Poke in a white (= 255) pixel.
```

This function runs from start to stop. If stop is less than start, it just steps backward and *no error is reported.* Maybe we want this kind of error to be "fixed" during the run—buried—but I think we should at least print a warning that the range is coming in backwards. Maybe we should abort the program.

Given matrix A, we refer to the individual elements (a_{ij}) by the (i = row, j = col) convention. Similarly, when we read a page of text, we first fix on a row, and then read along a column. Unfortunately, there is competing convention: In the xy-plane we plot points by (x =col, y = row), and we also plot points on the computer screen using (col, row), but starting our "first quadrant" from the upper left, not the bottom left. Consequently, we have a tendency sometimes to use the matrix (row, col) scheme, and sometimes the point-plotting (col, row) scheme. Here is an example of a crossover. I start with (r = row, c = col) for the matrix, and then switch to (x = col, y = row) for plotting.

```
for r in range(8):
    for c in range(8):
        if M[r][c] == 1:
            x = c*70 + 85
            y = r*70 + 105
            canvas.create_oval(x-25,y-25, x+25, y+25,
            fill = 'BLACK')
```

There is no problem, because the code is clear. I only show this to illustrate that competing conventions sometimes occur in the same code chunks.

In the next example, I switched *x* and *y*, in two different calls to the same function, but the Python code still returns the same correct answer. How is this possible? Answer: I named the indices (keywords) *before* I passed them. Moral: Know your language.

```python
def sub(x, y):
    return x-y
#-----------------------------
def main():
    print(add(x = 2, y = 1)) # Output: 1
    print(add(y = 1, x = 2)) # Output: 1
```

> One YouTube commentator suggested never using
> x and y for matrix coordinates, but rather use row
> and col. Why? Because it is too easy to write (x,y)
> for what should be (y,x), whereas (row, col) are
> unlikely to be interchanged.

CHAPTER 12

Refactoring

WHEN YOUR PROGRAM is finished, don't walk away. Consider redesigning it—as long as a deadline is not looming. Redesigning, not to optimize, but to make working code easier to understand, to debug, to modify, and to integrate with other code is common enough to have a name: ***refactoring***.[1] Refactoring is reconsidering both variable and function names, breaking multi-tasking functions into single-task functions, applying stepwise refinement, reconsidering the choice of data structures, considering cohesion versus coupling, and rewriting code to make it clearer and more efficient.

I once wrote a simple function that received a string and a Boolean variable. An alarm immediately sounded in my head. Is this function doing two different tasks? Not really. The Boolean just told the function to print the string characters either alphabetically or ordered by frequency. I later discovered that I needed the function to also print the characters as they appeared in the string. It occurred to me that I could pass the Booleans True, False, or let the receiving parameter default to None.

---

[1]Breaking complex code into parts that are easier to understand is called "factoring," (aka decomposition) a term invented by programmers in the 1980s. The first known use of the term "refactoring" was in 1990. See *Wikipedia*, s.v. Code refactoring.

© Michael Stueben 2018
M. Stueben, *Good Habits for Great Coding*, https://doi.org/10.1007/978-1-4842-3459-4_12

However, this is a terrible way to code. Have you ever seen a Boolean variable that results in *three* values? Coders need to assume that some situations will never occur, even if they are possible. My eventual solution was to pass an integer to the function, which expected *only* the values 0, 1, and 2. Other values would cause a warning message to appear, would default to 0, but not throw an exception—no aborting of the program.

Why have a default value? Because the user of the function may not care how the output is ordered, may not want to be bothered to pass a parameter, or may not know the options available. Thus, the function becomes more robust.

Assignment: Write a function to return the first index of a target element in an array, else return -1. The code that follows shows three different ways to do this:

```python
# Method 1 (ugh!)
def indx(array, target): # 11 lines
    if array == []:
        return -1
    n = 0
    found = -1
    length = len(array)
    while n != length:
        if array[n] == target:
            found = n
            break
        n += 1
    return found
```

This first method was as inefficient as I could make it using standard ideas. It is the code produced by an imaginary student who never asks if the code can be written in a cleaner form (refactored).

```
# Method 2 Refactored
def indx(array, target): # 3 lines
    for n in range(len(array)):
        if array[n] == target: return n
    return -1
```

This second method is my best attempt. I assumed the built-in index function would make the code even shorter. (I was wrong.)

```
# Method 3  built-in (Easiest to understand)
def indx(array, target): # 4 lines
    try:
        return array.index(target)
    except:
        return -1
```

These examples show why students need to look at other students' code, or at least the teacher's code. The lessons that are learned this way stick with the student.

Refactoring offers you experience in design that helps on the next project. Never redesigning keeps you at the novice level. Sometimes function A calls function B. Later we have function A call function C and use the stuff from function B. Well, then function C should be calling function B, not function A. But if we do this redesign, then we may later drop function C, and have to backtrack. So for a while we live with inefficient design. Only when the program is finished, or is getting out of control, do we think about a redesign.

I don't think it is possible—or at least efficient—to finish a program with a well-crafted design. Too much will change along the way. Some problems are so difficult that until you see your program crash and burn, you are unlikely to have understood the difficulties of the assignment, or thought about all of the special cases, or realized you are better off with *strings* of digits, rather than *lists* of digits.[2]

> The picture of the software designer deriving his design in a rational, error-free way from a statement of requirements is quite unrealistic. No system has ever been developed in that way, and probably none ever will. Even the small program developments shown in textbooks and papers are unreal. They have been revised and polished until the author has shown us what he wishes he had done, not what actually did happen.—David Parnas and Paul Clements, Found in Steve McConnell, *Code Complete*, 2nd Ed. (Microsoft Press, 2004), page 74.

> If we have learned anything over the last couple of decades, it is that programming is a craft more than it is a science. To write clean code, you must first write dirty code *and then clean it*. Most freshmen programmers don't follow this advice particularly well. They believe that the primary goal is to get the program working. Once it's "working," they move on to the next task. Most seasoned programmers know that this is professional suicide.—Robert C. Martin, *Clean Code* (Prentice Hall, 2009), page 30.

---

[2]My earliest reference to this observation is 1965: "It is a truism in computing that only when a routine is debugged and tested, and some production has been run, does the programmer really know how he should have attacked the problem in the first place."—Fred Greunberger (RAND) and George Jaffray (Los Angeles Valley College), *Problems for Computer Solution* (John Wiley, 1965), page xvi. This is still an excellent book for C.S. teachers. These authors used the DEC Corporation's 12-bit PDP-8 minicomputer, the most commercially successful computer up to that date. It used variously a paper tape reader and a punched-cards reader. The earliest personal computers (microcomputers) were not introduced until 1975, and then only in crude form.

We are unlikely to get the design of a library
or interface right on the first attempt. As Fred
Brooks once wrote, "plan to throw one away; you
will, anyhow." Brooks was writing about large
systems but the idea is relevant for any substantial
piece of software. It's not usually until you've
built and used a version of the program that you
understand the issues well enough to get the
design right.—Brian W. Kernighan and Rob Pike,
The Practice of Programming (Addison-Wesley,
1999), page 87.

To put it crassly, top-down design is a great way
to redesign a program you already know how to
write.—P.J. Plauger, *Programming on Purpose*
(Prentice Hall, 1993), page 2.

There is a doctrine in the hard sciences that says if you can't measure
something by a number, then it doesn't exist.[3] Some people believe
this idea is false. You can't measure love by a number, and love exists.
Personally, I'm not so sure that someday love won't be measured by a set
of numbers. But it doesn't matter if this doctrine is false, because belief

---

[3] I often say that when you can measure what you are speaking about and express
it in numbers you know something about it; but when you cannot measure
it, when you cannot express it in numbers, your knowledge is of a meager
and unsatisfactory kind: it may be the beginning of knowledge, but you have
scarcely, in your thoughts, advanced to the stage of *science*, whatever the matter
may be.—Lord Kelvin (William Thompson (1824–1907). From an 1883 lecture.
Found in *Popular Lectures and Addresses* Vol. I (London: Macmillan and Co.,
1894), page 73.

in the doctrine fosters productive thinking.[4] So we ask: In what units can readability be measured? Decide before checking the footnote.[5]

Refactoring is hard work. Some programs are so exhausting to write that I just want to be done with them when they finally work, and don't redesign them. Of course, when I return to them the following year, I have difficulty understanding my own code.

> Doing a refactoring based on a couple of early uses, then having to undo it soon after is fairly common.—Kent Beck, *Test-Driven Development* (Addison-Wesley, 2003), page 102.

Before we leave this topic, an `if-else` should never be used in a case like this:

```
if x > 0:
    return True
else:
    return False
```

This construction is sometimes called an **anti-idiom** (poor design). Instead, we should write this:

```
return x > 0
```

---

[4]We hold mere falsity no ground for rejecting a judgment. The issue is: To what extent has the conception preserved and furthered the life of the race? The falsest conceptions—and to these belong our synthetic judgments *a priori*—are also those which are the most indispensable. Without his logical fictions, without measuring reality in a fictitious absolute and immutable world, without the perpetual counterfeiting of the universe by number, man could not continue to live. The renunciation of all false judgment would mean a renunciation, a negation of life.—Friedrich Nietzsche, *Beyond Good and Evil* (originally published in Germany in 1866), part I, §4; this translation is found in Tobias Danzig, *Number the Language of Science,* 4th ed. (Doubleday Anchor, 1956), page 249.

[5]The answer is time. We try to refactor our code to minimize the time necessary for someone else to understand it.

QUIZ 7. Refactor the following code. The answer is in the footnote.[6]

```
if x > 0:
    if ch in {'A','B','C'}:
        return True
    else:
        return False
else:
    return False
```

The following code is a shell program that I occasionally use.

```
"""+===========+=======-=======*=======-=======+============+
  ||                        TITLE                          ||
  ||                  by M. Stueben (DATE)                 ||
  ||                                                       ||
  ||    Description:                                       ||
  ||    Language:    Python Ver. 3.4.                      ||
  ||    Graphics:    None                                  ||
  ||    References:  None                                  ||
  +===========+=======-=======*=======-=======+============+
"""

####################<START OF PROGRAM>####################
def fn():
    pass
#==========+====<GLOBAL IMPORTS AND CONSTANTS>=================
None
#=======================<MAIN>===========================
```

---

[6]QUIZ 7 ANSWER: return (x > 0) and (ch in {'A','B','C'}).

```python
def main():
    pass
#-----------------------------------------------------------------
if __name__ == '__main__':
    from math import sqrt; from random import random, randint,
    uniform, shuffle
    from sys import setrecursionlimit; setrecursionlimit(100)
    from time import clock; START_TIME = clock(); main();
    print('~-'*16)
    print('PROGRAM RUN TIME:%6.2f'%(clock()-START_TIME),
    'seconds.')
#   import winsound; winsound.Beep(1500,500) # Frequency,
    milliseconds
#########################<END OF PROGRAM>#########################
```

Notice the five lines at the bottom. The first line imports the math functions often needed in school algorithms. The second line sets the possible recursive depth to 100 instead of the default 1000. Rarely is a greater depth needed. And infinite recursion, which is a common bug in my code, takes too long to fail with 1000 recursive calls. The next two lines calculate and print the program run time. The final line makes a beep (if desired) to announce the program is finished.

Suppose you need to have the user enter one of four choices. Here is one way to do it:

```python
input('Enter PUsh, pOp, View, or Quit. Choice (U,O,V,Q):')
```

Here is another way to do it:

```python
def userChoice():
    msg = ''
    pr = """
Enter u for push.
Enter o for pop.
```

```
Enter v for view.
Enter q for quit (or push the enter key).

Enter choice: """
    while True:
        try:
            choice = input(msg+pr).strip()[0].lower()
        except:
            return 'q'
        if choice not in 'uovq':
            msg = 'ERROR: "' + choice +'" is an invalid choice.
            Try again.\n'
        else:
            return choice
```

The second method takes more space and is harder to debug,
but gives the program a prettier interface and is more robust code. Is it
worth the extra effort? If you have the time and if others will be using
your program, then maybe it is. For the first draft, the single line of code is
better.

With simple if statements, avoid negative if-tests where you can,
because negations are harder to parse than positive statements. I hope you
have memorized DeMorgan's laws:

```
not (A and B) → (notA)  or  (not B).
not (A  or B) → (not A) and (not B).
```

QUIZ 8. Apply DeMorgan's laws and refactor the following loop body.
My solution follows.

```
for n in range(5):
    if not A or x >= 10:
        doSomething
```

QUIZ 8 ANSWER:

```
for n in range(5):
    if A and (x < 10):continue
    doSomething
```

The second version eliminated a not and reduced the indenting.

Some experts prefer to use "<" over " > " in if tests, because this is consistent with the number line, which keeps the smaller numbers to the left. This seems reasonable, unless, for psychological reasons, ">" does fit in better with an expression—e.g., if x > 0.001: doSomething(). Recall that in English classes you are advised to avoid passive writing ("The ball was hit by the boy."), and prefer active writing ("The boy hit the ball."). Yes, of course. But if the ball is more important in the story than who hit it, then don't we prefer the so-called passive version? Anyway, in the if test, it is x that is probably significant, not so much the 0.001, which perhaps is just an arbitrary small number.

Beware of multiple ifs, especially with a final else. Consider replacing nested else if statements with a set of if statements, perhaps by turning the structure up-side down or by ending each if with a return, break, or a continue. Why? Simple ifs are easier to debug than else ifs.

```
# LOGIC error (beginner's error 1, bleeding ifs)
    x = 1
    if x == 1: x = 2
    if x == 2: x = 3
    if x == 3: x = 4
    print(x) # output: 4 (but the programmer expected 2)

# LOGIC error (beginner's error 2, back-stabbing else)
    x = 1
    if x == 1: x = 2
    if x == 3: x = 4
    else:      x = 5
    print(x) # output: 5 (but the programmer expected 2)
```

```
# Using returns, breaks, and continues can make code easier to
debug.
def doIt(x):
    if x == 1:
        return 2
    if x == 2:
        return 3
    if x == 3:
        return 4

# Here is the useful subscripted list trick:
def doIt(x):
    return['-',2,3,4][x]
```

> During our many years of analyzing programming
> problems in industry, we found complications
> resulting from multiple nested if statements were
> the single most common cause of logic bugs.—Tom
> Rugg and Phil Feldman, *Turbo Pascal Tips, Tricks,*
> *and Traps* (Que, 1986), page 132.

Tangled code: if, elif, and else statements, indented to several
levels, sometimes can be refactored in dramatic ways. It takes some
practice to skillfully apply the tricks, so maybe you should cover up the
solution following each quiz until you can think of a refactor.

QUIZ 9. Refactor the body of this function to make it more readable:

```
def doIt(a,b,c):
    if a == 1:
        if b == 1:
            if c == 1:
                print ('abc')
```

```
        else:
            print('ab')
      else:
          print('a')
    else:
        print('-')
```

QUIZ 9 ANSWER:

```
def doIt(a,b,c):
    if a != 1:
        print('- '); return
    if b != 1:
        print('a '); return
    if c != 1:
        print('ab'); return
    print('abc')
```

Here, the refactor made the tests negative, which violates the advice given earlier. General rules have exceptions.

QUIZ 10. Refactor this code. Two solutions follow.

```
#---BLOCK 1 (22 lines).
    if a == 1:
      if b == 1:
          if c == 1:
              print ('abc')
          else:
              print ('ab-')
      else:
          if c == 1:
              print('a-c')
          else:
              print('a--')
```

```
else:
    if b == 1:
        if c == 1:
            print ('-bc')
        else:
            print('-b-')
    else:
        if c == 1:
            print('--c')
        else:
            print ('---')
```

Tangled code (multiple if else statements) can often be improved by repeated and statements with vertical alignment.

QUIZ 10 ANSWERS:

```
#---BLOCK 2 (8 lines).
    if a == 1 and b == 1 and c == 1: print('abc')
    if a == 1 and b == 1 and c == 0: print('ab-')
    if a == 1 and b == 0 and c == 1: print('a-c')
    if a == 0 and b == 1 and c == 1: print('-bc')
    if a == 0 and b == 0 and c == 1: print('--c')
    if a == 0 and b == 1 and c == 0: print('-b-')
    if a == 1 and b == 0 and c == 0: print('a--')
    if a == 0 and b == 0 and c == 0: print('---')

#---Block 3 (8 simpler lines)
    if (a,b,c) == (1,1,1): print('abc')
    if (a,b,c) == (1,1,0): print('ab-')
    if (a,b,c) == (1,0,1): print('a-c')
    if (a,b,c) == (1,0,0): print('a--')
    if (a,b,c) == (0,1,1): print('-bc')
    if (a,b,c) == (0,1,0): print('-b-')
    if (a,b,c) == (0,0,1): print('--c')
    if (a,b,c) == (0,0,0): print('---')
```

The previous two solutions are a bit contrived. If the identifiers were function calls, the code wouldn't look so impressive. Here is the same quiz again with the same answer.

```
#---BLOCK 1 (again).
    if inStock(item):
        if name in customerList:
            if price-1 < payment <= price:
                print ('abc')
            else:
                print ('ab-')
        else:
            if price-1 < payment <= price:
                print('a-c')
            else:
                print('a--')
    else:
        if name in customerList:
            if price-1 < payment <= price:
                print ('-bc')
            else:
                print('-b-')
        else:
            if price-1 < payment <= price:
                print('--c')
            else:
                print ('---')

#---BLOCK 2 (again).
    if (   inStock(item) and
           name in customerList and
           price-1 < payment <= price):  print('abc')
    if (   inStock(item) and
```

```
            name in customerList and
       not(price-1 < payment <= price)): print('ab-')
   if (    inStock(item) and
       not name in customerList and
          price-1 < payment <= price):  print('a-c')
   if (    inStock(item) and
       not name in customerList and
       not(price-1 < payment <= price)): print('a--')
   if (not inStock(item) and
          name in customerList and
          price-1 < payment <= price):  print('-bc')
   if (not inStock(item) and
          name in customerList and
       not(price-1 < payment <= price)): print('-b-')
   if (not inStock(item) and
       not name in customerList and
          price-1 < payment <= price):  print('--c')
   if (not inStock(item) and
       not name in customerList and
       not(price-1 < payment <= price)): print('---')
```

QUIZ 11. Here the unimproved Block 1 seems easier to debug than the refactored Block 2. Is there no way to improve Block 1? Yes, the improvement (Block 3) is at the end of this chapter.

QUIZ 12. Refactor this code, significantly reducing the number of lines:

```
#---BLOCK 1 (13 lines).
   if a == 1:
      if b == 1:
         if c == 1:
            print(doIt())
         else:
            print ('error 3')
```

```
            return
        else:
            print('error 2')
            return
    else:
        print('error 1')
        return
```

My solution (Block 2) is at the end of this chapter.

QUIZ 13. Simplify/improve the code below:

```
def selectCourse(name):
    if name != '':
        courseName = name
    else:
        courseName = 'Computer Science 101'
    return courseName
```

QUIZ 13 ANSWER:

```
def selectCourse(name):
    assert type(name) == str
    return name or 'Computer Science 101'
```

The assert is necessary to guarantee that name is not None, (), [], **0**, or False. Is the "or trick" justified, or have I fallen into the "clever code" trap? One of the summer instructors at Colgate University in 2002 discouraged me from using tricks that take advantage of a language's eccentricities. He may not have approved of this code.

QUIZ 11 ANSWER:

```
#---Block 3 (6 lines)
    (item, payment, name) = (0,0,0)
    msg = ['-', '-', '-']
```

```
    if inStock(item):           msg[0] = 'a'
    if name in customerList:     msg[1] = 'b'
    if price-1 < payment <= price: msg[2] = 'c'
    print (''.join(msg))
```

QUIZ 12 ANSWER:

```
#---BLOCK 2 (4 lines).
    if a != 1:                        print ('error 1'); return
    if a == 1 and b !=1:              print ('error 2'); return
    if a == 1 and b ==1 and c != 1: print ('error 3'); return
    print (doIt())
```

Advice to remember: If your code has several returns, consider rewriting it to have early returns rather than later returns, even if you need to make your if tests negative.

CHAPTER 13

Write the Tests First (Sometimes)

> We've interviewed and hired a lot of testers. We have yet to meet a computer science graduate who learned anything useful about testing at a university.—
> Cem Kaner, Jack Falk, Hung, Quoc Nguyen, *Testing Computer Software* 2nd Ed. (Wiley, 1999), page ix.

*I*N INDUSTRY, the first step in testing is called **domain testing**: testing of variables, constraints, and correct types. Next is unit testing (aka functional testing aka **white-box testing**): the testing of individual functions. Finally there is **black-box testing**: the testing of the entire program. Industry also uses programs to test programs. In school, we generally test as we go by tracing data and checking for the expected answers. We don't usually write other functions to test our functions. This is fine, with one exception. For a complicated algorithm, a test function should be written first—*before* writing the algorithm, and then another test function should be written after the writing the algorithm. That is two different test functions. You must see an example to appreciate this advice. The following code is the first test function, a smoke test,[1] that I wrote prior to writing the binary search.

---

[1]A **smoke test** is a simple test for a common situation. The term "smoke test" evidently comes from hardware testing. Turn it on. If the device starts smoking, then turn it off. The test is finished.

© Michael Stueben 2018
M. Stueben, *Good Habits for Great Coding*, https://doi.org/10.1007/978-1-4842-3459-4_13

THE NOTORIOUS BINARY SEARCH

In case you have forgotten, the **binary search** is an algorithm to search for the index of a target number t in a _sorted_ list of numbers. If t is not in the list, then the algorithm returns -1. If t occurs more than once, the search returns any one of its indices. Because the algorithm can eliminate half of the indices with each probe, the binary search over a list of length L will take at most ceil($\log_2$(L)) probes. For a billion indices, this is 30 probes for the worst case. The algorithm sounds easy to write. It isn't.

```
def binarySearchTest():
    array = [0,1,2,3,4,6,7,8,9] # <--5 is missing
    print('array   =', array)
    print('Test -9 =', binarySearch(array,-9) == -1)
    print('Test  0 =', binarySearch(array, 0) ==  0)
    print('Test  4 =', binarySearch(array, 4) ==  4)
    print('Test  5 =', binarySearch(array, 5) == -1)
    print('Test  9 =', binarySearch(array, 9) ==  9)
    print('Test 10 =', binarySearch(array,10) == -1)
```

This test code is good enough to catch obvious errors, and that is all smoke tests should do. When I finally came to write the binarySearch, almost every logic error was immediately exposed by this test code. Of course, fixing one error would introduce another error, but the smoke test usually caught that error too.

The binarySearch function took me 70 minutes to write (passing the smoke tests) and to refactor. How confident was I about my binarySearch? Not very, because smoke tests are crude. The final step was to create and test 1000 random-sized sorted arrays of random integers. Then every possible number in each array, and some not in each array, were searched for. The following code does this.

```python
def binarySearchTest():
    runs = 1000 # The number of random arrays to be tested.

#---A function to verify the binarySearch for a single element.
    def check(array, value):
        valueIndex = binarySearch(array, value)
        if ((valueIndex == -1) and (value in array)) or \
           ((valueIndex != -1) and (array[valueIndex] !=
           value)):
            print('\nFALSE: array =', array)
            print('The position of', value, 'is returned as',
            valueIndex)
            exit()

#---Check all numbers in all random arrays created below.
    for i in range(runs):
#-------Create a random sized array each with different random
values.
        arrayLength = randint( 0, 30)
        sm          = randint(-5, 20)    # sm = smallest
                                         possible value in array.
        lg          = randint(20, 40)    # lg = largest possible
                                         value in array.
        array       = sorted([randint(sm,lg) for j in
        range(0,arrayLength)])
#-------Test every value possible in the array and many not in
the array.
        for value in range(sm-2, lg+2):
            check(array, value)
    print('True: The binarySearch function passed', runs,
    'tests.')
```

The only test my binary search failed was with the empty set. That was a quick fix, and now I was confident about my code.

My Binary Search

```
def binarySearch(array, target):
    # UNCHECKED preconditions: array is a list of sorted
      integers.
    left  = 0
    right = len(array)-1

    while left < right:
        mid = (left + right)//2    # rounds down.
        if array[mid] == target:
            return mid
        if array[mid] < target:
            if left == mid:
                left = left+1
            else:
                left = mid
        else:
            right = mid

#---Check for empty array or possible solution where left = right.
    if (array != []) and (array[left] == target):
        return left # left = right = index of target.
    return -1       # Either array = [], or target not in array.
```

When I compared this version to a published version of binarySearch, I realized that I made a poor design decision. My code used while left < right, when while left <= right would have produced a simpler design. It is difficult to identify every key relationship when you begin designing a complex function.

Digression. Below is a binary search that I found on the Internet. Notice the elif and else. I call this **tangled code**. There is a simple trick to untangle code: Just repeat the if tests.

```
def binarySearch(array, target): # A better design. 29.51
                                                seconds
    left  = 0
    right = len(array)-1
    while left <= right:
        mid = (left+right)//2     # rounds down.
        if array[mid] < target:
            left = mid+1
        elif array[mid] > target:
            right = mid-1
        else:
            return mid
    return -1
```

Here is the untangled code:

```
def binarySearchUT(array, target): # Untangled code. 39.33
                                                seconds
    left  = 0
    right = len(array)-1
    while left <= right:
        mid = (left+right)//2    # rounds down.
        if array[mid]  < target: left  = mid+1
        if array[mid]  > target: right = mid-1
        if array[mid] == target: return mid
    return -1
```

This is simpler and has three fewer lines. In a test of ten million runs, the tangled binarySearch finished in 29.51 seconds. The untangled binarySearchUT finished in 39.33 seconds. Is the refactored improvement worth the loss of speed? The untangled binary search is still lightning fast on almost any array. End of Digression.

A natural question is how do we test the tests? The answer is two-fold. First, we purposely pass bad data (aka **fault injection**) to our test code to verify that it can detect errors. Second, with simple code, the program verifies the tests at the same time that the tests verify the program.

Should all test results be reported or only the first case to fail? My preference is to report only the first case to fail, because the test code should be as simple and quick to write as possible. Consequently, when an error is discovered, the function prints information and then returns or exits on the spot. We do not want to climb out of nested for loops, unwind recursion, or carry error flags that tell us to ignore a default True.

Although the binary search is an instructive example, only a few school problems will benefit from writing the tests first—e.g., the quick sort. In writing the Traveling Salesman Problem, the A* searching algorithm, and the difficult back-propagation algorithm for a neural network, the student never gets beyond manually testing the program with fixed data—perhaps data required by the instructor. Consequently, when an assignment appears that can benefit from writing tests first, a student may not think about writing them.

Professor Donald Knuth claims that the first binary search was published in 1946, but the first bug-free binary search was not published until 1962.[2] In his courses at Bell Labs and IBM, Jon Bentley reported asking over a hundred professional programmers to write a correct binary search within two hours. Only 10 percent produced correct algorithms.[3] Incredibly, even Bentley's published binary search contained a tiny

---

[2]Donald Knuth, *The Art of Computer Programming*, Vol. 3, *Sorting and Searching*, 2nd Ed. (Addison-Wesley, 1998), Section 6.2.1.

[3]Jon Bentley, *Programming Pearls* (Addison-Wesley,1986), page 36. The most common error was an infinite loop. Bentley's students were probably hand-writing their code on paper and could not test their code on a computer.

error.[4] That being the case, how is it possible that I wrote a correct binary search in 70 minutes? First, I wrote smoke tests before I wrote the code, which exposed hard-to-find errors on every practice run. Second, I ran a thousand random tests on my finished code.

However, the 70 minutes did not include the time to write the testing code. That took another hour. And, of course, this extra time is one reason people do not want to write the tests first—or at all.

By the way, there are several attributes of the binary search that I missed. The first is the number of mid values (probes) calculated. With an array length of 2^n, there should be $n+1$ or fewer probes. I never checked this. The second is choosing an array so large that `mid = (left+right)//2` leads to overflow. This can't happen in Python, but it can in Java, C++, and other languages. The solution is `mid = left + (right-left)//2`. (This was Bentley's tiny error.) Third, I never explicitly tested an array with all equal values, except for the array of one element. Fourth, does it matter if the target element is at an even position versus an odd position? I never thought about this in my testing, but even and odd positions must have occurred multiple times in the thousand runs. Did I miss something else? I will never be sure.

---

[4]Andy Oram and Greg Wilson, Eds., *Beautiful Code* (O'Reilly, 2007), page 88. Here an entire chapter is devoted to the binary search.

CHAPTER 14

Expert Advice

> Of course, a chap can't expect to become a thorough backwoodsman all at once without learning some of the difficult arts and practices that the backwoodsman uses. If you study this book you will find tips in it showing you how to do them—and in this way you can learn for yourself instead of having a teacher to show you how.—Lord Baden-Powell, the Foreword in *Scouting for Boys* (1908), found on the Internet.

THIS CHAPTER IS A LIST of programming tips I have collected over the years. The most important tip is to read other people's code, especially well-written code.

1. **Fail fast**. For example, hard code your input data, because having to type in the same input on every run is needlessly time-consuming. I once assigned my students to write a program that ran a loop 100,000 times. This took about 20 seconds. Incredibly, some of the students were trying to debug their program with the 100,000 number. They should have reduced that number to 10 for debugging purposes, and later, when the program seemed to work, changed it to 100,000.

© Michael Stueben 2018
M. Stueben, *Good Habits for Great Coding*, https://doi.org/10.1007/978-1-4842-3459-4_14

2. Use **vertical alignment** to emphasize relationships, to make errors visually stand out, and to make look-up easier. This requires a mono-spaced font,[1] like Courier.

VERTICAL ALIGNMENT

```
M = [[0, 0, 0, 0, 0, 0, 0, 0,],
     [0, 0, 0, 0, 0, 0, 0, 0,],
     [0, 0, 0, 0, 0, 0, 0, 0,],
     [0, 0, 0,-1, 1, 0, 0, 0,],
     [0, 0, 0, 1,-1, 0, 0, 0,],
     [0, 0, 0, 0, 0, 0, 0, 0,],
     [0, 0, 0, 0, 0, 0, 0, 0,],
     [0, 0, 0, 0, 0, 0, 0, 0,],]
```

MORE VERTICAL ALIGNMENT

```
for c in range(1,length-1):
    ch = chr(32)                    # = blank space  = background
                                                       color
    if L[c]== 1: ch = chr(9607) # = solid square = foreground
                                                       color
    if maxx == max1:
        canvas.create_text(c*12 + 640-12*r, (r-1)*10,
        text = ch, \
                 fill = 'red', font = ('Helvetica', 8, 'bold') )
```

---

[1]The words *font* and *type* or *typeface* are often used interchangeably. A font is associated with an attribute of a typeface—e.g., Calibri italic, Calibri bold, or Calibri mono-spaced are all different fonts of the Calibri typeface. A typeface refers to the core shapes of the characters. Robert Harris in *The Elements of Visual Style* (Houghton Mifflin, 2007) claims that typefaces fall into four broad categories: **serif** (with extenders like Times Roman), **sans serif** (without extenders like the Calibri type face you are reading), **script** (cursive handwriting like Lucinda Handwriting), and **novelty** (like **Juice ITC**).

```
if maxx == max2:
    canvas.create_text(c*6 + 640- 6*r, (r-1)*4,
    text = ch, \
                fill = 'red', font = ('Helvetica', 4,
                'bold') )
if maxx == max3:
    canvas.create_text(c*4 + 640- 4*r, (r-1)*3,
    text = ch, \
                fill = 'red', font = ('Helvetica', 2,
                'bold') )
if maxx == max4:
    canvas.create_text(c*2 + 640- 2*r, (r-1)*2,
    text = ch, \
                fill = 'red', font = ('Helvetica', 1,
                'bold') )
```

3. Try to write **robust** code. Robust is the opposite of brittle and fragile. Robust code is code that either heals itself, allows the user to help it recover, or if it must, crashes gracefully.

4. Avoid global *variables*. Why? Variables with large scope are difficult to track down to detect unexpected changes. On the other hand, global *constants* are acceptable. One reason we write constant names in all capitals is so the programmer knows *not* to change their *constant* values.

   That being said, there are situations where global variables make sense—e.g., where the globals are not part of your code. Imagine you decide to introduce a temporary variable to count how many times a recursive function backtracks. You don't want to pass this variable to the function and increase an already long parameter list. The variable is needed only for debugging, and it doesn't affect how the program works. Make it global.

A global that holds the time for the start of the program and that can be used to print out incremental time steps in various functions is another acceptable global. This is a global that is never modified by other code and shares the attribute of a global constant. My rule is *never use global variables without a compelling reason.*

5. The acronym *SESE* refers to a function having a single entry point (don't drop in with a goto), and a single exit point. The single entry point makes sense. The single exit point is too restrictive. Rather than unwind multiple levels of loops, it is sometimes convenient to return or break on the spot. In Python, a function using yield will begin on the last iteration of the loop, so in a sense you can enter the function at two different points. I suspect the original motivation for the SESE rule was that it made proving program correctness easier.

6. Avoid writing a function that returns a single variable of two different data types. (Usually the second data type is the indication of an error.) Why? Because every time the function is called, it must be called with an if statement. This makes the function harder to use. Nevertheless sometimes you are required to return multiple datatypes. Consider the humble quadratic formula. Most students would write a fine 9-line version like this:

```
def quad(a, b, c):
    from math import sqrt
    disc = b*b-4*a*c
    if disc < 0:
        return 'There are no real roots.'
    x1 = (-b+sqrt(disc))/(2*a)
    x2 = (-b-sqrt(disc))/(2*a)
    if disc == 0:
        return x1
    return x1, x2
```

This code returns either a string, a tuple of two numbers, or a single number. Note that this version does not take care of the three cases that can arise if a = 0: all real numbers, no roots real or otherwise, and -c/b. Nor does it always get the correct answer for extreme numbers. If a = 6, b = 1073741900, and c = 7, then the computer has sqrt(b*b-4*a*c) = sqrt(b*b) =|b|. The two roots will be (0.0, -178956983.33333334). But zero cannot be an answer. By inspection all roots must be negative. The version that follows will print the correct answers:

```
(-178956983.33333334, -6.519257560871937e-09).
```

```
def quad(a, b, c):
#---Rescale all three coefficients to prevent overflow of b*b
and 4*a*c. (Python
#   has 16-17 digits of accuracy.) Underflow is still possible.
Mathematically
#   the roots are not changed by this process.
    m = max(abs(a),abs(b),abs(c))
    if m != 0:
        a1 = a/m
        b1 = b/m
        c1 = c/m # Now the largest parameter (a, b, c) is 1.
```

```
#---Special case 1: a = 0, b = 0, and c = 0.
    if a == 0 and b == 0 and c == 0:
        return 'All real numbers are roots.'
```

```
#---Special case 2: a = 0, b = 0, and c != 0.
    if a == 0 and b == 0 and c != 0:
        return 'There are no roots (real or otherwise).'
```

```
#---Special case 3: a = 0 and b != 0.
    if a == 0 and b != 0:
        x1 = -c/b # = the only root.
        #-Cast as int type if possible (optional).
        if x1 == int(x1): x1 = int(x1) # This turns -0.0 into 0.
        return  x1
```

```
#---Bookkeeping.
    from math import sqrt
    disc = b*b-4*a*c
```

```
#---Special case 4: sqrt of negative number.
    if disc < 0:
        return 'There are no real roots.'
```

```
#---Special case 5: a != 0, b = 0, c = 0 (Needed for case 6.)
    if a != 0 and b == 0 and c == 0:
        return 0
```

```
#---Special case 6: Rationalize the numerator in one of the
roots. Why? If b*b
#    is much much larger than 4*a*c, then sqrt(disc) = |b|.
Consequently,
#    -b + sqrt(b*b) will be zero for b > 0, and -b - sqrt(b*b)
will be zero
#    for b < 0. We need the "+" and "-" signs reversed in these
two situations.
```

CHAPTER 14   EXPERT ADVICE

```
if b > 0:
    x1 = (-b-sqrt(disc))/(2*a)
    x2 = (-2*c)/(b+sqrt(disc)) # = (-b+sqrt(disc))/(2*a)
else:
    x1 = (-b+sqrt(disc))/(2*a)
    x2 = (-2*c)/(b-sqrt(disc)) # = (-b-sqrt(disc))/(2*a)

#---Cast as int types if possible (optional). This turns -0.0
int 0.
    if x1 == int(x1): x1 = int(x1)
    if x2 == int(x2): x2 = int(x2)

#---Special case 7. Only one root.
    if disc == 0: return x1

    return x1, x2
```

And this is the problem with writing code to

1. take in *all* cases—e.g., a = 0,

2. to prettyprint the output—e.g., "-0.0" should print as "0", and

3. to maximize the limits of computing—e.g., scaling and rationalizing.

The code went from 9 lines to 56 lines, needing 19 lines of comments, and requiring rationalizing numerators to understand. Is it worth the effort? Maybe worse is better.

7. Know your order of operations (aka operator hierarchy, aka operator precedence) and your Boolean properties. Whoever wrote this:

```
a and b == True,
```

probably meant this:

```
(a and b) == True
```

There are multiple comments on the Internet to never write "== **True**". One reason is to avoid problems like the above. I take exception. The two expressions if x and if x == True are NOT always equivalent in Python (e.g., x = 'a'). And the two expressions if not x and if x == False are NOT always equivalent in Python (e.g., x = [], None, 'a').

In Python, empty strings and lists have a Boolean value of False. Naturally, this makes a programmer want to write

```
if stng: doSomething
```

instead of either

```
if len(stng) > 0: doSomething()
```

or

```
if stng != '': doSomething()
```

The longer versions are not only more readable, but protect the code from stng being None or a number.

Recall that the bit shift >>2 is equivalent to dividing an integer by 4. Since shifting is faster than division (unless the compiler is optimized), you might consider replacing

```
a + b/4
```

with

```
a + b >> 2.
```

But these two expressions are *not* equivalent. Parentheses are required.

```
a = 6
b = 4
print(a + b/4)      # output: 7.0
```

```
print(a +  b >> 2)   # output: 3
print(a + (b >> 2))  # output: 7
```

Give the output: `print(2**3**2)`. The answer is in the footnote.[2]

If you have to look up an order of operations, then use parentheses to make it clear to the reader.

8. Be aware that general code is easier to re-use, but specific code is easier to write. Unless you suspect that you will expand a function, it might *not* be worth your time to make it general. The following is my Python function to input an integer, which uses a try/except construct. That way I can catch *any* kind of run-time error.

```
def dataInput():
    s = 'Enter an integer:'
    posLimit =  float('inf')
    negLimit = -float('inf')
    while True:
        try:
            data = input(s)
            num  = int(data) # a non-int will raise exception.
            if not (negLimit < num < posLimit): raise Error
            #out-of-bounds?
        except:
            s = '"' + str(data) + '" is NOT an integer! \
                Try again. \nEnter an integer:'
        else:
            print('input = ', num)
            return num
```

---

[2] `2**3**2 = 2**(3**2) = 512`. Stacked exponents are the only algebraic expressions I know of that are evaluated from right to left.

I decided to rewrite the above function to print two kinds of error messages, and to accept parameters for input bounds—instead of hard-coding them. The result was a more complicated function. This is a common predicament in coding. Do we accept the more powerful, and/or the more general[3] (**extensibility**, where future growth is taken into consideration in the initial design) at the cost of increased time to write, increased size, and increased complexity? The answer is often personal. In this case, I went back to the simple version, above. (For me, worse is sometimes better.)

I once wrote a Sudoku solver for a 9×9 grid. Then I re-wrote part of it for an *n*×*n* grid. The general case was much shorter than the specific case. Unfortunately, it was also *much* harder to debug. Below is the 9x9 code followed by the *n*×*n* code. Which would you rather debug?

```
#---Build list of 9x9 blocks.
    block = [[],[],[], [],[],[], [],[],[],]

    block[0] = [matrix[0][0].value, matrix[0][1].value,
                matrix[0][2].value,
                matrix[1][0].value, matrix[1][1].value,
                matrix[1][2].value,
```

---

[3]Sometimes you want to design code so that it is general, and can easily be extended to work with bigger data sets. This makes sense only if the code is also **scalable**. If a program or algorithm works well with a small data set, but is significantly inefficient with a larger data set, then the program/algorithm is not scalable. For example, the insertion sort $O(n^2)$ is more scalable than the bubble sort $O(n^2)$, but less scalable than an $O(n\log(n))$ sort when the data size in increased. The binary search $O(\log(n))$ is extremely scalable and the hash table $O(1)$ is perfectly scalable for any sized data set. (Unfortunately, the memory required to hold the searchable data in a hash table must be 50% to 100% more than the space actually needed to hold the data. As the data set is increased, the hash keys must be changed.) Python is great for small programs (under 1000 lines), but not large programs—i.e., the language is not scalable—this is mainly due to lack of type checking, and being an interpreted language. See *Wikipedia*, s.v., scalability.

```
                matrix[2][0].value, matrix[2][1].value,
                matrix[2][2].value,]

block[1] = [matrix[0][3].value, matrix[0][4].value,
                matrix[0][5].value,
                matrix[1][3].value, matrix[1][4].value,
                matrix[1][5].value,
                matrix[2][3].value, matrix[2][4].value,
                matrix[2][5].value,]

block[2] = [matrix[0][6].value, matrix[0][7].value,
                matrix[0][8].value,
                matrix[1][6].value, matrix[1][7].value,
                matrix[1][8].value,
                matrix[2][6].value, matrix[2][7].value,
                matrix[2][8].value,]

block[3] = [matrix[3][0].value, matrix[3][1].value,
                matrix[3][2].value,
                matrix[4][0].value, matrix[4][1].value,
                matrix[4][2].value,
                matrix[5][0].value, matrix[5][1].value,
                matrix[5][2].value,]
block[4] = [matrix[3][3].value, matrix[3][4].value,
                matrix[3][5].value,
                matrix[4][3].value, matrix[4][4].value,
                matrix[4][5].value,
                matrix[5][3].value, matrix[5][4].value,
                matrix[5][5].value,]

block[5] = [matrix[3][6].value, matrix[3][7].value,
                matrix[3][8].value,
                matrix[4][6].value, matrix[4][7].value,
                matrix[4][8].value,
```

```
                matrix[5][6].value, matrix[5][7].value,
                matrix[5][8].value,]

    block[6] = [matrix[6][0].value, matrix[6][1].value,
                matrix[6][2].value,
                matrix[7][0].value, matrix[7][1].value,
                matrix[7][2].value,
                matrix[8][0].value, matrix[8][1].value,
                matrix[8][2].value,]

    block[7] = [matrix[6][3].value, matrix[6][4].value,
                matrix[6][5].value,
                matrix[7][3].value, matrix[7][4].value,
                matrix[7][5].value,
                matrix[8][3].value, matrix[8][4].value,
                matrix[8][5].value,]
    block[8] = [matrix[6][6].value, matrix[6][7].value,
                matrix[6][8].value,
                matrix[7][6].value, matrix[7][7].value,
                matrix[7][8].value,
                matrix[8][6].value, matrix[8][7].value,
                matrix[8][8].value,]

#---Build list of nxn of blocks.
    block = []
    for n in range(MAX):
        block.append([])
    for n in range(MAX):
        for r in range(blockHeight):
            for c in range(blockWidth):
                row = (n//blockWidth)*blockHeight+r
                col = (n%blockHeight*blockWidth) +c
                block[n].append(matrix[row][col].value)
```

9. Avoid so-called *magic numbers*. Magic
   numbers are numbers that are represented by
   constants. If you use 10 as the length of an array
   throughout a program, you may later find yourself
   hunting through your program changing every
   10-associated-with-an-array-length to 100. Better is
   to set all arrays to the length of MAX, which is set to
   10. There are some minor exceptions. We don't need
   `TWO = 2` in `area = PI * radius ** TWO`. We don't
   need `FEET_PER_MILE = 5280`, but maybe we do
   need the comment `# 5280 = feet-per-mile`. If we
   need a pause of 10 seconds, and the 10 appears only
   once in the program, then perhaps 10 is better than
   `pause = 10`.

```
secondsInAnHour = 3600
time = round(clock() - START, 2) # START is global time in secs.
hours = int(time/secondsInAnHour)
time -= hours  * secondsInAnHour
```

Another exception is using a *fudge factor*. The word "fudge" here
means "cheat." If a program's results are always off by 2, then add 2 to all
of the results, *and document this in the code*. Perhaps this is acceptable
if a deadline has arrived. (Use the right tool for the right job.[4]) But this is
attending to symptoms, not causes.

That being said, there is one big exception—at least in my mind:
General can be significantly harder to understand than specific. When
writing my first artificial neural net program using back propagation,
I preferred magic numbers. That was the most difficult program I ever
wrote. I needed to make it as simple as possible (many fewer variables).

---

[4]This was the advertising slogan for True Temper Tools since at least 1907.

10. Do not repeat code (DRY: Don't repeat yourself).
      This is one of the big rules for professional
      programmers. Below is a function that tests for
      a win in a tic-tac-toe game. I prefer the second
      version. Why? A change to one part does *not* require
      a change to the repeated part. If the change is a
      bug fix, you might not think to make that bug fix in
      another line that wasn't executed.

FIRST VERSION

```python
def result(board):
    score = 'XXX'
    B = board
    if B[0] + B[1] + B[2] == score or B[3] + B[4] + B[5] ==
        score or \
        B[6] + B[7] + B[8] == score or B[0] + B[3] + B[6] ==
        score or \
        B[1] + B[4] + B[7] == score or B[2] + B[5] + B[8] ==
        score or \
        B[0] + B[4] + B[8] == score or B[2] + B[4] + B[6] ==
        score:
        return 'win'
    score = '000'
    if B[0] + B[1] + B[2] == score or B[3] + B[4] + B[5] ==
        score or \
        B[6] + B[7] + B[8] == score or B[0] + B[3] + B[6] ==
        score or \
        B[1] + B[4] + B[7] == score or B[2] + B[5] + B[8] ==
        score or \
        B[0] + B[4] + B[8] == score or B[2] + B[4] + B[6] ==
        score:
        return 'win'
    return 'unk'
```

SECOND (BETTER) VERSION

```python
def result(board):
    B = board
    for score in ('XXX', '000'):
        if B[0] + B[1] + B[2] == score or B[3] + B[4] + B[5] == score or \
            B[6] + B[7] + B[8] == score or B[0] + B[3] + B[6] == score or \
            B[1] + B[4] + B[7] == score or B[2] + B[5] + B[8] == score or \
            B[0] + B[4] + B[8] == score or B[2] + B[4] + B[6] == score:
            return 'win'
    return 'unk'
```

Not repeating yourself is factoring out commonality.

I once wrote a program to run four different depth-first searches to a particular goal node: Find any path, find the fewest-nodes path, find the path of least cost, and find all paths. The main function was a mess of function calls and printing results. What gave me the simplicity I wanted was a factoring out the common print code into a printResults function. My code follows.

```python
def printResults(root, goal, path1, path2, path3, distance,
pathsList):
    print('   == DFS SEARCHING ==')
    print('1. Random       path from', root, 'to', goal, 'is',
    path1)
#-------------------------------------------------------------
    print('2. Fewest-nodes  path from', root, 'to', goal, 'is',
    path2)
#-------------------------------------------------------------
```

```
    print('3. Shortest-dist path from', root, 'to', goal, 'is',
    path3,
        '(', distance,'Km.)')
#-------------------------------------------------------------

    if pathsList == []:
        print('4. There are no paths.')
        return
    print('4. All paths from', root, 'to', goal, 'are listed
    below.')
    count = 0
    pathsList.sort(key = len)
    for path in pathsList:
        count += 1
        print('--%2d'%count, '. ', path, sep = '')
    print('\n---TOTAL search time =', round(clock() -
    startTime, 2),
            'seconds.')
#============================<MAIN>===========================

def main():
    root = 'A'; goal = 'B'
    path1               = DFS_AnyPath            (root,  goal)
    path2               = DFS_FewestNodes        (root,  goal)
    path3, distance = DFS_ShortestCostPath (root,  goal)
    pathList            = DFS_AllPaths           (root,  goal)
    printResults(root, goal, path1, path2, path3, distance,
    pathList)
```

The point is that the main function is now simple to understand, because all of the printing has been pushed into the printResults function.

11. Do *not* optimize for speed or memory use as you go. This is one of the biggest mistakes a beginner can make. Optimize only *after* a program is written, if at all. If one is hill-climbing in 64 directions, maybe we could optimize by pre-computing the 64 sines and cosines and place them in a look-up table rather than re-computing them for every step. Then again, if your program is fast enough, why bother? On the one occasion I tried this, the time was reduced by only 23%.

Do we ever need the speed of binary representation in a file? In my experience, the answer is no. Text files are better, because they are so much easier to use and to visually inspect.

> It is not always a good idea to play the best moves, particularly when you have to use up a lot of time finding them.—Simon Webb, *Chess for Tigers* 3rd Ed. (Batsford, 2005), page 15.

If **optimization** (increasing speed, reducing memory needs, increasing accuracy, decreasing lines of code) will make a block of code much harder to understand, then you must do a cost/benefit analysis. Is the goal worth the effort? Couldn't your time be better spent doing something else? Better is the enemy of good enough. Sometimes, less really is more.

> What's my approach to code optimization? Ninety-nine percent of the time something simple and brute-force will work fine.—Ken Thompson (Bell Labs, creator of UNIX, designer of UTF-8), found in Peter Seibel, *Coders at Work* (Apress, 2009), page 470.

* * *

I think performance is greatly overrated in the computer science field, because what you need in performance is good enough performance. You don't need the best performance.—Barbara Liskov (2008 Turing Award winner), Found in Edgar G. Daylight, *The Dawn of Software Engineering* (Belgium: Lonely Scholar, 2012), page 155.

12.   Do not write clever code.[5] Clever code is a breeding ground for bugs. In the equivalent examples below, A is the best because it is the easiest to understand and the easiest to debug.

---

[5]The same advice is given for writing essays. When the writing becomes noticeable, it distracts from the ideas it expresses. This is one difference between prose and song lyrics.

1. "Whenever you feel an impulse to perpetrate a piece of exceptionally fine writing, obey it—whole-heartedly—and then delete it before sending your manuscript to the press. *Murder your darlings*."—Sir Arthur Quiller-Couch, *The Art of Writing* (G.P. Putnam's Sons, 1916), page 281.

2. "Kill your darlings, kill your darlings, even when it breaks your egocentric little scribbler's heart, kill your darlings."—Stephen King, *On Writing*, (Simon & Schuster, 2000), page 224.

3. "Look for *all* fancy wordings and get rid of them."—Jacques Barzun, *Simple & Direct, A Rhetoric for Writers* (Harper and Row, 1975), page 27. Read this book. Barzun is an acknowledged genius.

4. Read over your compositions, and wherever you meet with a passage which you think is particularly fine, strike it out. [This is a statement of a college tutor, recalled by Dr. Johnson in 1773. Source: James Boswell's *Life of Samuel Johnson* (1791).]

5. Every once in a while, you emit a phrase or a paragraph that seems to have a life of its own. It has just that mix of aptness and cleverness you wish you could pull off all the time. When you write stuff like that, swallow hard and throw it away. Two months later, you will recognize it for the irrelevant purple prose it really is.—P.J. Plauger, *Computer Language* (October 1991), "Technical Writing," page 32.

```
#---A.
    if random() < 0.8:
        theta += 0.3
    else:
        theta -= 0.1
```

```
#---B.
    theta = theta - 0.1 + (random()<0.8)*0.4
```

```
#---C.
    theta += [-0.1, 0.3][random() < 0.8]
```

```
#---D.
    theta += choice ([-0.1, 0.3, 0.3, 0.3, 0.3])
```

Simple code:

```
if x >  y: z = z + 3
if x <= y: z = z - 5
```

Clever code (avoid):

```
z = z + 3*(x > y) - 5*(x <= y)
```

There are several ways to simulate the non-existent "switch" statement in Python. It is a good question to ask if these constructs are clever code or not.

```
def fn0():
    print(0)
def fn1():
    print(1)
def fn2():
    print(2)
def fn3():
    print(3)
```

```
#===========================<MAIN>===========================

def main():
#---0. The standard if-elif-else construct:
    print('\nif-elif-else: ', end ='')
    x = 1
    if   x == 0: fn0()
    elif x == 1: fn1()
    elif x == 2: fn2()
    else: fn3() # output: if-elif-else: 1
#-------------------------------------------

#---1. The subscript trick to emulate a switch statement:
#      (Alas, it has NO default else.)

    doIt = [fn0, fn1, fn2]
    print('\nsubscript:    ', end='')
    doIt[1]()   # output: subscript:    1
#-------------------------------------------

#---2. The dictionary trick to simulate a switch statement:
#      It does have a default else, but it is complicated to call.
#      dict.get(2, fn3)() refers to dict[2] = fn2. However, if
#      there is no key 2, then the default (explicitly given in
#      the call as fn3) is the value.
    print('\ndictionary:   ', end ='')
    dict = {0: fn0, 1: fn1, 2: fn2, 3:fn3,}

    dict[1]()                          # output: dictionary:   1

    print('\ndefault else: ', end ='')
    dict.get(2, fn3)()                 # output: default else: 2
#--------------------------------------------------------------
```

Clever tricks that were necessary with older code may not be needed in a modern language. For example:

1. How many digits comprise the integer num?

    ```
    print('length =', 1 if num == 0 else
    floor(log10(abs(num))+1))
    print('length =', len(str(abs(num))))   # simpler
    ```

2. Determine the third digit from the RIGHT of integer num.

    ```
    print('third digit from right =', (abs(num)//100)%10)

    print('third digit from right =', int(str(num)[-3])
                                    # simpler
    ```

3. Determine the third digit from the LEFT of an integer num.

    ```
    length = 1 if num == 0 else floor(log10(abs(num))+1)
    print('third digit from left =', abs(num)//pow
                                (10, length-3)%10)

    print('third digit from left =', int(str(abs(num))
                                [2]))   # simpler
    ```

13. Beware the curse of Cambridge professor Charles Babbage (1791-1871)—or rather the curse that befell Professor Babbage. Charles Babbage was possibly the first person to conceptualize the modern computer. He solicited grants from the British Government to build difference engine 1. Part way through building the thing, he realized it could be made better. He scrapped his initial design and started over. Part way through difference engine 2, he had more insights and began anew (the analytic

engine). When the grant money (£17,000 in 1842) ran out, he still didn't have a computer. In fact, he never built a computer.[6] The lesson for the amateur programmer is to keep a log for improvements to build into the *next* design. Do not incorporate them into the current project (**feature creep**) or you may never finish.

14.   Consider **pair programming**, as opposed to the usual **solo programming**. This means taking on a partner. The **driver** types the code while the **navigator** looks on and makes suggestions. Eventually, they switch places. Many good programmers would rather write their own code and not be bothered with carrying along a weaker classmate.[7] And one source says industrial programmers need about 8–12 hours to become comfortable with this process. The disadvantage is that two programmers take about 15% longer to write one program than they each would have done by working alone.[8] The advantages of pair programming are: The programs have significantly fewer bugs and are more readable.

---

[6]See *Mathematics in the Modern World,* readings from the *Scientific American* (W.H. Freeman, 1968), pages 53–56. In 2002 the Babbage difference engine 2 was finally built. It took 17 years to complete, contains about 8,000 parts, and weighs nearly five tons.

[7]My father was an excellent poker player. He once mentioned that in his youth he had been an avid bridge player. When I asked him why he gave up the game, he replied "because my partner was always an idiot." (My father never worked well with other people.) This is one reason talented programmers may not want to be assigned partners. Also, the challenge and fun of doing it all by yourself is diluted.

[8]Andy Oram and Greg Wilson, editors, *Making Software* (O'Reilly, 2011), page 314.

The programmers learn much from each other, and student programmers gain some experience working others. Pair programming is popular in industry. Try it twice, with two different partners.

Brilliant programmers who can't do teamwork shouldn't get themselves in the position of being hired into a traditional programming position—it will be a disaster for all involved, and their code will be a nightmare for whoever inherits it. I actually think it's a lack of brilliance if you can't do teamwork.—Guido van Rossum (creator of the Python language), Found in Frederico Biancuzzi and Shane Warden, *Masterminds of Programming* (O'Reilly, 2009), page 28.

For most of my career I have required my students to write an essay based on reading Dale Carnegie's *How to Win Friends and influence People* (first published in 1936, and currently with over 6000 customer reviews on Amazon). My public justification was that computer science requires people to work in teams. But the real reason is that too many people have weak people skills and actually *need* to read this book. They need to be convinced to avoid arguments, to rarely criticize, to offer sincere—and *only* sincere—compliments, and to let other people do much of the talking. How many people have you and I met who needlessly cause friction and don't bother to give simple words of appreciation to those around them? I have had students thank me twenty years later for assigning this book.

15. Beware advice from experts.[9] Having just given you advice from experts, and much of it common sense, why the warning? Because professional software developers work in a significantly different world from the C.S. student. The software professional is part of an ever-changing *team* that works on the evolution of *huge projects* of *legacy code*. The software they write is often intended for end users who need *convenient interfaces. Team coordination* is vital. *Consistency* in coding style is necessary. The following questions asked by a software designer, are rarely asked by a student:

1. Is the program easy to install?

2. Does it adjust itself to the computer memory available?

3. Is the interface intuitive?

4. Can the user modify the interface?

5. Is the learning curve steep?

6. Can the user get results quickly?

7. Does the software offer the user performance warnings where needed?

8. Is bad input detected and the user notified?

9. Does the software depend on Internet sites, which may change or go down?

10. Does it work with files built by other software?

---

[9]If anyone ever creates a list of ten commandments for writing code, I have a suggestion for an eleventh commandment: Beware of gurus, priests, interpreters, and dogma. Thou shalt think for thyself.

11. Can updates be automatic?

12. Does it run on several operating systems?

13. Has it been well-tested by potential users?

14. Has it been designed to allow for future enhancements?

15. Is customer support easy?

16. Is its data secure and protected?

In contrast, the student programmer, especially in high school, is only trying to code up algorithms that will be run one time in front of the teacher.

PART III

Perspective

CHAPTER 15

A Lesson in Design

MR. SOKOLSKY ROSE from his desk and moved to the computer console in the front of the classroom. This was his fourth day of teaching the Advanced Computer Science class at Smallville High School. He had taken over for Pam Jones, who was on medical leave. Mr. Sokolsky faced a sea of unsmiling faces.

"I assume everyone has finished the first assignment. I'll come around later and examine each of your programs. But I would like to have one student demonstrate his or her program for the class. Can I have a volunteer?"

No one raised a hand. Mr. Sokolsky picked up his gradebook and scanned the student roster.

"Roger, pick a number between 1 and 26."

"Ok, seven," replied the student.

"Seven, that is, let's see, that's Anna. Anna, will you please come up and demonstrate your program?"

Anna was a bright junior. She had done well under Miss Jones, whose enthusiasm for teaching and love of programming was appreciated by all of her students. Mr. Sokolsky was different. That he had never been a high school teacher before was made apparent by his first assignment.

Anna came up to the console with her laptop. She attached the video cable, and typed in her program's name: `mult`. A question mark appeared on the screen. She typed in 2. Another question mark appeared. She typed in 3. The answer 6 appeared, followed by another question mark. Anna walked back to her seat without saying a word. By her curt manner, she obviously considered the assignment a waste of time.

© Michael Stueben 2018
M. Stueben, *Good Habits for Great Coding*, https://doi.org/10.1007/978-1-4842-3459-4_15

"I'm sorry Anna, but I can't give you any credit for this program. It's just lacking."

Anna looked both confused and annoyed. "But it's just what you asked for. A program that multiplies two numbers."

"Well, let's see," said Mr. Sokolsky. He pulled up a copy of the assignment and read it. "Write a program that takes two numbers as input and prints their product. Pretend this assignment is part of a larger commercial program—i.e., it needs a user-friendly interface and must contain significant functionality. And, of course, your program must be refactored. Always try to give more than is expected."

"I did it," said Anna. "What more did you want?"

"Ok, a user should know what program he is running. You needed a title and some user instructions. What do your question marks mean? Be explicit to the user. And your program seems to run forever. How is the user supposed to exit the program? Remove the battery from the laptop? So let me ask you a question. After the program prints the answer, do you think the user should see a message saying 'Enter X to exit,' or 'C to continue adding'? Would that be a good idea?"

"Well, yeah, I guess so. But it is such a simple program, who cares?" said Anna.

"The guy who is giving you a grade cares, for whatever that is worth. But anyway, my suggestion is actually a poor one. We don't want the user to have to enter more information than is necessary. When requesting the first number, the user instruction might be, 'Enter a number or "X" to exit.' Thus the user enters only another number to continue, not a 'C' and then a number."

Anna looked exasperated, but said nothing.

"Ok, maybe I didn't make the assignment clear enough. So I have an idea. Work on this during the period, and we'll meet back in the classroom in 30 minutes to discuss this program again. And be sure to give more than expected. If you finish early, then start on the second assignment."

Thirty minutes later, Anna was again demonstrating her revised program.

"Did you give me more than I asked for, Anna?"

"I gave you what you asked for," said Anna.

"Well, maybe that is enough. Anna, may I suggest the two numbers you enter?"

"Sure."

"OK, I want the first number to be a 1."

Anna entered the 1.

"And the second number is one-third, that is a 1 followed by a slash, followed by a 3."

"It won't work for numbers like that, Mr. Sokolsky. I already tried. You have to enter them like this."

Anna typed in 0.333333333. Her program printed 0.333333333.

"Ok, but suppose I don't want that many decimal places in the output. Why not give me a choice, Anna?"

"You said the user should not be pestered with questions, so I followed your advice."

"Actually, I said the user should not be required to enter any more information than is necessary. So why not make the default number of decimal places two, unless the output is an integer. And allow the user to enter either a number, an "X" to exit, or a "P" to change the default precision from 2. That way the user could ignore the options."

The class reaction was various forms of annoyance.

"OK, so fix this program, and I'll look at everyone's work on Monday. Have a nice weekend and think often of me."

Mr. Sokolsky's sarcasm did not go down well, but he had entered into one confrontation with a student on the first day and other students were weary of his anger.

On Monday, Anna was again demonstrating her program with the numbers Mr. Sokolsky had used before.

"So far so good, Anna. But did you give me more than I had requested?"

"You tell me, Mr. Sokolsky."

"Ok, enter 2 as your first number, then enter the string 'happy.' I want to know what 2 times happy is. Yeah, I want to know what number that is."

Anna entered the 2 followed by "happy."

The program responded "Not a number. Please re-enter a number."

"Ah, very good Anna. You anticipated my irrational and twisted request. But how about if I just hit the enter key and don't input anything at all?"

"It works for that, too. I tested it," said Anna.

"Ok, then this program is much improved. But an improvement would be instead of just printing a single-number output, print the first input, followed by a times sign, the second input, followed by an equal sign, followed by the product. That is better, because it allows the user to check for an input mistake. So that is now required."

He turned to the class.

"The first version of this program that you all wrote last week was probably a fine first draft. And I mean that. You can spend, no *waste*, a lot of time coding for special cases when the program won't correctly multiply 2 times 3. So first get a working basic version, and keep it working. Then code for special cases, like the two I just gave Anna. Sometimes you need to write the tests first, and sometimes automate them. But that's another lesson."

"There are four kinds of computer bugs. Most students know only one. Most students think that if their program does what it is supposed to do every time in all reasonable situations, then the program is finished. But that is so untrue. Programs like that have removed bugs only of the first kind: compile errors and logic errors. Errors of the second kind are code-readability or style errors. The worst thing you can say about someone's code is that to debug it, or modify it, you have to re-write it from scratch. Errors of the third kind are functionality errors. Does the program have all of the features a user desires? The fourth kind of error is the interface error. Is the program intuitive to use? Does the program give the user the information he or she needs at the right time? Since most of our school assignments are implementing algorithms, functionality and interface errors are rarely encountered."

"So, let me ask you. Can you think of giving our 'mult' program any more functionality? Why would a student fire up our program rather than reach for a calculator? What might our program do in multiplying two numbers that a calculator can't easily do?"

The class was silent.

"Ok, we'll just sit here until somebody thinks of something."

After a moment one student raised his hand. "We could let the user enter a big number with commas, because that makes the number more readable, if it was a giant number."

"Ok, we could do that, and it would make the program nicer. So that is a good suggestion, but for our purposes, I'm going to pass on bothering with commas. It would be a lot of work for a small feature. I think our time can be better spent. So what else can we get our program to do by keeping it limited to multiplying two numbers?"

Another student raised her hand. "You could put in '1/3'. I mean we could code for that."

"That is an excellent feature, but doesn't it seem like a lot of work? I mean you would have to scan the input for a slash and then try to read off the two numbers on each side. But still, I like your idea. What else could we add to this program?"

Again the class was silent.

"So, I guess, we'll think about this for tomorrow."

Anna raised her hand. "I suppose we could allow the user to change the base for each of the two input numbers."

"Yes, exactly. Each input number may have its own base. Of course, internally we work in base ten. We just have to translate an input in base b to base ten. How do we do this? Well, the process is pretty easy with **int** casting. Here is the code for 23 in base 6, which is 15 in base 10: int('23',6). That is a little awkward, but it is only needed when not working in base 10.

But the input of '1/3' will not directly translate to a number. So does anyone know how to do this without scanning, which would be too much work?"

Again the class was silent.

"I'm going to suggest a trick that most of you don't know about: the wonderful Python eval instruction, which is an expression parser. Look it up on the Internet, but here is an example that multiplies 23 in base 6 by '1/3':

```
input(x)       # x = "int('23',6)*1/3"
print(eval(x)) # Output: 5.0
```

"In fact, with eval you can evaluate any arithmetical expression. So, pick up my *How to Evaluate an Arithmetical Expression* handout in the corner, and then off to your computers."

When Anna sat down, she went to the Internet to get some more examples of the eval command. The problem was beginning to interest her. The impracticality of anyone ever needing to multiply numbers in different bases didn't occur to her. Elizabeth, who always sat next to Anna, leaned over. "Can you understand the assignment, Anna?"

"Yes, I think I will in a minute."

"Ok. I think I'll wait for you to finish, and then get your help."

Elizabeth's idea of help was to copy some of Anna's code. Anna had noticed that Mr. Sokolsky never seemed to observe any copying. He occasionally warned the class to beware of getting too much help from classmates, but encouraged students to help each other with code ideas. Anna briefly wondered why Elizabeth couldn't write much code on her own. It just didn't seem that hard. Anna stopped and looked around. Alice was reading about the eval function too. Yuri, the math whiz, was already coding. She heard Avi tell David, "You write the precision part, and I'll write the computation part." The other students were chatting or playing on the Internet. Too many of them were waiting on their classmates. It suddenly occurred to Anna that the class was only for a few students. The others just memorized and copied key parts of code, and seemed to be content in doing so. It was just one more strange thing in the world that didn't make sense to Anna.

Anna returned to her reading.

Elizabeth placed a fresh stick of gum next to Anna's keyboard.

The End

I ran across an interesting C.S. book titled *Testing Computer Software,* 2nd Ed. (Wiley, 1999) by Kaner, Falk, and Nguyen. The book contains an appendix of more than 340 common software errors. Most of those errors deal with interfaces and functionality, which are concerns more of industry than of students in C.S. classes. On page 1 the authors had an amazing example that intrigued me. They asked the reader to consider writing a program that did no more than add two numbers. Then they used this trivial example to show what Industry deems appropriate in design and testing.

First they considered the **interface**. Does the user know what the program is supposed to do? Do the users know where they are in the program? Are there on-screen instructions? Are they clear? Is there an obsession with security? How does a user stop the program? Are the inputs displayed with the final answer? Are they lined up or displayed in a visually attractive manner?

Next were questions about **functionality**. What happens with incorrect input? Does it abort the entire program or does the user have a chance to correct it? Can there be spaces before and after the numbers? Can the two input bases be changed? Can the precision be changed?

Since my school assignments both as a teacher and as a student myself rarely included questions about interfaces and functionality, I decided to write this program, changing addition to multiplication.

My first step was to write code to change from base b to base 10. I wrote the code to allow the user to enter a 'B' or a 'b' instead of a number if he wished to change a base. But this made the interface inconvenient. I scrapped the code and wrote new code to allow the user to enter either a number or a number-with-its-base as a tuple—e.g., (12,8). But this was too much typing for the user (parentheses and a comma). I again scrapped my code and wrote new code to allow the user to enter either in a number, or two numbers (a number with its base) or three numbers (a number with its base, followed by the decimal precision required). This would require me to separate the numbers either by spaces or commas. And if extra spaces were entered, I would have to strip them off.

All of this redesign and coding was spread over several days. What took the most time was thinking about how I was going to detect invalid user input. The coding was becoming both frustrating and time-consuming. Would I even dare to offer such a torturous assignment to students? The only lesson I was learning was how difficult a consumer program was compared to an academic program. In fact, two more days went by without any coding.

Eventually, I got the new idea of allowing both input numbers to be entered on the same line with only an asterisk separating them. Then suddenly I thought of the Python `eval` function. That function combined with a `try/except` block and an **int** cast to a base would make all these pesky problems go away. I wrote some test code and discovered that the Python built-in functions such as `sqrt`, and `log` were perfectly evaluated by `eval`. Even extra spaces were ignored by `eval`. My actual program suddenly became easy to write.

All of this took five days of thinking and coding. Why didn't I think of using `eval` immediately? The answer is that I had to become dissatisfied with my code before I went looking for a new idea. Only failure of some kind prompted me to look for a new design. I think that is perhaps the only way I ever do improve the designs of my code. There was much for me to learn personally over these five days. Unfortunately, the limited time that students have for each subject does not allow an assignment like this to be given to a class. Only

a few students could make progress, and most of those students probably
are making progress like this on their own. What can be given to students is
the kind of assignment that the imaginary Mr. Sokolsky gave. In almost all of
the first few C.S. classes, the essential ideas need to be given early, and the
students just build coding skills by putting the parts together, or by looking
up key topics. Mr. Sokolsky went a little further in allowing the assignment to
evolve after some simple versions were shown to be inadequate. Below is my
final program. Maybe you can see why this program took me five days.

```
"""+===========+========-========*========-========+===========+
   ||                The Multiplying Program              ||
   ||               by M. Stueben (October 8, 2017)       ||
   ||                                                     ||
   || Description:See printDirections().                  ||
   || Language:   Python Ver. 3.4.                        ||
   || Graphics:   None                                    ||
   || References: Cem Kaner, Jack Falk, Hung Quoc Nguyen, Testing||
   ||             Computer Software, 2nd Ed. (John Wiley, 1999), ||
   ||             pages 1-7.                               ||
   +===========+========-========*========-========+===========+
"""

####################<START OF PROGRAM>####################

def printDirections():
    print('+-------------------------------------------------+')
    print('|        == THE MULTIPLICATION PROGRAM ==         |')
    print('|       by M. Stueben (Ver. 1.0, August 2017)     |')
    print('|DIRECTIONS:                                      |')
    print('|1. Enter a first number, followed by an asterisk (*),|')
    print('|   followed by a second number. Examples:        |')
    print('|   5280 * 3.14, (-27 + 6) * (1/3), sqrt(100) *   ')
    print('      log(10).  |')
    print('|2. Push enter to see the output.                 |')
```

```
    print('|OPTIONS:                                            |')
    print('|3. Enter X to exit the program.                     |')
    print('|4. Enter P to change the precision (default = 2)
           of any                                                |')
    print('|    float output.                                   |')
    print("|5. To enter, say 21 in base 19, type
              int('21',19).                                      |")
    print('|    Special case: 0X12 and 0x12 both are 18 in
              base 10.                                           |')
    print('|6. The user will be requested to re-enter any bad
              input.                                             |')
    print('+----------------------------------------------------+')
    print('\n RESULTS:')
#---------------------------------------The multiplying program--

def requestPrecisionFromUser():
    msg ='Choose the decimal precision of your answer (from 0
    to 17):'
    while True:
        data = input (msg)
        ch = data.strip()
        if ch in {'X', 'x'}:
            print (' Goodbye.')
            return
        try:
            precision = int(data)
            if (precision < 0)or(precision> 17)
            or(type(precision) != int):
                raise Error
        except:
            msg = 'Bad input. Choose a non-negative integer
            (0 to 17).'
```

```
        continue
      return precision
#----------------------------------The multiplying program--

def requestAndMultiplyTwoNumbers():
#---Initialize.
    from math import sqrt, log, log10
    precision     = 2
    problemCounter = 0
    errorMsg      = ''

    while True:
        msg = errorMsg \
            + 'Enter expression * expression, P (precision),
            or X (exit).'
        data = input(msg) # Dialog box

#-------Check for 'X or x'.
        ch = data.strip()
        if ch in {'X', 'x'}:
            print (' Goodbye.')
            return

#-------Check for 'P or p.
        if ch in {'P', 'p'}:
            precision = requestPrecisionFromUser()
            errorMsg = ''
            continue

#-------Attempt to calculate an answer.
        try:
            answer = eval(data)
            if not isinstance(answer,(int, float)): raise
            exception
```

```
            errorMsg = ''
        except:
            errorMsg = '=========== BAD INPUT ===========\n'\
                    + 'You entered -->   ' + data +'.\n'
            continue

#-------Print the answer.
#       Sample output: "1. 1.23 * 4.56 = 5.61 [decimal
        precision = 2.]"
        problemCounter += 1
        if type(answer) == float:
            print('    ', str(problemCounter) + '. ',
            data, ' = ' , \
                    round(answer, precision), \
                    ' [decimal precision = ', precision, '.]',
                    sep ='')
        else:
            print('    ', str(problemCounter) + '.', data, '=',
            answer)
#==========================<MAIN>==========================

def main():
    printDirections()
    requestAndMultiplyTwoNumbers()
#============<GLOBAL CONSTANTS and GLOBAL IMPORTS>============
if __name__ == '__main__':
    from time import clock; START_TIME = clock(); main();
print('- '*12);
    print('RUN TIME:%6.2f'%(clock()-START_TIME), 'seconds.');
#####################<END OF PROGRAM>#####################
```

Question: Why allow, or even introduce, students to the eval function? There are warnings all over the Internet to stay away from this Python function. As a test of how dangerous eval can be, I made up a bogus file called filex.py in my Windows E directory. Then I destroyed the file by running this one line in Python.

```
eval("__import__('os').remove('e:filex.py')")
```

I imagine this line could be useful for having a trial program erase itself.

The eval function is dangerous only if it accepts user input from an untrusted source. Since the student is usually the only person who has access to his or her own code, this fear is unfounded for school problems. The eval function can work miracles in a program, as it did here. Introducing eval to students is an opportunity to discuss what eval can do with malicious code, and—much more interesting—what motivates people to be malicious.

Discussions of the eval function, and absolute adherence to certain programming styles can easily turn into arguments of emotion, not logic.

The following outline is a design methodology that I believe in, but as they say in Zen, it must be experienced to be appreciated.

How to Approach a Major Computer Science Project

1. Set aside more time than you think you will need. You can spend much time working on a program and have little to show for it, except some insights on how not to write the program.

2. Plan to focus. This means moving away from the seductive-but-chatty classmate. If you have a partner, then consider pair programming.

3. Understand the problem (= analysis + program specifications). This may mean constructing some examples. You are also searching for relationships and insights.

4. Choose your data types and then design/redesign your program.

    a. Produce a *minimum* design. The *must have* functions are written first, hence, an early working program. Later, the *should have* functions are added. Finally, the *could have* functions are written, if at all. [In a smart tic-tac-toe program, the first version would be a program where the computer plays legally, but moves randomly.]

    b. Expect that the initial design may be poor and that your datatypes may need to be changed.

5. Write the code.

    a. Use stepwise refinement and self-documenting code (few comments).

    b. Use asserts and error traps.

    c. Test each key function after you write it (white box testing).

    d. Consider writing a crude test function *before* a tricky algorithm is written.

    e. Consider testing a complicated algorithm with hundreds of random inputs, *after* it is written.

6. **Return to step 4** as often as needed to redesign the program and change datatypes based on new insights, coding difficulties, user feedback, and maybe changing specifications. Again, accept that the initial version often turns out to be a failure that insures success in the second or later versions.

7. Fix any final bugs by testing the entire program (black box testing). You may have overlooked some special cases or borderline cases.

8. Refactor the entire program. This is where you learn program design.

9. Reflect on your mistakes and the lessons you learned.

## CHAPTER 16

Beware of OOP

My opinion is that OOP is one of the great frauds perpetrated on the community. The truth of the matter is that the single most important aspect of OOP is an approach devised decades ago: encapsulation of subroutines and data. All the rest is frosting. I used to say that encapsulation is 70% of what object programming provides, but I think I'm changing that to 90%.—Thomas Kurtz, Found in *Masterminds of Programming* (O'Reilly, 2009), pages 91 and 93. [Dartmouth professors Thomas Kurtz and John Kemeny co-developed the BASIC language in 1963–64. Kemeny won the IEEE Computer Pioneer award in 1986, and, for the same work, Kurtz won it in 1991. At the time of this interview, the 80-year-old Kurtz had been retired for 15 years and no longer wrote code.]

A study by Potok, et al. has shown no significant difference in productivity between OOP and procedural approaches.—*Wikipedia*, s.v. Object-oriented programming.

© Michael Stueben 2018
M. Stueben, *Good Habits for Great Coding*, https://doi.org/10.1007/978-1-4842-3459-4_16

AFTER MANY YEARS, OOP is still controversial.[1] The C++ language (C with classes) did not replace the C language. A claimed justification for classes is **code reuse** through **inheritance** (an *is a* relationship). Of course, we already have code reuse through cut-and-paste and through importing library files (modules). Some classes get so coupled with their applications that they are not easily reused. The advantages of code reuse through classes are more appreciated in industry than in school problems. Coding in terms of objects and classes *without* inheritance is sometimes called **object-based programming**.

That being said, I once used inheritance to import four functions (methods) that worked with vectors into a Vector class. Those functions were only applicable to the particular problem I was coding using vectors, and I did not want my Vector class to be redesigned. But that was more of a **composition** (a *has a* relationship) of two classes than inheritance.

Another advantage of inheritance is that a single change to a parent is a change to all of its children, because the commonality of all the children's code resides only in one place: the parent. Yet, even for programs without classes, commonality can be factored out into functions.

The most useful advantage of classes is **encapsulation** (bundling functions and data into a new data type, an **abstraction,**[2] and creating a mini-language to manipulate them). If the class models something in reality or even the programmer's perspective on a problem, then the

---

[1]See *Wikipedia*/Object-oriented programming/criticism.

[2]An **abstraction** in programming is considered to have two parts: **interface** and **implementation**. A class interface is the collection of methods—e.g., getters, setters, finders, modifiers, reporters, etc.—that are used to manipulate the data. The implementation consists of the private methods, and the primitive statements in the body of all the class's methods. The benefit is that details are abstracted away from (hidden from) the interface. This makes coding easier. For all classes, the *minimum* number of method types you need is six: constructor, getter, setter, mutator (to change parts of an object), comparison of objects (=, !=, and maybe >), and a printer. In Python you don't actually need getters and setters—e.g., Oop.x = 5, an Oop.setX(5) is not necessary.

programmer can think and write code in terms of objects instead of their individual parts. Thinking in terms of objects is like thinking about music in terms of chords instead of individual notes. This sounds great, but I have never encountered worthwhile problems that benefited much from an abstract data type. What I have encountered are artificial problems designed to require encapsulation for student learning—e.g., cars and motorcycles inheriting from vehicles.

Encapsulation is design, and an efficient design often comes from throwing out several inefficient designs. You can spend much time trying to produce a generic class. The experts give us the following advice:

1. Try to write natural functions that closely correspond to reality. The whole point of classes (abstractions) is that they should make thinking and programming more intuitive. Rather than trying to design a near-optimal class, design it so that it is easy to extend.

2. Despite many claims that promise a smooth transition from object-oriented analysis to design, in practice the transition is anything but smooth.— Erich Gamma, Richard Helm, Ralph Johnson, and John Vlissides (the "gang of four"), *Design Patterns, Elements of Reusable Object-Oriented Software* (Addison-Wesley, 1995), pages 11 and 353.

With encapsulation comes **data hiding** with **private data**—i.e., data that either cannot be accessed or can be accessed only through **getters** and **setters**, which limit modifications. The user could rewrite the class so that the private data could be accessed with no limits, but then that would be a different class. If a class has been well tested, then the bugs in a program that uses the class are unlikely to be found in the class. Of course, the same can be said about the well tested functions in any library module.

What is rarely talked about with objects is the way the objects communicate with each other. According to some OOP gurus, **efficient messaging** is of paramount importance.

When I wrote my first neural network program, I thought making a Node class made sense, because a network is made up of nodes. Unfortunately, the Node class seemed to complicate matters. So I rewrote the network without any classes. Then I decided to re-write the network program again as a neural-network class with only one object. This shouldn't make any sense, because then that object would have no other objects to interact with. What's the point? But, in fact, it made the coding simpler. Because of the **semi-global** properties of the many internal instance variables, I didn't have to pass or return them in the class methods. Since the network was small, the negative side-effects of globalization didn't occur. Nevertheless, I eventually re-wrote the program again, without the class.

Polymorphism with classes supports operator overloading. For example, when working with vectors, we can overload all of the operators in a Vector class and end up writing this

```
F = 3*(B+C)/4 - A/2,
```

instead of:

```
F = vectMinus(scalarMult(3/4, VectAdd(B,C)), scalarMult(1/2, A)).
```

Now you see why I built a Vector class. The operator overloading made a positive difference—for about ten lines of code. This was worth the effort mainly because my students learned how to build a class and apply it to a serious problem: searching with the beautiful Nelder-Mead algorithm.

Java allows programmers to overload functions, but not operators. In Python, you can overload the operators, but not its functions. I think this is because in Python any function will accept parameter lists (signatures) of variable sizes and types using the star (*) operator. See the code below. The single doIt() function is in effect overloaded.

```
def doIt(*args):
    if len(args) == 1:
        print(args[0])
        return
    if type(args[1]) == list:
        print('list')
    else:
        print(args[1])
#------------------------------
def main():
    doIt(1)          # output: 1
    doIt(1,'A')      # output: A
    doIt(1,[1,2,])   # output: list
```

In both C++ and Python, you can overload operators that already exist, but cannot introduce new operators. Continuing with my vector example, if I want to write a line of code involving the cross product, I can NOT use the letter "x" as an operator. Instead I must write something like A = B.crossProd(C), or A = Vector.crossProd(B,C), or overload the star (*) operator.

Industry tells us that classes make sense in huge programs where code can be written in terms of the objects. In most school problems this sense seems lacking.

Digression. Can you think of a simple geometrical diagram that can *not* be drawn to scale? The answer is in the footnote.[3] End of digression.

---

[3]No cross product diagram with units can be drawn to scale. If vectors A and B have scalars in terms of meters, the perpendicular cross product vector C = AxB will have scalars in terms of square meters. Also note that scalars in a vector must all have no units or must all have identical units. Otherwise the magnitude will not exist. I was told this by a physics teacher, and curiously never found this fact in a math book. Later I found this mistake in David R. Causton's otherwise excellent book, *A Biologist's Mathematics* (London: Edward Arnold, 1977), page 37. The author tried to find the "distance" between two plant species by measuring both stalk lengths and the number of flowers.

CHAPTER 17

The Evolution of a Function

> The two things I have the most trouble with when I'm coding are what to name things and where to put things. And I've come to the conclusion that they are the same problem. Does each name represent everything I want to say about the named thing, and do the names that appear together evoke ideas that seem to go together? And if I'm having trouble naming things, I often discover that the problem is that things are together that shouldn't be, or they aren't together that should be.—Dale Emery, *Understanding Coupling and Cohesion,* YouTube video.

I'M GOING TO SHOW YOU a trivial problem I once worked on: replacing a character in a string. Since Python strings are immutable (cannot be changed), a line of code must be written to work around this limitation. So why not just use a mutable type instead, like a list? A list cannot be a key to a dictionary. All languages have their limits and imperfections.

The nine-character string in this problem represents a tic-tac-toe board. The empty board looks like this:

```
board ='---------'.
```

© Michael Stueben 2018
M. Stueben, *Good Habits for Great Coding,* https://doi.org/10.1007/978-1-4842-3459-4_17

After two moves, the board might look like this:

```
board = '----X---O'.
```

So, how do we proceed from `'---------'` to `'----x----'`? Answer: We break the string apart, replace a hyphen character, and then glue the string back together:

0. My first try immediately solves the problem:

```
board = board[:position] + char + board[position + 1:]
```

Justification: The author could not make the line any simpler.

1. The first improvement: Make the line into a function:

```
def insertMove(board, position, char):
    return board[:position] + char + board[position + 1:]
```

Justification: The function call `insertMove(board, position, char)` is more descriptive than the instruction itself.

2. The second improvement: Stuff the board into a list.

```
def insertMove(board, position, char, boardCollection):
    newBoard = board[:position] + char + board[position + 1:]
    boardCollection.append(newBoard)
    return newBoard
```

Justification: It turns out that every new board needs to be stored in a list called `boardCollection`, hence the append line. (Later, the boards would become dictionary keys. At this moment in the program construction, I didn't have any values to go with the keys. So, I just loaded the keys into a list, instead of a dictionary.)

By placing both instructions in the same function, two lines of code (inserting and storing) are reduced to one function call. However, the function now does two tasks, not one. An alarm should go off in any programmer's head, that this (two tasks in one function) makes modification more difficult and bugs more difficult to detect.

3. The third improvement: Change the name of the function.

```
def insertMoveAndStoreBoardInDictionary(board, position,
char, boardCollection):
    newBoard = board[:position] + char + board[position + 1:]
    boardCollection.append(newBoard)
    return newBoard
```

Justification: The function's name must change as the function evolves.

4. The fourth improvement: Split the function into two functions.

```
def insertXAndStoreBoardInDictionary(board, position,
boardCollection):
    newBoard = board[:position] + 'X' + board[position + 1:]
    boardCollection.append(newBoard)
    return newBoard
```

```
def insertOAndStoreBoardInDictionary(board, position,
boardCollection):
    newBoard = board[:position] + 'O' + board[position + 1:]
    boardCollection.append(newBoard)
    return newBoard
```

Justification: The program will be easier to debug if the name of the function tells us which letter ('X' or 'O') is being inserted into the board. An alarm goes off: This code is violating the DRY (do not repeat yourself) principle. Also, do these two functions really make the program easier to debug? Note that this improvement did remove char from the parameter list.

5. The fifth and FINAL improvement: Return to the one-task-per function principle, which still violates the DRY principle.

```
def insertX(board, position):
    return board[:position] + 'X' + board[position + 1:]
```

```
def insertO(board, position):
    return board[:position] + 'O' + board[position + 1:]
```

205

Justification: I became tired of alarms going off in my head every time I looked at my code. I was breaking two principles DRY, and one-task-per-function. I continued to break the DRY principle because I fell in love with the readability of this code. I told myself that because the two functions were physically close to each other, it was less likely that I would forget to make two changes instead of just one.

6. Attempt to improve: Change the function's name (REJECTED):

```
def insertXInBoard(board, position): ...
```

Justification: The InBoard makes the name longer and adds little to the understanding, mainly because board is the name of the first parameter. This is a nice example of how a well chosen parameter can combine with a function name to improve understanding.

7. Attempt to improve: Use OOP (REJECTED).

I considered combining the data and its functions into a class object. Then, instead of writing

```
insertX(board, position),
```

I would write

```
board.insertX(position).
```

Does this help? My guess is no, but in many cases, a programmer cannot know if encapsulation brings an advantage unless the program is written once with encapsulation and once without encapsulation. The general rule is that objects will not confer a benefit unless they interact with each other and have effective communication.

So what is the point of all this fiddling with the code? Is this function call

```
insertX(board, position)
```

significantly better than the original single line:

```
board = board[:position] + char + board[position + 1:] ?
```

I feel the function call is better because it helps us understand more and faster and with less effort. It may seem that this discussion is an obsession with details. But obsession with details is exactly the appropriate attitude for coding, for communicating complicated ideas, for chess playing, and for anything creative. If we rarely re-think our designs, because they are "good enough," then we don't gain enough experience doing quality design.

CHAPTER 18

Do Not Snub Inefficient Algorithms

IN THE EXCELLENT popular mathematics book *The Golden Ticket* (*P, NP, and the Search for the Impossible*), the reader is asked to partition the 38 numbers below into two distinct sets of 19 numbers that each sum to 1,000,000.

```
Lst = [14175, 15055, 16616, 17495, 18072, 19390, 19731,
       22161, 23320, 23717, 26343, 28725, 29127, 32257,
       40020, 41867, 43155, 46298, 56734, 57176, 58306,
       61848, 65825, 66042, 68634, 69189, 72936, 74287,
       74537, 81942, 82027, 82623, 82802, 82988, 90467,
       97042, 97507, 99564]
```

The author made the comment, "Not so easy, is it. There over 17 billion ways to break these numbers into two groups." The programming solution the author had in mind is "dynamic programming." This method is so difficult to apply that whole books of examples have been written just to help programmers build their skills.

© Michael Stueben 2018
M. Stueben, *Good Habits for Great Coding*, https://doi.org/10.1007/978-1-4842-3459-4_18

That said, there is another, much easier way to solve this problem, a method that every programmer should have in his or her toolkit: **fail-fast guessing**. My code follows.

```
Lst =  [See above.]
count = 0
flag = True
while flag:
#----Initializing.
    count += 1
    s = set() # = empty set

#----Randomly assemble 19 different indices.
    while len(s) < 19:
        s.add(randint(0,37)) # Duplicates are never added.

#----Check the total.
    if sum(Lst[n] for n in s) == 1000000:

    #--Print the solution.
        s = sorted(s)
        print('Answer =', end = ' ')
        for n in s:
            print(Lst[n], end =', ')
        print('\ntotal =', sum(Lst[n] for n in s))
        print('This took', count, 'tries.')
        flag = False
```

My code solved this problem in less than ten seconds (about 220,000 guesses). Evidently, there are many solutions to the original problem. If there had been only one solution, then methodically checking every possibility could take almost nine days (with 22,000 unique probes per second) for the worst case. When we need a numeric solution quickly and do not have an algorithm to find it, fail-fast guessing can sometimes quickly find a decent answer, and sometimes the best answer.

The following is the infamous bubble sort, or at least my six-line version of it:

```python
def bubble(x):
    leng = len(x)
    for i in range(leng-1):
        for j in range(leng-i-1):
            if x[j] > x[j+1]:
                x[j], x[j+1] = x[j+1], x[j]
    return x
```

> The bubble sort seems to have nothing to recommend it, except a catchy name and the fact that it leads to some interesting theoretical problems.—Donald Knuth, *The Art of Computer Programming*, Vol. 3.

Is the bubble sort good for anything, except introducing sorting algorithms to beginners? We will see. [This bubble sort can be made more efficient. Do you see how?[1]]

The return x is not needed. I put it in for two reasons. First, the call x = bubble(x) explicitly tells the reader that x is being modified, without having to look at the function's code. Second, if the function code is later modified so that the address of x is reassigned, then the code will still work.

The first pass of the bubble sort will place the final element in place. The second pass will place the next-to-last element in place, etc. With each pass we sort one-less element. This explains the leng-i expression.

---

[1]The j+1 computation is done three times. Let k = j+1 and then let k replace j+1. A student had to point this out to me.

I have read that the bubble sort is the world's fastest sort for four-or-fewer elements. That seems reasonable, and I had been sharing that fact with my students for years. One day I decided to compare the bubble sort to the built-in Python sort. To sort four random floats a million times, the Python built-in sort took an amazingly short time: 0.63 seconds. The bubble sort above took 2.93 seconds. I wasn't expecting such a large difference in time, and I was upset that my decades-long claim seemed false. Then I realized I could cheat. Behold the bub1 function, below.

```
def bub1(x):
    if x[0] > x[1]:
        x[0], x[1] = x[1], x[0]
    if x[1] > x[2]:
        x[1], x[2] = x[2], x[1]
    if x[2] > x[3]:
        x[2], x[3] = x[3], x[2]
    if x[0] > x[1]:
        x[0], x[1] = x[1], x[0]
    if x[1] > x[2]:
        x[1], x[2] = x[2], x[1]
    if x[0] > x[1]:
        x[0], x[1] = x[1], x[0]
    return x
```

This is much faster (1 second), but not fast enough. Could I cheat anymore? Yes, behold bub2.

```
def bub2(x):
    [a,b,c,d] = x
    if a > b:
        a, b = b, a
    if b > c:
        b, c = c, b
```

```
if c > d:
    c, d = d, c
if a > b:
    a, b = b, a
if b > c:
    b, c = c, b
if a > b:
    a, b = b, a
return [a, b, c, d]
```

The result is 0.52 seconds. My claim was verified. Or was it? My code omitted loops, changed the data type (list variables are slower to access than primitive variables), and copied the list elements to a new list instead of in-place sorting. Is this what people think of as the bubble sort? Also, the Python built-in sort is probably running C-code (40-50 times faster than Python code).

My little experiment was not convincing. I needed to run the standard bubble sort (bubble above) against the quick sort also written in Python. On the *Stack Overflow* site, I found the following clever and fast quick sort version

```
def quickSort(array):
    if len(array) < 2:
        return array
    less, equal, greater = [], [], []
    pivot = array[0]

    for x in array:
        if x <  pivot:
            less.append(x)
        elif x == pivot:
            equal.append(x)
```

```
    else:
        greater.append(x)

return quickSort(less) + equal + quickSort(greater)
```

This code took a whopping 3 seconds to run. When coded up in a similar way, the standard bubble sort is *slightly* faster than the quick sort for four elements. You may not be impressed. Who cares about sorting four elements?

Suppose you needed to sort a large list in place (almost no extra memory). What sort would you use? Maybe not the quick sort, because that needs extra stack memory in both the iterative and recursive versions. Would you reject the bubble sort as being too slow? That would be making a big mistake. The quick sort is only about twice to three times as fast as a well-tuned bubble sort, and the bubble sort is much easier to code. Let us assume a million random integers. Look again at this bubble sort line:

```
for j in range(leng-i-1).
```

The -i makes the bubble sort more efficient, because elements moved to the end do not have to be re-examined. Suppose we exchange the -i with -gap, where the variable gap (initialized to leng = len(x)) would reduce in size (by being divided by 1.3) on every pass until it became 1.

This clever trick (first published in 1980) produces the so-called **comb sort.** The comb sort has a speed of half to a third of the quick sort, is *much* easier to code, and (because it is an exchange sort) needs almost no extra memory. [See *Wikipedia*, s.v. comb sort.]

So is the comb sort a bubble sort or a close relative? The question has no answer, because the definition of the bubble sort is not precise. My point in this chapter is that even otherwise inefficient ideas may be efficient in certain contexts.

As simple as the comb sort sounds, it took me over two hours to write, debug, test, and refactor the code. What took so long? Why not write this sort on your own and compare your code and coding time with mine. My code follows:

```
def combSort(array):
    aLength    = len(array)
    recentSwap = False
    gap        = aLength
    while recentSwap or gap > 1:
        gap        = max(1, int(gap/1.3))
        recentSwap = False
        for i in range(aLength-gap):
            j = i+gap
            if array[i] > array[j]:
                array[i], array[j] = array[j], array[i]
                recentSwap = True
    return array
```

I wrote the following code to test my creation:

```
def sortTest(trialRuns, sortFunct):
#---This sub function checks if an array is sorted or not.
    def arraySorted(x):
        for i in range(len(x)-1):
            if x[i] > x[i+1]:
                print('NOT SORTED! at positions', i, 'and', i+1)
                return False
        return True

#---Create random-sized array of random integers, then sort and
check if sorted.
    for n in range(trialRuns):
        listSize = randint(0,50)
        array = []
        r = randint(0,20)
```

```
    for i in range(listSize):
        array.append(randint(-r,r))

    sortFunct(array)

    if not arraySorted(array):
        exit()
    print('\nTested', sortFunct)
    print('Passed test of', trialRuns, 'random trialRuns.')
    print('-'*46)
#============<GLOBAL CONSTANTS and GLOBAL IMPORTS>=============

from random import shuffle, randint
#=======================<MAIN>================================

def main():
    sortTest(trialRuns = 10000, sortFunct = combSort)
#- - - - - - - - - - - - - - - - - - - - - - - - - - - - - - - - - - - - - - -
```

To test that the combSort actually sorted an array, I had to write a Boolean arraySorted function to examine every element in the array. I embedded this function in the sortTest function. The sortTest function then created 10,000 random-sized arrays with random integers and tested the combSort 10,000 times. The assignment was to write one function, the comb sort, but I felt I had to write two more functions to trust my code. Hence, the two hours.

The fastest sorts are of order $n\log(n)$. This is actually $kn\log(n)$, where the k is dependent on the efficiency of coding, the speed of the processor, etc. This expression makes it looks like the base of the log function must be 10. But it doesn't matter what the base is, because there is only one log function (your choice). All the others are just multiples of what you choose as *the* logarithmic function—e.g., $\log_{10}(x) = c\log_2(x)$, where c

does *not* vary as *x* varies. Can you calculate the numerical value of *c* in this equation? The answer is in the footnote.[2]

In special cases we can sort *n* numbers faster than *n*log(*n*) order time. Suppose I need to sort a list of 10,000 random numbers. Why can't I just read in a list of 10,000 random numbers that I sorted last week. In that case, the sorting is of constant, order $O(1)$. Suppose I have to sort 10,000 integers in the range of 1 to 100. In that case I can just count how many there are of each value and generate a sorted list. That is a sort of linear order, $O(n)$. As a challenge, write this countSort now. You can compare your code's readability to mine. The sortTest code can be reused. My code follows:

```
def countSort(array, max):
#---This array is assumed to take values in the range of 0 to
max (inclusive).
    counters = [0] * max

    for number in array:
        counters[number] += 1

    array = []
    for (number, count) in enumerate(counters):
        array.extend([number]*count)

    return array
```

---

[2] $c = \log_{10}(x)/\log_2(x) = \log_{10}(x) \div (\log_{10}(x)/\log_{10}(2)) = \log_{10}(2) = 0.30102\ldots$

There are certain questions we always need to ask while programming, and I asked them here:

1. If our function is going to be an algorithm, should the tests be written first?

2. If we need both a list element *and* its index, should we use the Python enumerate function?

3. If a for loop produces a list, should we use a list comprehension?

The three answers for the countSort are YES, YES, and NO. By using the built-in enumerate function and using extend instead of append, I was able to write this code with only two loops. Although we have a for loop producing a list, I could not get the list comprehension to work without an additional flattening of the sorted array, which I thought would complicate the function.

The moral here is that certain otherwise inefficient algorithms may work well in certain cases, or have an advantage—e.g., quick to code—that makes it a good choice in a particular situation.

Somewhere I read that on a data size of 50 elements or less all algorithms are efficient. Even the humble—and trivial to write—bubble sort looks good with such a data set.

PART IV

Walk the Walk

CHAPTER 19

Problems Worth Solving

> In a well-run computer course, the student does many exercises. He should also do at least one problem. The distinction is this: An exercise relates to a specific technique, and the approach is usually spelled out. A problem, on the other hand, will involve a broad goal, using many techniques, and with very little spelled out.—Fred Greunberger (RAND) and George Jaffray (Los Angeles Valley College), *Problems for Computer Solution* (John Wiley, 1965), page xv.

SEVERAL OF MY former students who became programmers later returned and gave talks about professional programming. One of them mentioned that he had set up short, after-work classes to help the newer programmers improve their skills. He told me that he was disappointed to discover that instead of trying to solve the problems he gave them, some of the new programmers would find a solution on the Internet and turn it in as their own work. My guess is that these programmers had gone through school relying on too much help from their friends, the Internet, and perhaps grade inflation.

© Michael Stueben 2018
M. Stueben, *Good Habits for Great Coding*, https://doi.org/10.1007/978-1-4842-3459-4_19

The following interview-type questions[1] are graded not only on the code working, but also on their designs and readability. Good luck.

Problem 1. Microsoft programmer Steve Maguire used to ask perspective programmers to write code for him.[2] This is daunting, because there are many algorithms that are hard to code on the fly. Once, Maguire asked his candidates to write a function that only uppercased a character. Ignore the fact that there is already a built-in function to do this. As simple as this sounds, more than half the programmers interviewed did not do a satisfactory job. Since every candidate probably submitted code that worked, what were Maguire's objections? Write up your own code function and compare it to the several designs that follow.

```
#                       Problem 1 Answers
#====================<FIVE POSSIBLE ANSWERS>==================

def upper1(ch): # Bad. It should ignore non-lowercase letters.
    return chr(ord(ch) - 32)
#-----------------------------------------------------------

def upper2(ch): # BAD: It aborts program.
    if 'a' <= ch <= 'z':
        return chr(ord(ch) - 32)
    exit('ERROR: Bad input = ' + str(ch))
#-----------------------------------------------------------

def upper3(ch): # BAD: It returns TWO different data types.
    if 'a' <= ch <= 'z':
        return chr(ord(ch) - 32)
    return -1
```

---

[1]Currently on the Internet you can find a wonderful set of C.S. articles and book reviews by computer scientist and journalist Brian Hayes. Just type in `Brian Hayes - American Scientist` or go to `http://www.americanscientist.org/authors/detail/brian-hayes`.

[2]Steve Maguire, *Writing Solid Code* (Microsoft Press, 1993), pages 100–101.

```
#----------------------------------------------------------------

def upper4(ch): # OK, however, the error traps are unnecessary.
    assert type(ch) == str and len(ch) == 1, ch
    if 'a' <= ch <= 'z':
        ch = chr(ord(ch) - 32)
    return ch
#----------------------------------------------------------------

def upper5(ch): # Best: 1. It ignores non-lowercase letters.
               #       2. It returns only one data type.
               #       3. It has no needless error traps.
    if 'a' <= ch <= 'z':
        ch = chr(ord(ch) - 32)
    return ch
```

The important question to ask is, "What is the context?" Probably this function will be used to help parse a string, where the user needs letters in only one form (capitals). What happens if a digit or punctuation mark is passed to the function? The function should probably just ignore it. What happens if a multi-character string is passed to the function? That is such a huge error that an exception should be thrown.

Problem 2. In your favorite language, or in pseudo-code, write a function named equal that will accept two numbers num1 and num2 (floats, integers, or one of each). The function will return False if the numbers are a trillionth or more apart, or else True. The one-trillionth was chosen because in Python you can add a tenth (0.1) nearly a 1000 times before you have a round-off error of plus or minus a trillionth.[3] When you finish, compare your work to my Python solutions below.

```
#                   Problem 2 Answers
#
def equal1(num1, num2): # Terrible code
#---Check the data
    if not isinstance(num1, (int, float)) or \
        not isinstance(num2, (int, float)):
        return None
#---Return equality (True or false)
    if abs(num1 - num2) < 0.000000000001:
        return True
    return False
```

---

[3]Did this justification of the trillionth seem valid to you? It did to me when I first wrote it, but later I realized that it is little more than nice-sounding words. I classify stuff like this as metaphysics, which in my opinion is another word for nonsense. "Metaphysics, that fertile field of delusion propagated by language... "—J.S. Mill. "Commit it [any book of metaphysics] then to the flames: for it can contain nothing but sophistry and illusion."—David Hume. The following is a metaphysical joke, which, I think, shows metaphysics is one step away from crazy. When the great French philosopher Jean-Paul Sartre was young, he asked his uncle if he could work as a waiter Saturday afternoons in his uncle's café so he could make some pocket change. The uncle, who already knew young Sartre to be strange, was hesitant, but decided to give his nephew a practice run. "Memorize today's menu and I'll test you," said the uncle. Sartre took an unusually long time to study the menu, and even insisted on verifying it with the kitchen. But eventually he completed the task. "Put on this apron, wait on the customer over there, and I will watch you," said his uncle. Sartre complied and approached the customer. "How may I help you, sir?" queried the young Sartre. "Bring me a cup of coffee, without cream," replied the customer. "We are out of cream," said Sartre. "May I bring you a cup of coffee without milk?"

```
def equal2(x, y):  # Ex.: equals2(0.000 000 000 01,  0) is False,
                   # but  equals2(0.000 000 000 001, 0) is True.
    return abs(x-y) <= 1e-12 # 1e-12 = 0.000 000 000 001
    (eleven decimal zeros)

def equal3(x, y): # Ex.: equals3(0.000 000 000 01,  0) is False,
                  # but  equals3(0.000 000 000 001, 0) is True.
    return round (x, 11) == round (y, 11) # 1e-12 = 0.000 000
    000 001 = 1 billionth
```

Notice that the first version returns TWO different data types: Boolean and None. This is usually a mistake. The error trap in the first version is unnecessary, because the compiler will catch this error in a run. The comments help in the next two versions. The final function seems easiest to debug.

Problem 3. Consider the famous Bertrand's Box Paradox (1889).[4]

> A chest contains three drawers. Each drawer has two coins. One drawer has two gold coins. Another drawer has a gold coin and a silver coin. The last drawer has two silver coins. You go to the chest and randomly pull out a drawer. You reach in and randomly take out a coin. It is a gold coin. What is the probability (a number between 0 and 1) that the other coin is also a gold coin?

Write the code fragment to solve this problem by computer simulation. In other words, make an abstract model in computer code to reproduce the situation described in the puzzle. Then run the situation 100,000 times

---

[4]For a readable and interesting discussion, see *Wikipedia* s.v." Bertrand's box paradox." This article references other simple-to-state puzzles with counterintuitive answers, which make excellent practice problems for high school computer science students.

to discover how often the second coin is gold, when the first coin chosen is gold. Next, print this ratio, which is the answer. My solution follows.

```
#                     Problem 3 My Answer


def solveBertrandsParadox():
#---Initialize.
    from random import randint
    trials    = 100000
    goldFirst = 0
    goldMatch = 0
    coin      = [['gold',  'gold'  ],
                 ['gold',  'silver'],
                 ['silver','silver'],]

#---Run many simulation trials.
    for n in range(trials):
        drawer   = randint(0,2)
        position = randint(0,1)
        if coin[drawer][position] == 'silver':
            continue
        goldFirst += 1
        if coin[drawer][position] == coin[drawer][1-position]:
            goldMatch += 1

#---Print labeled answer.
    print('Six coin answer for', trials, 'trials:',
            round(goldMatch/goldFirst * 100,  1), '%')
```

The output answer should be 2/3, not 1/2. Notice that the continue statement answers the question, "What happens if the silver coin is chosen first?" This design closely mirrors physical reality; you do not want to abbreviate or condense in a simulation.

Note on Proof by Computer (Simulation and Verification): How important is computer simulation? As far as I can tell, there are only five ways to make progress in the sciences: 1) abstract modeling (with mathematical proof), 2) field observation, 3) experimentation, 4) mathematical calculation of measurements, and 5) computer simulation. In some cases some people will prefer simulation to a mathematical proof, especially if they cannot understand the mathematical proof. But even the most rigorous proof has some philosophical objections.[5]

> **Problem 4a.** From the 1700s until 1910, Cambridge University held examinations on pure and applied mathematics called "the Tripos." These examinations were exceptionally difficult and lasted for several days. In the morning session of January 18, 1854, the following question was posed: A [straight] rod is marked at random at two points, and then divided into three parts at these points; determine the probability of forming a triangle with the three pieces.[6]

Your job is to answer the Tripos problem using *computer simulation*— i.e., translate physical reality into a virtual world formed by computer code. Then repeatedly run your counterfeit reality (10,000,000 times) and count

---

[5]**inference, rules of.** Methods of deduction (*which are assumed not to lead to error*), usually combined with axioms (*which are believed not to be inconsistent*) in a careful manner (*which is hoped not to involve a mistake*) that produce theorems (*which are presumed not to be paradoxical*) in the study of mathematics—*the science whose conclusions are considered absolutely certain.* [In other words, deduction is ultimately based on induction.]

[6]Source: Gerald S. Goodman, "The Problem of the Broken Stick," *The Mathematical Intelligencer*, Vol. 30, No. 3 (Springer, 2008), pages 43–49. I have slightly reworded the question for our purposes. The line after the semicolon originally read "shew that the probability of its being possible to form a triangle with the pieces is ¼."

how many times certain events occur or do not occur. By forming a ratio of these counts, you can obtain a probability (accurate to three decimal places) describing the real world.

> *Problem 4b.* Curiously, there is another definition of "random" that could be applied to this problem. A human would break the given stick once, and then break the longer of the two pieces. Your job is again to solve the Tripos problem using this definition of "random."

> *Problem 4c.* Surprisingly, there is a third definition of "random" that can be applied to this problem. A human might break the given stick once, and then randomly grab one of the two pieces to break next. Again, your job is to solve the Tripos problem using this third definition of "random."

> *Problem 4d.* Believe it or not, there is yet a fourth definition of "random" as applied to this problem. A human might break the given stick once, and then randomly grab one of the two pieces with a probability proportional to its length. [For example, if one piece was twice as long as the other, then that longer piece would have a probability of 2/3 of being chosen for the second break.] Then break the chosen piece into two parts. Once again, your job is to solve the Tripos problem using this fourth definition of "random."

```
#######################<START OF PROGRAM>####################
"""

    VERSION 4a. Two break points are randomly marked on the
                given stick, and the stick is broken into
                three parts.
"""
def puzzle4a():
    triangleCount = 0

    for n in range(TOTAL_RUNS):
        a, b  = random(), random()
        if a > b:
            a, b = b, a            # a   = length of left   piece
        if (a < 0.5 and b-a < 0.5 and b > 0.5):
                                   # b-a = length of middle piece.
            triangleCount += 1

                                   # 1-b = length of right  piece.

    print('Puzzle 4a: The probability of forming a triangle is',
                round( triangleCount/TOTAL_RUNS, 3) )
#---Output: Probability of forming a triangle is +------+ in 4.39
                                                           seconds.
#                                               | 0.25 |
#                                               +------+
#-------------------------------------------computer simulation--

"""

    VERSION 4b. One break point is randomly marked on the given
                stick. The stick is broken into two parts.
                A second break point is marked on the longer of
                the two sticks. That stick is broken.
"""

#-------------------------------------------computer simulation--
```

```python
def puzzle4b():
    triangleCount = 0

    for n in range(TOTAL_RUNS):
        a = random()
        if a < 0.5:
            b = uniform(a, 1)
        else:
            b = a
            a = uniform(0, b)
        if (a < 0.5 and b-a < 0.5 and b > 0.5): # a < b
            triangleCount += 1

    print('Puzzle 4b: The probability of forming a triangle is',
                    round( triangleCount/TOTAL_RUNS, 3) )
#---Output: Probability of forming a triangle is  +-------+ in 8.3
#                                                           seconds.
#                                                 | 0.386 |
#                                                 +-------+
#---------------------------------------------computer simulation--
"""

    VERSION 4c. One break point is randomly marked on the given
                stick.The stick is broken. One of the sticks
                is randomly chosen,and a second break point is
                marked on it. That stick is broken.
"""
def puzzle4c():
    triangleCount = 0

    for n in range(TOTAL_RUNS):
        r    = random()       # r = first break point
```

```
    if random() < 0.5:    # flip a coin
        a = uniform(0, r) # cut on the left side
        b = r
    else:
        a = r                # cut on the right side
        b = uniform(r, 1)
    if (a < 0.5 and b-a < 0.5 and b > 0.5): # a < b
        triangleCount += 1

print('Puzzle 4c: The probability of forming a triangle is',
            round( triangleCount/TOTAL_RUNS, 3) )
#---Output: Probability of forming a triangle is  +-------+ in 8.70
                                                                seconds.
#                                            | 0.193 |
#                                            +-------+
#----------------------------------------computer simulation--
"""
```

    VERSION 4d. One break point is randomly marked on the given
                stick. The stick is broken. One of the sticks
                is randomly chosen WITH A PROBABILITY
                PROPORTIONAL TO ITS LENGTH, and a second break
                point is marked
                on it. That stick is broken.
```
"""
def puzzle4d():
    triangleCount = 0

    for n in range(TOTAL_RUNS):
        r    = random()      # r = first break point
```

```
    if random() < r:      # break left stick
       a = uniform(0, r)
       b = r
    else:                 # break right stick
        a = r
        b = uniform(r, 1)
    if (a < 0.5 and b-a < 0.5 and b > 0.5): # a < b
       triangleCount += 1

 print('Puzzle 4d: The probability of forming a triangle is',
                round( triangleCount/TOTAL_RUNS, 3) )
#---Output: Probability of forming a triangle is  +-------+ in 8.68
                                                                seconds
#                                               | 0.25 |
#                                               +-------+
```

Notice that the answer to Problem 4d is the same as the answer to Problem 4a. One lesson to be learned here is to make sure you understand the problem before you code it, especially a probability problem. The word *random* can have different meanings.

> This branch of mathematics [probability theory]
> is the only one, I believe, in which good writers
> frequently get results entirely erroneous.—Charles
> S. Peirce, "The Doctrine of Chances," *Popular
> Science Monthly* (1878), Found in Justin Buchler,
> *Philosophical Writings of Peirce* (Dover 1955),
> page 157.

Problem 5. (Developing an algorithm.[7]) Occasionally we need to generate the rth permutation from some ordering of a sequence (n-choose-r = nPr). Write this function. In particular, write a RECURSIVE function called permute(Lst, r) to accept a sequence like Lst = [0,1,2,3,] and a positive integer, like r = 13. Then the permute function returns the rth permutation of the given sequence. Of course the "ordering" is arbitrary, but fixed for a particular problem. [I recall taking 45 minutes to write this function.]

EXAMPLE: There are 24 permutations of [0,1,2,3,], as shown below. Under this ordering, which is excellent for this problem, the 13th permutation is [2,0,3,1,]. GOOD NOTATION CAN MAKE A PROBLEM EASIER TO SOLVE. We start counting at 0 (not 1).

```
+-----------------------------------------------------------------+
|                  ==> Lst = [0,1,2,3,] <==                       |
|                                                                 |
| 0 [0, 1, 2, 3,]   6 [1, 0, 2, 3,] 12 [2, 0, 1, 3,] 18 [3, 0, 1, 2,] |
| 1 [0, 1, 3, 2,]   7 [1, 0, 3, 2,] 13 [2, 0, 3, 1,] 19 [3, 0, 2, 1,] |
| 2 [0, 2, 1, 3,]   8 [1, 2, 0, 3,] 14 [2, 1, 0, 3,] 20 [3, 1, 0, 2,] |
| 3 [0, 2, 3, 1,]   9 [1, 2, 3, 0,] 15 [2, 1, 3, 0,] 21 [3, 1, 2, 0,] |
| 4 [0, 3, 1, 2,] 10 [1, 3, 0, 2,] 16 [2, 3, 0, 1,] 22 [3, 2, 0, 1,] |
| 5 [0, 3, 2, 1,] 11 [1, 3, 2, 0,] 17 [2, 3, 1, 0,] 23 [3, 2, 1, 0,] |
+-----------------------------------------------------------------+
```

If we could extract the left-most digit (2 in [2, 0, 3, 1]), then we could recursively call our function to extract the left-most digit from a smaller list, etc. IMPORTANT: We would be passing up Lst = [0,1,3,]. That is, we would be passing up [0,1,2,3,] with 2 removed,

---

[7]My favorite way to describe computer science is to say that it is the study of *algorithms.*—Donald E. Knuth, "Computer Science and Its Relation to Mathematics," *American Mathematical Monthly* (April, 1974), page 323.

not [0,3,1,]. This counterintuitive fact tripped me up for a while. My code follows.

Problem 5 My Answer

```
def permute(Lst, r):
    from math import factorial

    L = len(Lst)
    assert L>=1 and r>=0 and r<factorial(L), ['L=', L, 'r=', r]
    Lst = Lst[:]
    if L == 1: return Lst

    d     = factorial(L-1)
    digit = Lst[r//d]
    Lst.remove(digit)
    return [digit] + permute(Lst, r%d)
```

Problem 6. Write a function called fizzBuzz(limit) that prints the positive integers from 1 to limit = 100 inclusive. But for multiples of 3, it prints "Fizz" instead of the integer; for multiples of 5 it prints "Buzz" instead of the integer; and for multiples of both 3 and 5 it prints the phrase "Fizz and Buzz" instead of the integer. See the *Wikipedia* article under "Fizz buzz."

Coding guru and Internet blogger Jeff Atwood used this test for coders applying for jobs at his company. Do you think he could make a good decision about a programmer based on such a simple test?

When I was in high school, I heard a restaurant inspector claim that he could rate a restaurant based on ordering a cup of coffee. I doubted his claim at the time. Now, years later, I consider his claim to be at least a half-truth. In poor restaurants, everything seems poor: the food, the service, the silverware, the china, and the environment. The entire staff doesn't seem to be sensitive to details.

Perhaps Mr. Atwood could eliminate the weakest programmers with this tiny test. After you write this code, I will show you several solutions. Most of them show some clever design, but a few are terrible. This is definitely a problem worth a student's time.

```
#                   Problem 6: Answers
#
#--Solution 1 Best, because it is so easy to debug.
    for x in range(1,101):
        if x % 15 == 0: print('Fizz and Buzz'); continue
        if x %  3 == 0: print('Fizz');          continue
        if x %  5 == 0: print('Buzz');          continue
        print(x)
#-------------------------------------------------------------

#--Solution 2  Mr. Stueben's solution.
    for x in range(1, 101):
        if x % 15 == 0:                      print('Fizz and Buzz')
        if x % 3  == 0 and x % 5 != 0: print('Fizz')
        if x % 5  == 0 and x % 3 != 0: print('Buzz')
        if x % 5  != 0 and x % 3 != 0: print(x)
#-------------------------------------------------------------

#--Solution 3 Not bad.
    for x in range(1, 101):
        if x % 15 == 0:
            print('Fizz and Buzz')
        elif x % 3 == 0:
            print('Fizz')
        elif x % 5 == 0:
            print('Buzz')
        else:
            print(x)
#-------------------------------------------------------------
```

```
#--Solution 4 Clever.
    for x in range(1, 101):
        stng = ''
        if x % 3  == 0: stng += 'Fizz'
        if x % 15 == 0: stng += ' and '
        if x % 5  == 0: stng += 'Buzz'
        print(stng if stng else x)
#----------------------------------------------------------------
```

```
#--Solution 5 Maybe too clever.
    for x in range(1, 101):
        stng =      'Fizz and Buzz' if x%15 == 0 \
               else 'Fizz'           if x% 3 == 0 \
               else 'Buzz'           if x% 5 == 0 \
               else ''
        print(stng if stng else x)
#----------------------------------------------------------------
```

```
#--Solution 6 # The "not" makes the code more difficult to
understand.
    for n in range (101):
        stng = str(n)
        if not(n%3): stng = 'Fizz'
        if not(n%5): stng = 'Buzz'
        if not(n%3 + n%5):
                    stng ='Fizz and Buzz'
        print(n, stng)
#----------------------------------------------------------------
```

```
#--Solution 7 This code says much about the programmer's lack
#            of experience in refactoring.
    for n in range(1,101):
        flag = True
```

```
  if n%3 == 0:
      print('Fizz', end = '')
      if n%15 == 0:
          print(' and Buzz', end = '')
      print()
      flag = False
  if flag and n%5 == 0:
      print('Buzz')
      flag = False
  if flag:
      print(n)
#----------------------------------------------------------------

#--Solution 8 Why would anyone work with x+1 instead of x? Why
would
#             anyone write "if (x+1) % 3 == 0: if (x+1) % 5 == 0",
#             instead of a single "if (x+1) % 15 == 0"?
  for x in range(100):
      if (x+1) % 3 ==0:
          if (x+1) % 5 == 0:
              print('Fizz and Buzz')
          else:
              print('Fizz')
      elif (x+1) % 5 == 0:
              print('Buzz')
      else:
              print((x+1))
```

My students took between three to seven minutes to handwrite this loop (pencil and paper). In all, 45 (73%) students passed and 18 students (29%) failed. I did not fail any student for writing needlessly complicated code. The main cause for failure was not mentally double-checking the logic through a few examples. At least this exercise told me who I should not hire as a summer assistant. Thanks, Jeff Atwood.

> Quite frankly, I'd rather weed out the people who don't start being careful early rather than late. That sounds callous, and by God, it _is_ callous. But it's not the "if you can't take the heat, get out of the kitchen" kind of remark that some people take it for. No, it's something deeper: I'd rather not work with people who aren't careful. It's Darwinism in software development.—Linus Torvalds (Creator of Linux), found in Bill Blunden, *Software Exorism* (Apress, 2003), page 1.

Note to problem 4a. Actually, the mathematical proof is easy to follow, but difficult to construct unless one has some experience with proofs like this.

Consider the stick to be the interval from 0 to 1. The two cuts are two randomly chosen numbers on the interval. Let x be the smaller number and y be the larger number. We can consider the ordered pair (x, y) to be randomly chosen in the upper left part of the unit square. *See figure.* If three pieces are to form a triangle, then x must <u>not</u> be larger than ½. (Region I is eliminated.) And y must <u>not</u> be smaller than ½. (Region II is eliminated.) Finally the distance from x to y must not be larger than ½. (Region III is eliminated.) Since all four triangles in the upper left half are all congruent, the answer must be ¼. Source: Thomas J. Bannon, *The Mathematics Teacher,* Vol. 103, No. 1 (August 2009) pages 56-61.

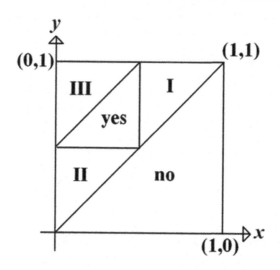

ASSIGNMENT: Write a program to simulate cutting of a circle into three pieces by three random cuts. What is the probability that one piece is larger than a semi-circle? [Alternate statement: What is the probability that three randomly chosen points on a circle are contained in a semicircle?] Surprise, this is the same question as dividing a stick into three pieces to make a triangle. Why? Because the first cut severs the circle into a segment. Then the next two cuts correspond to x and y in the previous problem. However, the answer to this re-formulation of the straight-stick problem is ¾.

CHAPTER 20

Problem Solving

The lame in the path outstrip the swift who wander from it.—Francis Bacon (scientific philosopher), *Novum Organum* (1620), section 61.

Writing code at midnight may be fun, but writing code at midnight the day the assignment is due is not fun.—a senior taking his fourth programming class (December 2011).

Another reason for the dullness of so many short pieces is that too few academic writers have had enough experience of writing. A good writer, like a good pianist, needs daily practice and a love of the art for its own sake. To keep in practice, he must write his weekly minimum of three to five thousand words.—G.B. Harrison *Profession of English* (Doubleday, 1962), page 111.[1]

---

[1] G. B. Harrison's short and wonderful book *Profession of English* (1967) is his attempt to answer what he should be trying to accomplish in teaching English at the university level. I think some of his ideas apply to the teaching of any subject or craft.

© Michael Stueben 2018
M. Stueben, *Good Habits for Great Coding*, https://doi.org/10.1007/978-1-4842-3459-4_20

WHAT DO YOU DO when you don't know what to do? Of course, you can
check the Internet, review books, and talk to others—if you can get them
to listen. After that, when no new ideas come, then what? It may seem that
there is nothing to do. But that is not correct.

First, start making up examples: Look for patterns, observations, and
relationships. ("Extreme cases are particularly instructive."—Polya) When
you notice relationships, you can think in terms of relationships. This is
called deep thinking. If you can find relationships among the relationships,
then you can do deeper thinking. Second, work related, but easier
problems. This way you train yourself to solve the original problem.

I have listed two actions to take. There is a third action that is even
more important than the first two: Come to the problem with a history
of trying to work challenging problems. That is the *key* to solving all hard
problems, and it is also why *practicing* problem-solving is important. Did I
say important? "Vital" is the better word.

So how does one learn or practice effectively? The first step is imitation
and memorization. The second step is trying to work out many challenging
problems *by yourself.*[2] If, after some considerable effort, you can't solve a
problem, then ask for help. But you may not omit the struggle. Otherwise,

---

[2]1. "How should we go about trying to improve? My guess is that chess skill
emerges from chess playing combined with chess training, where 'training'
means working things out for yourself."—(GM) Jonathan Rowson, *Chess for
Zebras* (Gambit, 2005), pages 28–29.

2. Japanese saying: "Ambition is the source of discipline."—Thomas P. Rohlen,
Japan's High Schools (University of California, 1983), page 266.

3. "The student is taught the *best* who is taught the *least*."—R.L. Moore, found in
John Parker, *R.L. Moore* (MAA, 2005), page 263. [The famous Moore method of
teaching is to make problem-solving almost the entire course experience. Little
lecturing, no tests, no quizzes, and–absolutely—no hints, just problems for each
student to work out for himself. I think Moore was mostly right, if one's goal is to
increase the student's problem-solving abilities. That is the best way to learn
mathematics. "The Moore method is, I am convinced, the right way to teach
anything and everything."—Paul Halmos, *I Want to be a Mathematician—*
Springer-Verlag, 1985), page 258.]

both skill and fact retention are retarded. The late mathematician George Polya tried to condense this advice into the following anecdote:

> The landlady hurried into the backyard, put the mousetrap on the ground (it was an old fashioned trap, a cage with a trapdoor) and called to her daughter to fetch the cat. The mouse in the trap seemed to understand the gist of these proceedings; he raced frantically in his cage, threw himself violently against the bars, now on this side and then on the other, and in the last moment he succeeded in squeezing himself through and disappeared in the neighbour's field. There must have been on that side one slightly wider opening between the bars of the mousetrap. The landlady looked disappointed, and so did the cat who arrived too late. My sympathy from the beginning was with the mouse; and so I found it difficult to say something polite to the landlady, or to the cat; but I silently congratulated the mouse. He solved a great problem, and gave a great example.
>
> That is the way to solve problems. We must try and try again until eventually we recognize the slight difference between the various openings on which everything depends. We must vary our trials so that we may explore all sides of the problem. Indeed, we cannot know in advance on which side is the only practicable opening where we can squeeze through.
>
> The fundamental method of mice and men is the same; to try, try again, and to *vary the trials* so that we do not miss the few favorable possibilities.
>
> —George Polya, *Mathematical Discovery*, combined edition (Wiley, 1981), pages 75–76.

The third step to learning is to reflect on both the result and the experience. You need to become philosophical every time you solve a tough problem: What should you have noticed to have found the solution sooner? Can the solution be simplified? Does the solution offer a key to solving other problems?

A curious method of self-reflection is called "the method of five whys."[3] Example:

1. Why did this happen? (I overlooked a special case.)

2. Why did I overlook the special case? (It never occurred to me.)

3. Why didn't it occur to me? (My thinking was superficial.)

4. Why was my thinking superficial? (I worked too fast.)

5. Why did I work too fast? (I wanted to be finished.)

The fourth and last step is to associate with smart people and get them to talk shop (or read the books they wrote).

Stanford computer science professor Donald Knuth made an interesting observation about common errors in programming.

> In volume 1 of *The Art of Computer Programming*, I wrote: "Another good debugging practice is to keep a record of every mistake that is made. It will help you learn how to reduce the number of future errors." But if you ask whether keeping such a log [916 errors in T_EX] has helped me learn how to reduce the number of future errors, my answer has to be No. I kept a similar log for errors

---

[3]This idea is from Kent Beck's *Extreme Programming Explained*, 2nd ed. (Addison Wesley, 2005), page 65.

in METAFONT, and there was no perceivable
reduction. I continue to make the same kinds of
mistakes.—Donald E. Knuth, *Literate Programming*,
CSLI Lecture Notes 27 (Center for the Study of
Language and Information, 1992), page 286.

I think Knuth is talking about the little problems that we all make and
we all quickly fix. Such errors are more embarrassing than a hindrance
to coding. Certainly some coders don't get much better after years of
coding, because they don't analyze their mistakes and forget too many of
their experiences. They are disconnected from their work. Others are the
opposite and become better with each difficult problem they solve.

The following is a compilation of common errors that I share with
my students. Does this list reduce their errors? Very little, because such a
list must be constructed from personal experience in order to be recalled
when needed. Again, each student must teach himself. The teacher simply
selects the problems and then offers insights when the student is ready to
appreciate them.

1. You interchanged parameters—e.g., (a,b)
   was passed as (b,a); coordinates x and y were
   interchanged; matrix row and column subscripts
   were interchanged.

2. You have a memory location error. Something
   got moved, overwritten, or your reference was
   accidentally changed.

3. You have an aliasing error—i.e., two variables access
   the same memory address (a deepcopy was not
   made). You have two functions with the same name.
   You have used a reserved word as a variable name
   or as a file name.

4. You were looking at one file (say, `lab99.py`), but running another file (`lab99`).

5. You never called the function in the first place.

6. An outer for-loop index was used as an inner loop index. [This cannot occur in Python.]

7. You dropped the parentheses pair from a function name.

8. You used == for =, or vice versa.

9. You wrote < for <= or vice versa. [This error has cost me hours of time on several occasions.]

10. You were ignorant of precedence—e.g., `a and b != True` means `a and (b != True)`, not `(a and b) != True`.

11. You failed to initialize a variable (not possible in Python).

12. Your numbers got too big (overflow).

13. You misspelled two similar words—e.g., the variable names `differenceInYears`, `differenceinYears`, and `differenceInYears` are all different.

14. Round-off accumulations produced a wrong number.

15. A list/array in a for-loop header was changed in the for-loop body.

16. You have an OBOE (off-by-one error).

17. You have an indenting or scope error.

18. You confused a list value (x[n]) with its position (n).

19. You assumed A += B always operates exactly like A = A + B. Not with lists.

20. You misunderstand how a built-in function works—e.g., a function may operate on data *in place* and does not return data as you think.

21. You compared floats for absolute equality.

22. You never mastered your language. A built-in function or clever syntax arrangement would have simplified your complex code.

23. You wrote the letter '0' for zero (0), or vice versa.

24. You were expecting [], "", or None in a function header, but got one of the others, instead.

25. Your if-else statements *appear* independent, but are connected. You may have

    a. a dangling else (an else connected to the wrong if),

    b. a back-stabbing else (two or more ifs followed by an else), and

    c. bleeding ifs that change the test data between if comparisons.

* * *

War Story 1. On a graphics program I assigned, a student copied my code from a handout and then told me she kept getting the error "Unassigned global variable...". The global variable was being imported and worked on all the other students' computers. After five minutes of inspecting the code, and comparing it to mine, I had nothing. What to do? What would you do? I never discovered what the problem was, but I was able to remove the error. I simply copied my working code, removing the functions I wanted the student to write, and e-mailed it to her. It worked. I later asked her to send me the defective code, but she had overwritten it. Too bad, because those are the errors that teach us something.

War Story 2. I once had a student construct a giant Python dictionary that would not compile. Compile errors are usually easy to remove, but not this one. The dictionary, made up of many lines, was viewed as one line by the computer. Consequently, the compiler could not give the actual physical line number of the error. After much disassembling of the dictionary, I found the error. On the second line of the dictionary, the student had written the letter 'o' for a zero (**0**).

War Story 3. My colleague Dr. Torbert once spent half a day (yes, half a day!) trying to debug a student's code. The student had used the reasonable identifiers getx and gety, which, unbeknownst to her and to Dr. Torbert, were reserved words in the inherited JPanel class. You would think the original designer would use more obscure identifiers, or even something like JPgetX or GETX.

War Story 4. I once wrote a program to solve a
Sudoku puzzle. I created a matrix of cell objects
to represent the Sudoku board. Each cell object
contained the address of its own matrix: the
matrix that contained all of the cells. This was
accomplished with a Python class variable. (See
below.) Thus, a change to the value in one cell could
be detected by the code referencing another cell.

```
class cell(object):
    matrix = None <-- class variable
#--constructor-----------------------
    def __init__(self, val, r, c, matrix):
      if val != 0:
        self.value = {val,}
      else:
        self.value = {1,2,3,4,5,6,}
      self.row    = r
      self.col    = c
      self.block  = self.blockNumber(r, c)
      cell.matrix = matrix <-- accessed with the
      class name.
```

The program worked fine for a simple Sudoku.
This made me confident about the class variable
and general design. But the program failed under
recursion. After about a week of debugging, I
finally realized the matrix was not being reset in
backtracking, even though the code to reset the
matrix was being executed. How was this possible?

Eventually I copied the code and threw out all of the lines that seemed irrelevant to the bug. This gave me a simpler structure with which to examine the bug. To my surprise, the bug didn't appear. I decided to think about this later and got up from my desk to get my lunch. As I was walking down the hall, the complete answer hit me. Evidently my brain had been thinking about this problem without my being aware.

The problem occurred with copying of the matrix. When the data structure was copied, the copy resided at a *new* address, but each cell contained the address of the original matrix. Remember, I had used a class variable, not an instance variable, to hold the initial address of the matrix. Those cell addresses needed to be changed, or the values of the copied matrix needed to be fed back into the original matrix to reset it. I discussed this error with my students and concluded with the following remarks.

Recursive errors can take hours to fix if there is no bug-effect until deep into the recursion. If we throw enough time at the problem, we usually can fix it. This process can take a lot out of us emotionally. Some people can handle the unending frustration and not let it take away from the more enjoyable and creative aspects of coding. Yet, there are many smart people who have no patience for this kind of mental struggle. For them, coding seems torturous. The only general piece of advice I can give you is to ask how each big error you discover could have been prevented, and then change the way you write code based on your analysis.

Having given you this piece of advice, you might ask me how I could have avoided spending a week looking for the matrix bug that I discussed earlier. Could I have set up an error trap? Could I have tested earlier? In fact, I don't know what I could have done that would have either avoided the bug, or exposed it earlier. I had never before worked with a class variable used in recursion.

It is not unreasonable to think that with every line of code a student writes, the student is becoming a worse coder, by reinforcing bad habits. Couldn't a good teacher help here? Not beyond offering worthwhile assignments and making many insightful remarks, some about life. It is vanity to think we can save others—they can only save themselves.[4]

So, again, how do we become good coders, especially if errors are impossible to eliminate? The answer is to learn the details of our computer language, work many challenging problems that offer insight, don't easily quit on these problems, practice refactoring, reflect over both solutions and errors, and talk shop with other good coders.

And now for a surprise. If there is any advice that will help you develop your programming skills, then you must discover it *on your own*, or at least you must identify coding problems so that you can seek out advice from others by asking them *explicit* questions. To beginners, this book must necessarily be just so much background noise. My perspective cannot be yours. Even telling you about my perspective is not enough to make it meaningful. The goal of this book is to inform you that professional programmers (and chess players and pianists) believe that certain habits have increased their productivity and reduced their frustrations. My words can only be a weak guide to finding your own personal perspective in coding. Good luck.

---

[4]Paraphrased from the French film *Queen to Play* (2009).

The Evolution of a Programmer

Disconnected from the programming experience, superficial efforts, failure to avoid distractions, procrastination, lack of style, little review, little reflection over mistakes, no self-study of the language, no analysis of other's code, quick to give up, dependence on classmates.

Programming = typing.

Confusion, annoying bugs, programs taking forever to complete, missing deadlines.

Repeated failure, frustration, bugs from hell, *misery*.

Give up and quit.

 OR

How can this be? *As God is my witness*, this will stop happening to me! My successes and failures are *not* predetermined.

Resolve (change is painful), self-analysis, seek advice, read the code of others, learn the language more deeply, change perspective, ask questions, and reflect over the causes of errors.

New habits, serious focus, extra-time commitment, self-documenting code, well-chosen descriptive names, structured code, error traps, early testing of functions, deep final testing of program, and much REFACTORING.

Success (maybe).

CHAPTER 21

Dynamic Programming

PREFACE. A PREFACE to a chapter is unusual, but dynamic programming requires some motivation.

The Most Profound Academic Joke Ever Told

A professor was searching near a lamppost for his dropped keys when one of his former students walked by. "Did you lose your keys, Professor?" asked the student.

"Yes, I did," replied the professor.

"Well, I'll help you look," said the student.

After a few minutes of search, the student asked, "Do you know on which side of the lamppost you most likely dropped them?"

"Oh," said the professor, "I dropped them somewhere over there by the side of the building."

"What!" exclaimed the student. "Then why are you looking for them here?"

"Oh, the light is so much better here that the search is easier."

© Michael Stueben 2018
M. Stueben, *Good Habits for Great Coding*, https://doi.org/10.1007/978-1-4842-3459-4_21

A Memoir by Richard Hamming

Alan Chynoweth mentioned that I used to eat at the physics table. I had been eating with the mathematicians, and I found out that I already knew a fair amount of mathematics; in fact, I wasn't learning much. The physics table was, as he said, an exciting place, but I think he exaggerated on how much I contributed. It was very interesting to listen to Shockley, Brattain, Bardeen, J.B. Johnson, Ken McKay, and other people, and I was learning a lot. But unfortunately a Nobel Prize came, and a promotion came, and many of them left. Over on the other side of the dining hall was a chemistry table. I had worked with one of the fellows, Dave McCall; furthermore he was courting our secretary at the time. I went over and said, "Do you mind if I join you?" He couldn't say no, so I started eating with them for a while. And I started asking, "What are the important problems of your field?" And after a week or so, "What important problems are you working on?" And after some more time I came in one day and said, "If what you are doing is not important, and if you don't think it is going to lead to something important, why are you at Bell Labs working on it?" I wasn't welcomed after that; I had to find somebody else to eat with! That was in the spring.

In the fall, Dave McCall stopped me in the hall and said, "Hamming, that remark of yours got underneath my skin. I thought about it all summer, i.e. what were the important problems in my field. I haven't changed my research," he says, "but I think it was well worthwhile." And I said, "Thank you, Dave," and went on. I noticed a couple of months later he was made the head of the department. I noticed the other day he was a Member of the National Academy of Engineering. I noticed he has succeeded. I have never heard the names of any of the other fellows at that table mentioned in science and scientific circles. They were unable to ask themselves, "What are the important problems in my field?"—Richard

Hamming (An excerpt from a formal talk "You and Your Research" given by Richard Hamming given on March 7, 1986. The entire talk is on the Internet. Read it.)

The Wayfarer

The wayfarer,

Perceiving the pathway to truth,

Was struck with astonishment.

It was thickly grown with weeds.

"Ha," he said,

"I see that none has passed here

In a long time."

Later he saw that each weed

Was a singular knife.

"Well," he mumbled at last,

"Doubtless there are other roads."

—Stephen Crane, *War Is Kind and Other Lines* (1899).

INTRODUCTION. Welcome to dynamic programming, and to the most difficult chapter in this book. Why is such a difficult topic placed in a book for still-developing programmers? The answer is that we build skills for deriving and coding difficult algorithms by trying to derive and code difficult algorithms. That is the only way.

HISTORY. In the late 1940s and early 1950s, mathematician Dr. Richard Bellman[1] was one of many mathematicians employed by the RAND Corporation to solve military and industrial problems. He observed that he and some of his coworkers often used the same methods to solve certain kinds of problems. He coined the term **dynamic programming** to describe these methods.[2] His technical book *Dynamic Programming* was published

---

[1] In 1979 Richard Bellman received the IEEE Medal of Honor (the highest award in electrical engineering) for his work in dynamic programming. In 1985 the Bellman Prize in Mathematical Bioscience was established to honor his contributions.

[2] The earliest use of the term "dynamic programming" I have found is Richard Bellman, "On the Theory of Dynamic Programming," *Proceedings of the National Academy of Sciences*, 38 (8), 716–719 (1952), which is available online. Here he stated, "The theory of dynamic programming is intimately related to the theory of sequential analysis (1947) due to Wald [Wald's *Statistical Decision Functions*, John Wiley & Sons, 1950.]" Abraham Wald died in 1950 at age 48 in an airplane crash. In this paper, Bellman referenced several other technical papers dealing with decision processes—e.g., Arrow, K.J., Blackwell, D., and Girshick, M.A., "Bayes and Minimax Solutions of Sequential Decision Problems," *Econometrica*, 17, 214–244 (1949).
In the DVD *the bellman equation* (Shami Media, 2013), one of Bellman's wives said Bellman told her that dynamic programming was in the wind at the time. And if he had not discovered it (actually formalized the method, named it, and wrote a book expounding its use), then someone else would have. Harold J. Kushner, one of Bellman's colleagues at RAND, once stated in a speech, "Bellman did not quite invent dynamic programming, and many others contributed to its early development. But no one grasped its essence, isolated its essential features, and showed its full potential in control and operations research as well as in applications to the biological and social sciences, as did Bellman."

in 1957, the same year Fortran, the first high-level programming language, was introduced.[3] In 1962, he and co-author Stuart Dreyfus published a second exposition: *Applied Dynamic Programming*.[4]

---

[3]Fortran replaced assembler language in many programs, thereby reducing the size of those programs by an average factor of 20. See *Wikipedia*, s.v. Fortran. There were few computers in 1957, partly because they were so expensive, and the ones that existed were computationally feeble. Processing speed and memory size were both extremely limited. Computer memory was being converted from mercury tubes to iron cores. The operating systems and editors were crude. The machines were programmed in assembly languages. The first commercial computer (the UVIVAC I with 5000 vacuum tubes) was not shipped until 1952, and was priced at $159,000. Eventually the price rose to $1,500,000. As a comparison, I remember my mother complaining in the late 50s that she had difficulty buying groceries for a family of four on twenty dollars a week. Bellman worked at the RAND Corporation and their computer was the JOHNNIAC, hand-built by their engineers with funds from the Air Force and first working in 1953. The mean free time between (machine) failures was 500 seconds. It is not easy to communicate how difficult it was to run a complicated program on such a machine. Search the Internet for the 20-page *History of the JONNIAC* by Fred Joseph Gruenberger (1968).

[4]In 1973 Bellman developed a brain tumor, which when removed left him severely disabled. Nevertheless, he continued to publish at a high rate until he died in 1984 at age 63.
"Hal Shaperio asked me [Bellman], do you think you will be a better mathematician than Erdős?" "Far better," I said. Immediately four pairs of incredulous eyes fastened upon me. I explained. "Erdős has great talent, even genius, but he has no judgement. He does not match the problems he works on with his ability." I doubt whether at the time those listening got the point. I think they understand now.—Richard Bellman, *Eye of the Hurricane* (World Scientific, 1984), page 109.
This statement was made around 1946. Bellman (pre-PhD) was 26, and the Hungarian Paul Erdős was 35. Erdős later became one of the world's most prolific, respected, and admired mathematicians. His field was analytic number theory, one of the most difficult areas of mathematics. Bellman who initially specialized in the same field eventually gave it up for applied mathematics. In my opinion, the two mathematicians cannot be compared. The world needs both. Notice that Bellman's 1946 comment echoes this chapter's preface.

The term "dynamic programming" is not particularly descriptive, but "linear programming" was then a new term for a process that solved problems by working with systems of linear inequalities. Dynamic programming solved problems by working with systems of recursive functional equations. Plus, Bellman, in his interesting autobiography, admitted that he liked the term "dynamic."

DEFINITION. The term **dynamic programming** in operations research refers to the mathematical theory of multi-stage decision making—i.e., making the best decisions at different stages of a process, usually by creating an **optimal policy function**. That is its defining characteristic. The word "programming" in "dynamic programming" means scheduling, or planning, both when the term was coined and even today. Sometimes the policy function is used to find a single (usually optimal) value—e.g., the length of a shortest path instead of the path itself (directions to the goal).

Since calculus is famous for finding maximums and minimums by way of vanishing derivatives, what does dynamic programming bring to the study of optimization? Applied problems, common in industry and the military, are often discrete and not continuous, and hence, have no derivatives. Applied problems often have so many variables that calculus expressions become too difficult to compute, even for a computer.

THE METHOD OF DYNAMIC PROGRAMMING (DP)

1. Reduce a problem to **subcases** by reducing the number of parameters, choices, decisions, capacity, objects, or the size of an integer domain—i.e., reduce the problem's dimensionality at each step. Then reduce those subcases to more subcases, and those to even more subcases. Do this until the subcases are easy to solve.

2. All of the subcases must be produced in a similar (**recursive**) way.

3. The value of any case or stage must be determined by some combination of the values of its immediate subcases, often (but not always) as a maximum or minimum of the subcases. This is called the **principle of optimality**, and leads to an **optimal policy function**.

4. Pruning is usually necessary in practice. Find a way to **compute overlapping (shared) subcases (if they exist) no more than once**. [Each subcase will be only slightly simpler than its parent. If each subcase were significantly simpler than its parent, then there would be no need for dynamic programming. Just breaking up a problem into subcases in any way and solving them by brute force would work.]

Note well: In computer science, DP has come to mean a recursive algorithm that does not evaluate a subproblem twice. See *Wikipedia*. Choose your definition based on the problem you are trying to solve.

Dynamic programming has three (many say two) forms:

Form *a*) an iterative algorithm that builds a table of past calculations, which it uses to make new calculations (called the **bottom-up** approach)

Form *b*) a recursive algorithm with no reference to accumulating memory, just repeatedly calculating the same subcases (called the top-down approach)

Form *c*) a recursive algorithm that remembers previously computed subcases (also called the **top-down** approach).

Notice that form *b* above violates the fourth attribute of dynamic programming. Consequently, some people do not consider form *b* to be dynamic programming. Nevertheless, form *b* satisfies the defining characteristics of operations research DP, is the simplest DP function to write, is sometimes adequate to solve a problem at hand, and is the first step to writing form c, which in turn often helps to produce the faster form a. So, form b is at least part of the dynamic programming toolbox.

FUNCTIONAL EQUATIONS. The subcases of DP usually involve *functional equations*—i.e., equations that contain at least one function. Here is a simple example (Denardo, page 28). Suppose you wanted to know the probability of throwing a 3 before throwing a 7 with a pair of fair dice: $f(3,7)=?$. The probability of getting a 3 in one roll is $\dfrac{2}{36}$. The probability of getting a 7 is $\dfrac{6}{36}$. The probability of getting neither is $1-\dfrac{2}{36}-\dfrac{6}{36}$. Then our answer is the infinite geometric series:

$$f(3,7)=\frac{2}{36}+\left(1-\frac{2}{36}-\frac{6}{36}\right)\frac{2}{36}+\left(1-\frac{2}{36}-\frac{6}{36}\right)^2\frac{2}{36}+\left(1-\frac{2}{36}-\frac{6}{36}\right)^3\frac{2}{36}+\dots(1)$$

This series can be solved with the precalculus formula:

$$a+ar+ar^2+ar^3+\dots=\sum_{k=0}^{\infty} ar^k=\frac{a}{1-r},\text{ for } |r|<1$$

What if you can't recall the formula? A simple idea is to consider the series as a functional equation (1):

$$f(3,7)=\frac{2}{36}+\left(1-\frac{2}{36}-\frac{6}{36}\right)f(3,7)$$

And now just solve for x: $x=\dfrac{2}{36}+\dfrac{28x}{36}\Rightarrow\dfrac{8x}{36}=\dfrac{2}{36}\Rightarrow x=f(3,7)=\dfrac{1}{4}$.
Thus, if you know about functional equations, then you never need to remember the infinite geometric series formula., except for $|r|<1$. Incidentally, how would you check the validity of equation (1)? The answer is in the footnote.[5] Functional equations are handy tools that can help us solve problems as well as simplify calculations.

---

[5]By the same reasoning, the probability of $f(7,3)$ should work out to be ¾, which it does.

BOTTOM-UP, TOP-DOWN AND MEMOIZATION. Consider trying to generate the fifth Fibonacci number. A natural solution is in terms of DP—i.e., embedding the original problem in terms of recursive functional equations with reduced dimensionality:

$$(5)\ f[5] = f[4] + f[3]$$

$$(4)\ f[4] = f[3] + f[2]$$

$$(3)\ f[3] = f[2] + f[1]$$

$$(2)\ f[2] = f[1] + f[0]$$

$$(1)\ f[1] = 1$$

$$(0)\ f[0] = 0$$

In this example, working bottom-up, we would need to compute $f[2]$ only once on line (2) and then use it on lines (3) and (4). If we wanted to work top-down, we would need to make calls to $f[2]$ on lines (3) and (4). But when we finally calculated $f[2]$ on line (2), we could save the result and not need to recalculate it on lines 3 and 4.

If you asked a beginner to write a Python function that would print the nth Fibonacci number, he or she would probably write a simple iteration function, like this:

```
def fib1 (num): # ITERATION, bottom-up (form a)
    if num < 3: return 1
    a = b = 1
    for i in range(2, num):
        a, b = b, a+b
    return b
#----------------------------------------------------------------
```

If you asked the beginner to solve the same problem recursively, you would get something like this:

```
def fib2 (num): # RECURSION, top-down (form b)
    if num < 3: return 1
    return fib2(num-1) + fib2(num-2)
#----------------------------------------------------------------
```

It is important to note that the top-down (actually recursive) approach refers to the initial function calls starting at one end and not obtaining values until the calls reach the other end, then bouncing back with numbers. Since the actual computations cannot begin until the top-down calls reach the other end, embedded in the top-down approach is the bottom-up approach. In that case, why would anyone choose the top-down approach? Answer: The slower top-down approach is simpler to write than the faster bottom-up approach.

Here (fib2) the top-down approach is grossly inefficient. It *repeatedly computes the exact same subcases*. We can improve fib2 by introducing a dynamic (changing) look-up table. This trick is called **memoization**.[6] Below are two versions. The first keeps the earlier numbers in a semi-global list. The second version keeps the earlier numbers in a Python dictionary whose address is being passed along with each recursive call.

```
def fib3 (num): # RECURSION with memoization, top-down (form c)
    if num < len(fibNums): return fibNums[num]
    fibNums.append(fib2(num-1) + fib2(num-2))
    return fibNums.pop()
fibNums =[0,1,1]
#----------------------------------------------------------------
```

---

[6]The word "memoization" was coined from the root word "memo" by British AI pioneer Donald Michie in 1968.

```
def fib4 (num, Dict): # RECURSION with memoization, top-down,
(form c)
    if num in Dict: return Dict[num]
    Dict[num] = fib4(num-1, Dict) + fib4(num-2, Dict)
    return Dict[num]

    print(fib4(12, {1:1, 2:1})) # The call.
#-----------------------------------------------------------------
```

There is a significant observation to be made by examining the tree of recursive calls leading to the nth Fibonacci number. Every level (except the bottom few) has twice as many nodes as the level above it. With memoization, the computer goes down only one side of the tree and never branches away, except to recall one previously computed number for each level. This is extreme pruning. This is changing an exponential run time into a linear runtime. This is why recursive dynamic programming is usually combined with memoization.[7]

A PROBLEM FROM OPERATIONS RESEARCH. Whenever we realize that a problem can be reduced to a simpler case and that case can again be reduced in the *same way* to a simpler case, then we are probably talking about dynamic programming. Consider the famous jeep problem (aka the desert-crossing problem). You are not asked to solve this difficult problem, just notice the form of the solution.[8]

---

[7]Those who cannot remember the past are condemned to repeat it.—George Santayana, (1905) *Reason in Common Sense*, p. 284, volume 1 of the *Life of Reason*.

[8]I found the solution in Martin Gardner, *My Best Mathematical and Logic Puzzles* (Dover, 1994). The solution had appeared in an earlier book of Gardner's (1961). I met Martin Gardner twice and found him to be an extraordinarily warm and modest person. Gardner died in 2010. To this day (2017), there are meetings each called Gathering4Gardner.

THE PROBLEM. (RAND 1946) Suppose that we have a jeep that can carry enough gasoline to go a distance of d miles. In order to traverse a distance of $2d$ miles over a flat and barren terrain, it is necessary to establish intermediate caches of gasoline. The jeep's fuel consumption is assumed to be constant, and at any point the jeep may leave any amount of fuel that it is carrying in a cache, or may collect any amount of fuel that was left in a cache on a previous trip, as long as its fuel load never exceeds one full tank. The home depot has an infinite amount of gasoline. Two questions naturally arise: 1) How should the caches be located so as to minimize the total expenditure of gasoline required to travel $2d$ miles, and 2) what is the total distance traveled by the jeep to reach its destination?—R. Bellman, *Dynamic Programming* (Princeton, 1957), page 103, problem 54 (paraphrased here).

Comment. There are many different schemes to travel $2d$ across the desert. Consider the following. Suppose we start with 11 tanks of gasoline and move back and forth a distance of $d/4$, dropping off a half-tank every time. On the eleventh trip we arrive at $d/4$ with 5-3/4 tanks remaining. By repeating the process we move to $d/2$ with 3 tanks left. Then we move to $3d/4$ with 1-3/4 tanks left. Then we move to d with one tank left, just enough fuel to go the final distance to $2d$. This is one solution (11 tanks), but we can do better.

SOLUTION BY DYNAMIC PROGRAMMING (N.J. Fine, *American Mathematical Monthly*, Vol. 54, 1947, pages 458-462). Let us think in terms of recursive functional equations. We define $f(t) = d$, where t is one full tank of gasoline and d is in terms of miles.[9]

---

[9]*Tech. Note.* Any physics teacher insists on writing $f(t) = d$, with both letters containing units (fuel tanks and miles). Most math teachers tend to keep the units implicit to focus more on the mathematical structure: $f(1) = d$. The physics teachers are correct.

Then $f(2t) = d/3 + d$. Why? The jeep advances $d/3$ miles, deposits a third of its tank, and returns to the home depot. On the second trip it arrives at the cache and refills to a full tank, and the problem reduces to $f(t)$.

Next $f(3t) = d/5 + d/3 + d$. Why? The jeep advances to $d/5$ and deposits $3/5$ of a tank and returns. It then repeats this trip. On the third and final trip, the jeep arrives at the cache with $4/5$ of a tank and has $6/5$ of a tank waiting for it. This is 2 full tanks, and the problem reduces in the *same way* to the previous case.

Next $f(4t) = d/7 + d/5 + d/3 + d$. Why? The jeep begins by advancing $d/7$ miles and depositing $5/7$ of a tank. It repeats this trip two more times. On the fourth trip, the jeep arrives at the first cache with $6/7$ of a tank and finds the equivalent of $15/7$ fuel tanks waiting. This is 3 full tanks, and the problem reduces in the *same way* to the previous case.

Consequently, we see the pattern of caches for n full tanks: $f(nt) = d$, $d/3$, $d/5$, $d/7$, $d/9$, $d/11$, ..., $d/(2n-1)$. The distance traveled forward into the desert with n tanks of fuel is expressible as a recursive functional equation:

$$f(nt) = d/(2n-1) + f((n-1)t), \text{ with } f(t) = d.$$

So, with 8 tanks in the home depot, the jeep can travel forward $f(8t) = d + d/3 + d/5 + d/7 + d/9 + d/11 + d/13 + d/15 \approx 2.02d$. And, of course, with 8 tanks of fuel, the jeep will travel a total distance (back and forth) of $8d$. The key idea is that the solution to the original problem is repeatedly embedded in a family of recursive functional equations of smaller and smaller dimensionality (integer domain, here).

Distance in miles	Fuel measured in full jeep tanks
2*d*	8
3*d*	57
4*d*	419
5*d*	3092
6*d*	22,846
7*d*	168,804
8*d*	1,247,298
9*d*	9,216,354
10*d*	68,100,151

Because the sequence of fractions with odd denominators is divergent, there is no limit (in theory) as to how far the jeep could travel. Check out the table on the right. The distance traveled with n tanks of fuel can also be given in closed form:

$$1+\frac{1}{3}+\frac{1}{5}+\cdots+\frac{1}{2n-1}=\sum_{k=1}^{n}\frac{1}{2k-1}$$

N.B. This is not a proof ("we can see the pattern") for the general nth case, and neither was optimality proved. Bellman's book contains many pages of existence and uniqueness proofs for DP theorems, which are understandable only by the mathematical expert.

We now will examine four classic dynamic programming problems. The ideal way to proceed is to try to make some progress on each problem before looking at my solution. Other solutions and problems can be found on the Internet.

***Problem 1.* Shortest Path.**

In the following (acyclic and directed)[10] graph we seek the shortest path from any node to node 9.

Or do we? Don't we seek a function (an optimal policy) that given a node just tells us the next node to move to for an optimum path? Isn't that in the spirit of DP? Both yes and no. Producing a function to guide us in choosing the next node is how Bellman first described DP. And that is what is needed in industry. However, to find the next optimum node from any current node, we must first find the *entire optimum path* from the current node. So, we can't have one without the other.[11]

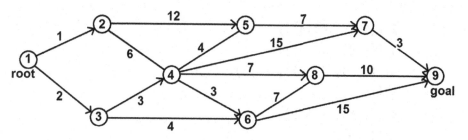

---

[10]The term "acyclic" means a loop (cycle) is impossible, and "directed" means all links are one way. Here we use the terms *nodes* and *links* (*arcs*) instead of *vertices* and *edges,* and we use *graph* instead of *network.* Any acyclic directed graph may have its nodes labeled so that any link (i,j) [from node i to j] will have the property that $i < j$. Why? If the graph is acyclic, then there must be at least one node with no incoming links. Label that node 1 and remove all outgoing links from that node. Then the remaining network must have at least one node with no incoming links (for the same reason as before). Then repeat.

[11]Reference: R. Bellman and S. Dreyfus, *Applied Dynamic Programming* (Princeton, 1962), page 229, A Routing Problem.

This figure was taken from Eric V. Denardo, *Dynamic Programming Models and Applications* (Dover, 2003), page 9. The shortest of the eleven possible paths is through nodes 1, 3, 4, 5, 7, 9, with a total length or cost of 19. Curiously, the greedy (myopic) algorithm produces the longest path (1,2,4,6,8,9) of length 27.

First, translate the graph picture into computer data. That will be an associative list—i.e., a list of lists: a list of nodes with each node having its own list of immediate forward neighbors and the distances to those neighbors. Python offers a built-in dictionary data type to help us work with this information. The following data structure can be used (unchanged) for both the top-down and bottom-up algorithms:

```
graph = {1:[(1,2), (2,3)], # (d,n) = (distance to next node,
next node)
        2:[(12,5),(6,4)],
        3:[(3,4), (4,6)],
        4:[(4,5), (15,7), (7,8), (3,6)],
        5:[(7,7)],
        6:[(7,8), (15,9)],
        7:[(3,9)],
        8:[(10,9)],
        9:[(0,0)], }
```

Now ask yourself what information you would need at any node to proceed by an optimal path to our goal (node 9, here). You would need a list of immediate forward neighbors and the distance to each neighbor from your current location (node). This information is already given in the statement of the problem (the graph data structure). The final piece of information you need is the optimum distance $f(i)$ from each neighbor (i) to the goal. This is where recursion comes in. Finding the shortest distance from a neighbor node to the goal node is exactly the same question we are asking at our present node, except the dimensionality (length of the remaining path in nodes) has been slightly reduced. Finding such a recursive function often requires much ingenuity. If it can be found and solved, then the would-be solver will be able to make the optimal decision at each stage. Although the thinking is recursive, the function we write could be either iterative or recursive, as we saw with the two Fibonacci functions.

Our function $f(i)$ represents the minimum (optimal) distance between node i and node 9. Clearly, $f(9) = 0$. But then

* $$f(i) = \min_{j}\left(d_{ij} + f(j)\right), \text{[The Bellman equation]}$$

where d_{ij} is the distance from node i forward to an immediate neighbor node j. Note that $i < j$, and $f(j)$ is the minimum distance from node j forward to node 9. In DP theory, technically when the recursive function is derived, the optimization problem is solved.[12]

The concise wording above needs to be more concrete. Consequently, by looking at either the graph picture, or at the graph data structure, write out, by hand, the nine equations f(9) = 0 to f(1) = 19 using formula (*). Warning: Do not skip this step. The answer (check after you finish) is given later.

The next paragraph contains the key idea behind determining the minimum path length *without* having to examine every possible path's length. We must, however, associate every node with a number (the minimum distance from that node forward to node 9).

When we come to node 6, we must evaluate two (short) distances to the goal. When we come to node 4, we need only examine four (not five) distances, because node 6 is now associated with only one distance (the optimal distance), not two distances. When we come to node 3, we need only examine two distances, not seven distances,

---

[12]*Tech. Note.* This particular recursive functional equation (*) is called a **Bellman equation** or, more accurately, the Bellman equation for this problem. See *Wikipedia*, s.v. Bellman equation. Some problems in dynamic programming do not require a max or a min—e.g., the Fibonacci function, the jeep problem, and Problem 3, given later.

because node 4 is associated with only one distance, and node 6 is associated with only one distance. This is the pruning power of dynamic programming with memoization. And it brings us to your first assignments. My code (the solution) follows the assignments.

ASSIGNMENT 1. Write an <u>iterative</u> function named fa (form *a*) to receive only a node (the graph data is global), and return the distance from that node to the goal node (9). The key idea for this short function is the recursive functional equation (*). You must create a local data structure to hold the optimum distances from each node to the goal node. I named my data structure data. My notes tell me this first function took me 50 minutes to write and another 10 minutes to refactor.

ASSIGNMENT 2. Write a <u>recursive</u> function (no pruning by memoization) named fb (form *b*) to receive only a node (the graph data is global), and return the distance from that node to the goal node (9).

ASSIGNMENT 3. Write a <u>recursive</u> function named fc (form *c*) that is a modification of function fb to include memoization.

ASSIGNMENT 4. Write a function determineMinimumPathAndDistance to call either fb, fc, or fa, and to return *both* the shortest path and the length of that path.

The Nine Equations

$$f(9)=0$$
$$f(8)=10+f(9)=10$$
$$f(7)=3+f(9)=3$$
$$f(6)=\min\begin{cases}7+f(8)=7+10\\15+f(9)=15+0\end{cases}=15$$
$$f(5)=7+f(7)=10$$

$$f(4)=\min\begin{cases}4+f(5)=4+10\\15+f(7)=15+3\\7+f(8)=7+10\\3+f(6)=3+15\end{cases}=14$$

$$f(3)=\min\begin{cases}3+f(4)=3+14\\4+f(6)=4+15\end{cases}=17$$

$$f(2)=\min\begin{cases}12+f(5)=12+10\\6+f(4)=6+14\end{cases}=20$$

$$f(1)=\min\begin{cases}1+f(2)=1+20\\2+f(3)=2+17\end{cases}=19$$

The Author's Four Solutions

```
"""+===============-========-========-========-========-======+
 ||      DYNAMIC PROGRAMMING (shortest route problem)       ||
 ||           by M. Stueben (October 8, 2017)               ||
 ||                                                         ||
 || Description: This program contains three functions (fa, ||
 ||              fb, and fc) which each determine the next  ||
 ||              node to move to in proceeding by the shortest ||
 ||              path to goal node 9. Then each of these    ||
 ||              functions is used to find the shortest route ||
 ||              and its distance from node 1 to node 9.    ||
```

```
|| Reference:    Eric V. Denardo, Dynamic Programming    ||
||               (Dover, 2003), pages 6-19.              ||
|| Language:     Python Ver. 3.4                         ||
|| Graphics:     None                                    ||
  +===========-========-========-========-========-==========+
""" 
```

```python
####################<BEGINING OF PROGRAM>####################
#============<GLOBAL CONSTANTS and GLOBAL IMPORTS>============
graph = {1:[(1,2),  (2,3)], # Each neighbor node moves us
                            towards goal node 9.
         2:[(12,5), (6,4)], # (d,n) = (distance to next node,
                            next node)
         3:[(3,4), (4,6)],
         4:[(4,5), (15,7),(7,8),(3,6)],
         5:[(7,7)],
         6:[(7,8), (15,9)],
         7:[(3,9)],
         8:[(10,9)],
         9:[(0,0)], }
count = 0                   # Counts the number of recursive calls.
#===========================================================
```

```python
def printResults(distance, path, func):
    print('--', func.__name__,'min path:', path)
    print('   distance =', distance, 'recursive calls =', count)
#================================================================
def fb(node):                       # Recursion with NO memoization.
    global count; count += 1
    if node == 9: return 0
    shortest = min([dist + fb(neighbor) for (dist, neighbor)
    in graph[node]])
    return shortest             # = shortest distance from current
                                    node to goal node.
#================================================================
def fc(node, dict = {}):        # Recursion with memoization.
    global count; count += 1;
    if node == 9: return 0
    data = []                   # data = [(dist to goal,
                                    neighbor),...]

    for (dist, neighbor) in graph[node]:
        if neighbor in dict:
            data.append((dist + dict[neighbor], neighbor))
        else:
            neighborsDistToGoal = fc(neighbor, dict)
            data.append((dist + neighborsDistToGoal, neighbor))
            dict[neighbor] = neighborsDistToGoal

    shortest = min(data)[0]
    return shortest # = shortest distance from current node to
                        the goal node.
#================================================================
```

273

```
def fa (node):
    data = ['-',0,0,0,0,0,0,0,0,0,] # = distances of each node
                                            to goal node (9).
    for n in range (8, 0, -1):
        data[n] = min([dist + data[neighbor] for (dist,
        neighbor) in graph[n]])
    return data[node]
#================================================================

def determineMinimumPathAndDistance(func, node):
    global count; count = 0
    minimumPath        = [node]
    shortestDistance   = 0

    while node != 9:
        (_, dist, node)  = min([(dist + func(neighbor),
                            dist, neighbor)
                                for (dist, neighbor) in graph
                                [node]])
        minimumPath.append(node)
        shortestDistance += dist
    return shortestDistance, minimumPath
#========================<MAIN>===============================

def main():
    for func in (fb, fc, fa):
        distance, path = determineMinimumPathAndDistance
                            (func, node=1)
        printResults(distance, path, func)
#---------------------------------------------------------------
```

```
if __name__ == '__main__':
    from time import clock; START_TIME = clock();
    main(); print('- '*16);
    print('Program run time:%6.2f'%(clock()-START_TIME), 'seconds.')
######################<END OF PROGRAM>######################
```

Output:

```
-- fb min path: [1, 3, 4, 5, 7, 9]
   distance = 19 recursive calls = 63
-- fc min path: [1, 3, 4, 5, 7, 9]
   distance = 19 recursive calls = 16
-- fa min path: [1, 3, 4, 5, 7, 9]
   distance = 19 recursive calls = 0
- - - - - - - - - - - - - - - - -
Program run time:  0.06 seconds.
```

The times for one million calls follow:

fb function run time: 16.5 seconds with 63 recursive calls and a max recursive depth of 27.

fc (function run time: 8.5 seconds, with16 recursive calls and a max recursive depth of 4.

fa function run time: 6.5 seconds.

It has always been my experience that *iterative* DP is faster than *recursive* DP. However, when I first ran this test, fc was many times faster than fa. I knew I had made some mistake in comparing the times, but what was it? Perhaps the reader can guess before looking at the footnote.[13]

---

[13]I had forgotten to deconstruct the dictionary (dict) before the beginning of each call. Consequently, neighbor was always in dict after the first call. A Bellman equation never had to be evaluated for the final 999,999 calls. Oops!

Code comments:

1. This is a rare case when a `for` loop in the main function actually simplifies the reading of the code. However, the purpose of this code is to demonstrate the three functions, not to solve a problem.

2. The function `determineMinimumPathAndDistance` includes the throw-away underscore variable ('_').

3. Why did I place the distance before the neighbor in the graph, instead of the other way around? Answer: The `min` function examines only the first element in a tuple or a list. This is a useful design trick when the `min` or `max` function is to be called in Python with tuples or lists.

4. Notice I used so-called magic numbers instead of assigning these numbers to identifiers—e.g., `rootNode = 9`. This made the code easier to understand, but harder to extend or debug if placed in a much larger program.

Although memoization makes a function harder to write, memoization (with recursion or iteration) gives dynamic programming its power. If the reader has reached this point without writing any code, then it is time to put the book aside, go back and write the code from both memory and understanding. Peek if you get stuck.

And now for a surprise. Having written the easy `fb`, we can define `fc` as `fb` with a decorator:

```
def memoize(function):
    from sys  import setrecursionlimit; setrecursionlimit(100)
    # default = 1000
    dict = {}
```

```
def wrapper(num):
    if num not in dict:
        dict[num] = function(num)
    return dict[num]
wrapper.__name__ = function.__name__  # In case we need the
                                         function's name.
    return wrapper
#================================================================

@memoize
def fb(node):                 # Recursion with NO memoization.
    global count; count += 1
    if node == 9: return 0
    shortest = min([dist + fb(neighbor) for (dist, neighbor)
    in graph[node]])
    return shortest       # = shortest distance from current
                            node to goal node.
```

The disadvantages of decoration are 1) it places the code in two different locations, 2) it requires more recursion, 3) it is slower, and 4) the code is harder to understand if you have not mastered the decorator syntax.

Here is something curious. It is possible to construct graph like this:

```
graph = {9:[(10,8), (3,7), (15,6)],
         8:[(7,6), (7,4)],
         7:[(7,5), (15,4)],
         6:[(3,4), (4,3)],
         5:[(4,4),(12,2)],
         4:[(3,3), (6,2)],
         3:[(2,1)],
         2:[(1,1)],
         1:[(0,0)], }
```

So, the new neighbors (i) are the nodes that feed into a given node (j) instead of neighbors following from a given node. Then the Bellman equation looks like this: $f(j) = \min_i \left(d_{ij} + f(i) \right)$, where $i < j$, $f(i)$ is the distance from node i back to node 1, and $f(1) = 0$. Which form is better? Neither, as far as I can see. Here is the code for the three forms, if you are interested:

```
#---1. Returns distance only (form a).
def f(n): # ITERATIVE, bottom-up, memoization.
    ff = [0,0,0,0,0,0,0,0,0,0,]
    for i in range(1, n+1):
        ff[i] = min([(ff[j]+d) for (d,j) in graph[i]])
    return ff[n] # = dist. from node n down to node 1.
#------------------------------------------------------------
```

```
#---2. Returns distance only (form b).
def f(n): # RECURSIVE, top-down, no memoization.
    if n == 1: return 0
    return min([ d+f(neighbor) for (d, neighbor) in graph[n] ])
# Bellman equation
#------------------------------------------------------------
```

```
#---3. Returns distance only (form c).
def f(n): # RECURSIVE, top-down, memoization.
    dist = []
    for (d, neighbor) in graph[n]:
        if neighbor not in f.dict: f.dict[neighbor] =
        f(neighbor)
        dist.append( d + f.dict[neighbor] )
    return min(dist)
f.dict = {0:0, 1:0} # A global dictionary makes the code easier
                    to understand.
#------------------------------------------------------------
```

Bellman wrote a second book on dynamic programming with Stuart E. Dreyfus. Fifteen years later Dreyfus wrote another book on dynamic programming, which included 187 solved problems. Dreyfus and his co-author offered the following advice:

> It is our conviction, based on considerable experience teaching the subject, that the art of formulating and solving problems using dynamic programming can be learned only through active participation by the student. No amount of passive listening to lectures or of reading text material prepares the student to formulate and solve novel problems. The student must first discover, by experience, that proper formulation is not quite as trivial as it appears when reading a textbook solution. Then, by considerable practice with solving problems *on his own*, he will acquire the feel for the subject that ultimately renders proper formulation easy and natural. For this reason, this book contains a large number of instructional problems. The student *must do these problems* on his own. Any student who reads the solution before seriously attempting the problem does so at his own peril. He will almost certainly regret this passivity when faced with an examination or when confronted with real-world problems. Do not just read the solution and think "of course that is how to do them."—Stuart Dreyfus and Averill M. Law, *The Art and Theory of Dynamic Programming* (Academic Press, 1977), page xi.

A natural question is this: Why don't all textbooks contain a good number of worked-out examples? My opinion: 1) Finding good examples is difficult and time-consuming. 2) Authors fear that criticism may come from their non-optimal solutions. And 3) the authors either already have the examples in mind or can construct them without much effort, and do not realize that their text is not easily understandable to others without such examples.

It has been said that teaching by example is *not* just one way of teaching—it is the *only* way of teaching. I would go one step further. Students should be given many problems that they do not find easy, but which can be solved by principles illustrated in the given examples (See *Wikipedia*, s.v. Moore method). Our late friend George Polya said it this way:

> "Teaching to solve problems is education of the will. Solving problems which are not too easy for him, the student learns to persevere through unsuccess, to appreciate small advances, to wait for the essential idea, to concentrate with all his might when it appears. If the student had no opportunity in school to familiarize himself with the varying emotions of the struggle for the solution, his mathematical education failed in the most vital point."—George Polya, *How To Solve It*, 2nd Ed. (Doubleday, 1957), page 94.

Problem 2. The 0-1 Knapsack Problem (aka The Cargo-Loading Problem).

A knapsack has a maximum capacity of C lbs. A given set of items, each with a weight and a dollar value, may be placed in the knapsack. Determine the maximum total dollar value the knapsack can hold, constrained by its capacity. (Later we will determine the items to be placed in the knapsack to maximize the value. But as beginners, we do the easier problem first.)

The 0-1 refers to the fact that only 1 item of any particular weight may be loaded.[14] Thus, that item is either included (1) or not included (0) in the knapsack. Below are the values we will use:

```
value          cost (= weight); C = 8
v[1] = 15,     w[1] = 1
v[2] = 10,     w[2] = 5
v[3] =  9,     w[3] = 3
v[4] =  5,     w[4] = 4
```

Recall that in dynamic programming the original problem is to be recursively broken up into smaller problems. The knapsack could have a smaller capacity (j) or allow fewer items (indexed by i) into the knapsack. Thus, we can reduce the size (dimensionality) of the problem in two different ways. The numbers in the following table represent all possible

---

[14]An early reference to this problem is Richard Bellman, *Dynamic Programming* (Princeton, 1957), page 45, problem 21. Bellman referred to loading cargo on a ship, not a knapsack. On page 117 of *The Art and Theory of Dynamic Programming* (Academic Press, 1977), the authors (Dreyfus and Law) imply that the knapsack problem is only the 0-1 version of the cargo-loading problem. Today entire books have been written about the cargo-loading problem and its variants.

subcases. The order of the items we consider placing in the knapsack is irrelevant. The answer is found in the bottom-right corner. How was this table/matrix produced?

```
The matrix (M) is a table of values
    0  1  2  3  4  5  6  7  8 <--remaining
    capacity of knapsack

        +--------------------------
0th item | 0  0  0  0  0  0  0  0  0
1st item | 0 15 15 15 15 15 15 15 15
2nd item | 0 15 15 15 15 15 25 25 25
3rd item | 0 15 15 15 24 24 25 25 25
4th item | 0 15 15 15 24 24 25 25 29 Answer = max value
                                        = 29 = M[4][8]
                                   Best weight set: [4, 3, 1]
```

Note well: The j values are indices in the code that follows. Consequently, this scheme would not work for non-integer weight/costs.

Consider trying to place the i-th item (with weight w[i] and value v[i]) in the partially filled (or empty) knapsack of remaining capacity j. In other words, we seek the value of the cell M[i][j]. Only three cases can occur:

Case 1. (simplest). We CAN'T ever put w[i] in the knapsack, because w[i] alone is greater than C. The value currently in the knapsack is optimal. Consequently, M[i][j] = M[i-1][j].

Case 2. We should *not* put weight w[i] in the knapsack, because w[i] will push out other weights that give the knapsack greater value than with the w[i] weight in it. (How could we know this? You will see in a moment.) Again, M[i][j] = M[i-1][j].

Case 3. We should put the w[i] weight in the knapsack, but then we will have to take out some (or none) of the items already in the knapsack, and fill the remaining space (if any) with the optimal combination of smaller weights. This optimal combination has already been determined as M[i-1][j-w[i]]. Thus,

M[i][j] = v[i]+ M[i-1][j-w[i]].

We can combine cases 2 and 3:

M[i][j] = max(M[i-1][j], v[i]+M[i-1][j-w[i]])

Look at cases 2 and 3 again. Suppose there is not enough room left in the knapsack (capacity = C) to insert the current item (with weight w[i]) under consideration. This does *not* mean we cannot insert it. We simply empty the knapsack, place the item under consideration into the knapsack—which reduces the knapsack capacity to a number already considered (C - w[i])—and then reload the reduced capacity knapsack. How do we know which items to place into the knapsack? The answer to that question is already in the table under j = C - w[i]. Then we decide: Does inserting the item (which perhaps pushed out some other items) increase the value of the knapsack (compared with not inserting it) or not?

What will make this coding easier is to append two zeros to the data sets w and v.

```
if w[0] != 0 or v[0] != 0:
    w = [0] + w
    v = [0] + v
```

These zeros are needed because the index i-1 will eventually reduce to -1 if we aren't careful. If we don't put in the zeros, then we will need more if statements, which will make the code more complicated. To test your program, here are some data sets with their answers:

```
# Data set 1
w = [ 1,  5, 3, 4]      # weights with index i.
v = [15, 10, 9, 5]      # values  with index i, not j.
C = 8                   # Answer: max val = 29; weights =
                           [4, 3, 1]
#----------------------------

# DATA SET 2
w = [1,  2,  3,  4,  5,  6,  7,  8,  9,]   # w[i]
v = [7,  4,  5, 15,  9, 12, 11, 10,  3,]   # v[i]
C = 20                  # Answer: max value: 49; weights:
                           [7, 6, 4, 2, 1]
#----------------------------

# DATA SET 3
w = [1,2,3,4,5,6,7,8,9]
v = [5,2,8,1,9,7,4,3,6]
C = 20                  # Answer: max val = 31; weights =
                           [6, 5, 3, 2, 1]
                        # Note that 6+5+3+2+1 = 17, not C = 20.
#----------------------------
```

```
# DATA SET 4
w = [ 1,  2,  3,  4,  5,  6,  7,  8,  9,10,11,12,13,14,15,]
v = [12,  2,11,  1,  9,10,  4,15,  6,  7,  8,14,  3,  5,  9,]
C = 25          # Answer: max value = 59 weights =
                 [8, 6, 5, 3, 2, 1]
C = 50          # Answer: max value = 81 weights =
                 [12, 11, 8, 6, 5, 3, 2, 1]
C = 60          # Answer: max value = 88 weights =
                 [12, 11, 10, 8, 6, 5, 3, 2, 1]
#-----------------------------
```

Write the iterative function to return the maximum value for any data set. My iterative function follows. It references any one of the data sets w, v and C, previously given.

```
def knapsackI(w,v,C): # Iterative: returns max value.
#---Special case (impossible).
    if w == []:
        return (0, [])

#---Append zero weights and values to make the top row and left
col zeros.
    w = [0]+w
    v = [0]+v

#---Set matrix size.
    rowMax = len(w)
    colMax = C + 1

#---Create empty matrix, filled with zeros. Note: Because of
w[0] = 0 and
#    v[0] = 0, the top row and left col are complete as zeros.
    M = [[0 for j in range(colMax)] # j = col index.
             for i in range(rowMax)] # i = row index.
```

```
#This is what we have so far:
#                     0  1  2  3  4  5  6  7  8 <--capacities
                      of the knapsack (j)
#                    +---------------------------
#      i = 0th item | 0  0  0  0  0  0  0  0  0
#      i = 1st item | 0  0  0  0  0  0  0  0  0
#  M = i = 2nd item | 0  0  0  0  0  0  0  0  0
#      i = 3rd item | 0  0  0  0  0  0  0  0  0
#      i = 4th item | 0  0  0  0  0  0  0  0  0

#---Fill the matrix with values from the bottom-up, starting at 1.
    for i in range(1,rowMax):
        for j in range(1,colMax):
            if w[i] > j:          # Case 1: weight exceeds
                                    capacity C.
                M[i][j] = M[i-1][j]
            else:
                M[i][j] = max(  M[i-1][j],
                v[i]+M[i-1][j-w[i]]  ) # cases 2 & 3

#---Select the answer (lower-right corner) and return it.
    return M[rowMax-1][colMax-1]
#----------------------------------------------------------------
```

Now we write the same function recursively without memoization (form *b*). I have written this function two different ways:

```
def knapsackR(i,j,w,v): # RECURSIVE, NO MEMOIZATION
                         (returns max value only)
#---Special case.
    if w == []:
        return (0)
```

```
#---Append zero weights.
    if w[0] != 0 or v[0] != 0:
        w = [0] + w
        v = [0] + v
        i += 1

#---Base cases.
    if i == 0 or j == 0:
        return 0 # base cases

#---Recursive cases.
    if w[i] > j:
        return knapsackR(i-1,j,w,v)
    return max(knapsackR(i-1,j,w,v), v[i] + knapsackR
    (i-1,j-w[i],w,v))

# The call: print('Maximum value =', knapsackR(len(w)-1, C, w, v))
#---------------------------------------- Knapsack problem--
```

Notice how much shorter and simpler the form *b* recursive method
is than the iterative method. Unfortunately for every recursive call the
"Special case" is considered. This is inefficient. The special case needs
only to be considered on the first call. The next version remedies this
inefficiency. Maybe, before looking, you can determine how I did this by
design, and not by if statements. My code follows:

```
def knapsackRR(w,v,C): # RECURSIVE, NO MEMOIZATION (returns max
                        value only)
#---Special case.
    if w == []:
        return (0)

#---Append zero weights, if necessary.
    if w[0] != 0 or v[0] != 0:
```

```
    w = [0] + w
    v = [0] + v
#-----------------------------------------------------------------
    def f(i,j): # <-- Helper function. Remember this trick.
#------Base cases.
    if i == 0 or j == 0:
        return 0 # base cases

#------Recursive cases.
    if w[i] > j:
        return f(i-1,j)

    return max(f(i-1,j), v[i] + f(i-1,j-w[i]))
#-----------------------------------------------------------------
#---Call the recursive function with lower-left indices of the
    implicit matrix.
    return(f(len(w)-1,C))

# The call: print('Maximum value =', knapsackRR(w,v,C)
#-----------------------------------------------------------------
```

Which form (knapsackR or knapsackRR) is better? I prefer knapsackRR, because of the simpler call: knapsackRR(w,v,C) compared to knapsackR(len(w)-1, C, w, v)).

Next, we seek to return the optimal set of weights to go into the knapsack, not just the maximum value. We do this by backtracking. Let's do the iterative function first. Do you need some hints on how to do this? Maybe not, because it is the solving without hints that builds our skill. Hints are in the next paragraph if you want them.

Start at the bottom in the lower right-hand corner of the matrix: M[maxRow-1][maxCol-1]. If this number is larger than the number directly above it, then we include w[i], in our answer (list of particular weights), and move up one row, i = i-1, and left a distance of w[i] (j = j - w[i]), and repeat. If the number is NOT greater than the number above it, then

we just move up, and do not include w[i] in our set of optimal weights.
It is that simple. My code follows, which is just some add-on code to the
knapsackI function:

```
def knapsackII(w,v,C): # Iterative: returns both max value and
list of weights.
#---Special case:
   if w == []:
      return (0, [])

#---Append zero weights and values, then when the "empty"
   matrix is created, the top row and left column are correct
   as zeros.
   w = [0]+w
   v = [0]+v

#---Set matrix size.
   rowMax = len(w)
   colMax = C + 1

#---Create empty matrix with top row and left col correct as
   zeros.
   M = [[0 for j in range(colMax)] # j = col index.
           for i in range(rowMax)] # i = row index.

#---Fill the matrix with values from the bottom-up.
   for i in range(rowMax):
       for j in range(colMax):
           if w[i] > j:
               M[i][j] = M[i-1][j]
           else:
               M[i][j] = max(  M[i-1][j],
               v[i]+M[i-1][j-w[i]]  )
   maxValue = M[rowMax-1][colMax-1]
```

```
#---Backtrack through matrix to find weights to give the
    maxValue. Without the w[0] = 0 (and v[0] = 0), this code
#   would ignore the first weight. Thefinal value if i-1
#   in M[i-1][j] would refer to the last row of M,
#   instead of the first row.

    i = rowMax-1
    j = colMax-1                    # i,j is the lower-right
                                      corner of M.

    bestWeights = w[1:]             # Ignore the 0th weight
                                      element.

    wPtr = len(bestWeights)-1       # wPtr is a pointer to
                                      the weight
                                    # currently under
                                      consideration.

    for n in range(len(bestWeights)):
        if M[i-1][j] < M[i][j]:
            j -= bestWeights[wPtr]      # Keep this weight.
        else:
            bestWeights.pop(wPtr)       # Remove a weight from
                                          bestWeights list.

        wPtr -= 1
        i    -= 1
    return maxValue, bestWeights
#------------------------------------------------------------
```

Only one more function to write and we are done with the 0-1
knapsack problem. This is a recursive function with memoization. We
want to find both the optimal set of weights and the maximum value
without constructing the matrix. Since the backtracking is exactly the same

as was done with the matrix, this should be easy, right? I had made an assumption that turned this assignment into a nightmare. I quickly wrote a function that worked well with *all* of the previous test cases, but failed if there was one item whose weight was greater than the capacity of the empty knapsack.

```
w = [0,  1,  5,  3,  8]    # weights with index i.
v = [0, 15, 10,  9, 50]    # values  with index i, not j.
C = 8                      # Answer: max val = 50; weights = [8]
```

My recursive function kept claiming either that there was an out-of-range list index error, or that the dictionary of previously computed values did not hold a necessary value. The solution was to place *the top row and the left column of the matrix into the memoization dictionary* before *the recursion began.* This is another example as to why programming (debugging) algorithms can be so extremely difficult. The coder is not aware of a subtle relationship that *must* be reflected in the code. Here is the corrected code:

```
def knapsackRR(w,v,C): # Recursive: returns both max value and
                       list of weights.
                    # Uses a dictionary (dict) for memoization.
#---This function recursively finds the max value while
building a dictionary.
    def f(i,j, dict): # <-- Helper function
        if i == 0 or j == 0:
            return 0 # Base cases
        if w[i] > j:
            if (i,j) not in dict:
                dict[i,j] = f(i-1,j, dict)
            return dict[i,j]
```

```
    if (i-1,j) not in dict:
        dict[i-1,j] = f(i-1,j, dict)
    a = dict[i-1,j]

    if (i-1,j-w[i]) not in dict:
        dict[i-1,j-w[i]] = f(i-1,j-w[i], dict)
    b = v[i] + dict[i-1,j-w[i]]

    dict[i,j] = max(a,b)
    return dict[i,j]
#        ---------------<End of helper function>------------------

#---Special case:
    if w == []:
        return (0, [])

#---Having w[0] = 0 and v[0] = 0 simplifies the code.
    if w[0] != 0 or v[0] != 0:
        w = [0] + w
        v = [0] + v

#---Make (i,j) the lower right-hand corner of table.
    i = len(w)-1
    j = C

#---Set up dictionary base cases (top row and left column).
    dict = {}
    for ii in range(i+1):
        dict[(ii,0)] = 0 # <-- Necessary (Omitting this was my
                                    3-day mistake.)
    for jj in range(j+1):
        dict[(0,jj)] = 0 # <-- Necessary (Omitting this was my
                                    3-day mistake.)
```

```
#---Find max value.
    maxValue = f(i,j, dict)

#---Backtrack through dictionary to find best weights.
    bestWeights = w[1:]                    # Ignore the 0th weight.
    wPtr = len(bestWeights)-1              # = weight pointer
    for n in range(len(bestWeights)):
        if (dict[(i-1, j)] < dict[(i,j)]):
            j -= bestWeights[wPtr]
        else:
            bestWeights.pop(wPtr)    # Remove a weight from
                                     bestWeights.
        wPtr -= 1
        i    -= 1
    return maxValue, bestWeights
#-----------------------------------------------------------------
```

In industry, tests are sometimes written before the functions to be tested. In a way I did that. I had a simple data set with an obvious answer:

```
w = [0,  1,  5, 3, 4]    #
v = [0, 15, 10, 9, 5]    #
C = 8                    # Answer: max val = 29; weights =
                         [4, 3, 1]
```

But that is not enough of a test. The knapsack function needs to be tested a thousand times:

```
def runKnapsackTests(runs = 10):
    print('Wait. Now running tests.')
    from random import randint, random
    for n in range(runs):
        if n % 100 == 0: print('.', end = '') # crude animation
                                                      for time.
```

```
    arrayLength = randint( 0, 30)
    sm          = randint( 1, 20)   # sm = smallest
                  possible value in array.
    lg          = randint(20, 40)   # lg =
                  largest  possible value in array.
    w           = list({randint(sm,lg) for j in
                  range(arrayLength)})
    C           = int(random() * sum(w))
    v           = [randint(1,40) for j in range(len(w))]
    ans1 = knapsackII(w,v,C)
    ans2 = knapsackRR(w,v,C)
    if ans1 != ans2:
        print('\n==FAILED!: w =', w, 'v =', v, 'C =', C )
        print('Iterative results =', ans1)
        print('Recursive results =', ans2)
        return
  print('\nPassed', runs, 'tests.')
#--------------------------------------------------------------
```

With a complicated algorithm you can never trust your thinking. The thousand random tests *must* be run to claim the code is finished.

Notice the crude animation, which tells the user of the progress made. We can sound an alarm at the end of a Python program using Windows.

```
def noise():
    import winsound
    winsound.Beep(1500,500) # Frequency, milliseconds
    winsound.MessageBeep()
    soundfile =  'c:/windows/media/chimes.wav'
    soundfile =  'c:/windows/media/tada.wav'
    soundfile =  'c:/windows/media/Alarm10.wav' # 01 to 10
    soundfile =  'c:/windows/media/Ring01.wav'  # 01 to 10
    winsound.PlaySound(soundfile, winsound.SND_FILENAME)
```

How much space does the recursive form save over the iterative form? Very little: The larger the matrix, the larger the dictionary needs to be. The iterative form was a little faster than the recursive form, even when the recursive code was tweaked.

The knapsack problem is a good problem to memorize, because its solution is typical of dynamic programming strategy. How easy did the genius Richard Bellman find these problems? We know:

> These problems, although arising in a multitude of diverse fields, share a common property—they are exceedingly difficult.—Richard Bellman, *Dynamic Programming* (Dover, 2003), reprinted from the 1957 edition, page viii.

We, however, have the benefit of personal computers, faster computers, the Internet, more convenient operating systems, languages with simple syntax, powerful built-in instructions, and useful data types, etc.

Problem 3. **Matrix Parentheses Count.**

Suppose we have several matrices to multiply in fixed order—e.g., A×B×C×D×E×F. There are many different ways (actually 42) to insert parentheses to get our answer—e.g., ((((A×B)×C)×D)×E)×F and (A×((B×C)×(D×E)))×F. Here is our problem:

Given *n* matrices to be multiplied in fixed order, how many ways are there to parenthesize the matrices?

The first four numbers are easy

A	→ f(1)	= 1
A×B	→ f(2)	= 1
A×B×C	→ f(3)	= 2
A×B×C×D	→ f(4)	= 5
A×B×C×D×E	→ f(5)	= ?
A×B×C×D×E×F	→ f(6)	= ? etc.

295

We can solve this problem by splitting it into two groups in all possible ways, thereby reducing the dimensionality to previously solved cases. If there are 4 matrices (A×B×C×D), then we need only to consider A×(B×C×D), and (A×B)×(C×D), and (A×B×C)×D. Here, the expression A×(B×C)×D has not been ignored. It is derived from splitting (A×B×C) into all possible pairs in (A×B×C)×D. In other words,

f(4) = f(1)*f(3) + f(2)*f(2) + f(3)*f(1) = 1*2 + 1*1 + 2*1 = 5.

Determine how many ways there are to insert parentheses for f(5) now, in your head, without pencil and paper. The answer follows.

Mathematically we can state our splitting-into-pairs observation like this:

$$f(n) = \begin{cases} 1, \text{if } n = 1 \text{ or else} \\ \sum_{k=1}^{n-1} f(k)f(n-k) \end{cases}$$

$f(1) = 1$

$f(2) = f(1) \times f(1) = 1 \times 1 = 1$

$f(3) = f(1) \times f(1) + f(2) \times f(1) = 1 \times 1 + 1 \times 1 = 2$

$f(4) = f(1) \times f(3) + f(2) \times f(2) + f(3) \times f(1) = 1 \times 2 + 1 \times 1 + 2 \times 1 = 5$

$f(5) = f(1) \times f(4) + f(2) \times f(3) + f(3) \times f(2) + f(4) \times f(1) = 14$

$f(6) = f(1) \times f(5) + f(2) \times f(4) + f(3) \times f(3) + f(4) \times f(2) + f(5) \times f(1) = 42$

Our recursive functional equation $f(n)$ is the sum of products of previous cells. There are no maximums or minimums involved, yet it is still considered dynamic programming, just like the Fibonacci functions, and the jeep problem. Your job is to write a recursive function (no memoization) to return this number. My code follows:

```
def f(n): # recursive only
#---base case
    if n == 1:
        return 1
```

```
#---recursive cases (n >= 2).
    total = 0
    for k in range(1, n):
        total += f(k)*f(n-k)
    return total
#-----------------------------------------------------------------
```

Incidentally, the resulting numbers are called Catalan numbers: 1, 1, 2, 5, 14, 42, 132, 429, 1430, 4862, 16796, 58786, 208012, 742900, 2674440, 9694845, 35357670, 129644790, 477638700, 1767263190, 6564120420, 24466267020, 91482563640, 343059613650, 1289904147324, 4861946401452, etc. The first number is indexed at 1, not 0—e.g., $f(1) = 1$, $f(2) = 1, f(3) = 2, f(4) = 5$, etc. The zeroth Catalan number is zero: $f(0) = 0$.

My code is form b. We need the memoization of dynamic programming to make this a faster function. Rewrite it both iteratively and with recursion. My code follows.

```
def f(n, ff = [0, 1]): # recursive with memoization
#---base case
    if n == 1:
        return 1

#---recursive cases (n >= 2).
    total = 0
    for k in range(1, n):
        if n-k >= len(ff):
            ff.append(f(n-k))
        total += ff[k]*ff[n-k]
    return total
#-----------------------------------------------------------------
```

```
def f(n): # iterative
    ff = [0, 1]
    for i in range(2, n+1):
        total = 0
        for k in range(1, i):
            total += ff[k]*ff[i-k]
        ff.append(total)
    return ff[n]
#-------------------------------------------------------------
```

Problem 4. Matrix Parenthesization. We now come to a famous problem in dynamic programming. You probably recall that matrix multiplication is not commutative—i.e., A×B is usually not the same as B×A. But matrix multiplication is associative—e.g., A×(B×C) = (A×B)×C. If you multiply a 4×3 matrix (A) by a 3×2 matrix (B), you end up doing 24 (= 4×3×2) multiplications to get A×B. And if you multiply that result by a 2 by 5 matrix C, you end up doing 64 (= 4×3×2 + 4×2×5) multiplications to get (A×B)×C. If we multiply these three matrices in a different order: A×(B×C), then we need to do 90 (= 3×2×5 + 4×3×5) multiplications. The first order is better. Here is our problem:

Place parentheses around a set of matrices that are about to be multiplied in fixed order to minimize the number of multiplications.

It is necessary to check that every pair of matrices that are to be multiplied are conformable—i.e., the number of the columns of the left matrix is equal to the number of rows of the right matrix. Otherwise, we are coding nonsense.

For 20 matrices, using brute force, we would have to consider about 1.7 billion cases. If we use memoization, then many of those subcases overlap and do not need to be recalculated, just recalled. Note that we are not asked to multiply any matrices in our code.

If you don't know how to apply recursion to a particular problem, there is a psychological trick that may help. Just start writing out one base case after another. (That is what I had to do with this problem.) When I worked out the case for three matrices, I suddenly saw that case as reducible to two cases of two matrices each. At that point, I saw the recursive pattern for all large sets of matrices.

Choosing the notation took some time. The following is one of my inputs with the output. Matrix A is 4×3; matrix B is 3×2, matrix C is 2×5, matrix D is 5×10, and matrix E is 10×4. The 0s are to be used for the number of multiplications necessary to obtain the particular matrix. For ABC this number is 64 in the optimum form of (AB)C.

```
initialMatrixList = [(0, 'A', 4, 3), (0, 'B', 3, 2),
                     (0, 'C', 2, 5), (0, 'D', 5, 10),
                     (0, 'E', 10, 4)]
```

```
#   Output: expr = (AB)((CD)E) value = 236 # optimum placement
of parentheses
```

Then my dictionary (associated with initialMatrixList) came to look like this (sorted by hand):

```
dictionary (dict)
num    key      value
1.     A: (0,    'A',         4,  3)
2.     B: (0,    'B',         3,  2)
3.     C: (0,    'C',         2,  5)
4.     D: (0,    'D',         5, 10)
5.     E: (0,    'E',        10,  4)
6.     AB: (24,  '(AB)',      4,  2)
7.     BC: (30,  '(BC)',      3,  5)
8.     CD: (100, '(CD)',      2, 10)
9.     DE: (200, '(DE)',      5,  4)
10.    ABC: (64, '((AB)C)',   4,  5)
```

```
11.   BCD:   (160,  '(B(CD))',        3, 10)
12.   CDE:   (180,  '((CD)E)',        2,  4)
13.  ABCD:   (204,  '((AB)(CD))',     4, 10)
14.  BCDE:   (204,  '(B((CD)E))',     3,  4)
15. ABCDE:   (236,  '((AB)((CD)E))', 4,  4)
```

For the key ABCD, the minimum number of multiplications is 204, but only when the four matrices are multiplied like this (AB)(CD). My code follows:

```
def f(M): # Recursive chain matrix multiplication with NO
MEMOIZATION
#    Example:
#    M = [(0, 'A',4,3), (0, 'B',3,2,),  (0, 'C',2,5,),
     (0, 'D',5,3,)]
#         (0 = value (multiplications), 'A' = expression,
4 = rows, 3 = cols)
#    answer = 'expr = (AB)(CD) value = 78'

    n = len(M)       # = 4 in the example above.
    if n == 1:       # A trivial, but necessary, base case.
        return M[0] # M[0] = (0, 'A',4,3) in the example above.

    if n == 2:   # This base case combines two previously
                    computed expressions.
                 # Almost all of the function's work is done
                    here, because the
                 # magic line (for n > 2) repeatedly calls this
                    base case.
    value = M[0][0]+M[1][0]+M[0][2]*M[0][3]*M[1][3]
    key = '(' + M[0][1] + M[1][1] + ')' # Insert parentheses =
                                    (AB) in ex. above.

    rows = M[0][2]
    col  = M[1][3]
    return (value, key, rows, col)
```

```
if n > 2:  # Recursive case.
    best = []
    for k in range(1,n):
        best.append(  f([ f(M[:k]), f(M[k:]) ])  )
        # The magic line.
    return min(best) # min evaluates on the first component of
                                    each tuple.
#-------------------------------------------------------------------
```

If you did not solve this problem on your own and cannot understand my code, then you may have to copy my code, load it with print statements, and then run it to understand how it works. I have needed to do this many times with code I found on the Internet or in books.

```
def f(M, dict = {}): # Recursive chain matrix multiplication
with memoization.
    n = len(M)
    if n == 1:
        return M[0]
    if n == 2:
        key = '('+ M[0][1]+'x'+M[1][1]+')'
        if key not in dict:
            result = M[0][0]+M[1][0]+M[0][2]*M[0][3]*M[1][3], \
                     '('+M[0][1]+'x'+M[1][1]+')',   M[0][2],
                     M[1][3],
            dict[key] = result
        return (dict[key])
    if n > 2:
        best = []
        for k in range(1,n):
            best.append(  f([ f(M[:k], dict), f(M[k:], dict) ],
            dict) )
    return min(best)
#-------------------------------------------------------------------
```

Next is the iterative function, which uses the same notation. You may not have enough time to attempt this problem. Glance at the length of my code before you commit yourself. Good luck.

```
def f(matrices): # Iterative using memoization
#---Check data format.
    for m in matrices:
        assert len(m) == 4 #  example: m = (0, 'A', 4, 3)
        assert m[0]    == 0
        assert 65 <= ord(m[1]) <= 90
        assert type(m[2]) == type(m[3]) == int
    for n in range(len(matrices)-1):
        assert matrices[n][3] == matrices[n+1][2]

#---Calculate the number of matrices
    limit = len(matrices)

#   HELPER FUNCTION
    def insertInDict (A,B,dict):
        # Example: if A = (0, 'A', 4, 3) and B = (0, 'B', 3, 2),
        then
        # key = 'AB' and result = (24, '(AB)', 4, 2)
        key        = A[1]+B[1]
        value      = A[0]+B[0]+A[2]*A[3]*B[3]
        expression = '('+A[1]+B[1]+')'
        result     = value, expression, A[2], B[3]
        dict[key]  = result

#   HELPER FUNCTION
    def dictKey(Lst):
        # Example: Lst =[(0, 'B', 3, 2), (0, 'C', 2, 5)]
        returns key = 'BC'.
        key = ''
        for x in Lst:
```

```
        key += ''.join(x[1])
    return key

#   HELPER FUNCTION
    def mult (key1, key2, dict):
        # This function multiplies two matrix expressions
        (denoted by their
        # keys) and puts the result in the dictionary with a
        new key.
        newKey = key1 + key2
        A = dict[key1]
        B = dict[key2]
        value  = A[0]+B[0]+A[2]*A[3]*B[3]
        expression = '('+A[1]+B[1]+')'
        # Below, we tack on the newKey with the result and
        return both.
        result = value, expression, A[2], B[3], newKey
        return result

#---Create empty dictionary.
    dict = {}

#---Insert singles into dictionary--e.g., (0, 'A', 4, 3) with a
    key of 'A'
    for n in range(0,limit):
            key = matrices[n][1]
            dict[key] = matrices[n]

#---insert the rest (doubles, triples, quads, etc.) into
    dictionary.
#   This is a complicated function/algorithm with FOUR loops.
    for i in range(2,limit+1):        # i = len(Lst)
```

```
    for j in range(0,limit-i+1): # Lst below starts at
    position j.
        Lst = [matrices[j+n] for n in range(0, i)]
#       Example: Lst = [(0, 'A', 4, 3), (0, 'B', 3, 2),
        (0, 'C', 2, 5)]
        candidates = []
        # Strategy: Split any Lst into two consecutive
        parts. (This can be
        #       done several ways.) Then multiply the
                two parts and
        #       place the result in the candidates
                list. Then only the
        #       candidate with the least value goes
                into the dictionary

        for k in range(1,len(Lst)):
            key1 = dictKey(Lst[:k]) # = left  part of Lst.
            key2 = dictKey(Lst[k:]) # = right part of Lst.
            candidates.append(mult(key1, key2, dict))
        best = min(candidates)
        dict[best[4]] = best[:-1] # The key is at the
        end (index 4).
    printDictionary(dict)

#---Return dictionary value with key equal to all matrix
letters.
    finalKey = ''
    for tuple in matrices:
        finalKey += tuple[1]
    return dict[finalKey]
#------------------------------------------------------------------
```

Perhaps the reader can improve, or at least code it in less than the 10 days it took me. Could I have written this program in five days? Maybe, if I were motivated by a deadline. Could I assign this problem to my high school students? I always have a few students who are much faster at coding than I am. Only those few students could solve this problem.

I could break the assignment up into little parts, and later have the students put these parts together to solve the big problem. Occasionally I do this, but there are two shortcomings with this teaching strategy.

First, the teacher is doing the assignment for the students. They are just solving the easy parts. Still, they do see the big picture. Second is the fact that when time comes to put the completed pieces together, some of the students will not have finished even the first part. This is usually not due to lack of intelligence. Some students have severe problems with procrastination and disconnect with any small distraction. Aging sometimes remedies this problem.

To give adequate instruction in an advanced programming course, or an honors math course, I have always felt it necessary to teach to near the top, not the middle, and adjust the grades so that there were more As than any other grade, and that few students, if any, receive a D or F. This, of course, is grade inflation, which has its downside. It also keeps me from handing out assignments that do not challenge the top students. Is this the best way to teach? For me in teaching students in advanced classes, yes; for other teachers, and with other students, definitely not, and for good reasons. The world needs both easy teachers and hard teachers. Even the same course taught in the same school needs both easy teachers and hard teachers. One size does not fit all.

In conclusion, I hope the reader has found something of value in these pages, if no more than the philosophy that we must *do* our subject to adequately and confidently teach it. (G.B. Harrison was right.) I wish you the best of luck in your future programming.

Index

A

Anti-idiom, 132
Arguments, 80
Arithmetical expression, 186
Atwood, J., 234, 235

B

Babbage, C., 173
Bad code, 97
Baden-Powell, Lord, 153
Beck, K., 244
Bellman equation, 269
Bentley, J., 150
Bertrand's Box Paradox, 225–226
Binary search, 146
    fault injection, 150
    number of mid values
        (probes), 151
    smoke test, 146
    tangled code, 149
Binary system, 40
Binet's formulas, 21
Boolean functions, 68, 95
Boolean variable, 127–128
Bottom-up design, 92
Boundary conditions, 111
Built-in functions, 9
Built-in index function, 129

C

Carnegie, D., 175
Chess, 15, 96, 169, 207, 242, 251
    Joel Johnson, 15
Clever code, 170–173
Code-readability, 184
Coding-on-the-fly, 106
Cohesion *vs.* coupling, 6
Comb sort, 214
Comments, 96
    docstrings, 103
    in-line, 96
    outline, 98
    printBoard(), 96
Compile errors, 184
Computer arithmetic, 22
    integers to floats, 25
Computer bugs
    compile errors and logic
      errors, 184
    functionality errors, 184
    interface error, 185
    style errors, 184
Computer science project,
    steps, 193–195
    rollover, 23
Computer simulation, 225, 227
    Monte Carlo method

© Michael Stueben 2018
M. Stueben, *Good Habits for Great Coding*, https://doi.org/10.1007/978-1-4842-3459-4

Get the eBook for only $5!

Why limit yourself?

With most of our titles available in both PDF and ePUB format, you can access your content wherever and however you wish—on your PC, phone, tablet, or reader.

Since you've purchased this print book, we are happy to offer you the eBook for just $5.

To learn more, go to http://www.apress.com/companion or contact support@apress.com.

Apress®

All Apress eBooks are subject to copyright. All rights are reserved by the Publisher, whether the whole or part of the material is concerned, specifically the rights of translation, reprinting, reuse of illustrations, recitation, broadcasting, reproduction on microfilms or in any other physical way, and transmission or information storage and retrieval, electronic adaptation, computer software, or by similar or dissimilar methodology now known or hereafter developed. Exempted from this legal reservation are brief excerpts in connection with reviews or scholarly analysis or material supplied specifically for the purpose of being entered and executed on a computer system, for exclusive use by the purchaser of the work. Duplication of this publication or parts thereof is permitted only under the provisions of the Copyright Law of the Publisher's location, in its current version, and permission for use must always be obtained from Springer. Permissions for use may be obtained through RightsLink at the Copyright Clearance Center. Violations are liable to prosecution under the respective Copyright Law.

Printed in the United States
By Bookmasters

Printed in the United States
By Bookmasters